Pricing and Profitability Management

A PRACTICAL GUIDE FOR BUSINESS LEADERS

Pricing and Profitability Management

A PRACTICAL GUIDE FOR BUSINESS LEADERS

Julie M. Meehan
Michael G. Simonetto
Larry Montan, Jr.
Christopher A. Goodin

WILEY

John Wiley & Sons (Asia) Pte. Ltd.

Copyright © 2011 John Wiley & Sons (Asia) Pte. Ltd.
Published in 2011 by John Wiley & Sons (Asia) Pte. Ltd.
1 Fusionpolis Walk, #07-01, Solaris South Tower, Singapore 138628

This publication is designed to provide accurate and authoritative information in regard to the subject matter covered. It is sold with the understanding that the publisher is not engaged in rendering professional services. If professional advice or other expert assistance is required, the services of a competent professional person should be sought.

Neither the authors nor the publisher are liable for any actions prompted or caused by the information presented in this book. Any views expressed herein are those of the authors and do not represent the views of the organizations they work for.

Other Wiley Editorial Offices
John Wiley & Sons, 111 River Street, Hoboken, NJ 07030, USA
John Wiley & Sons, The Atrium, Southern Gate, Chichester, West Sussex, P019 8SQ, United Kingdom
John Wiley & Sons (Canada) Ltd., 5353 Dundas Street West, Suite 400, Toronto, Ontario, M9B 6HB, Canada
John Wiley & Sons Australia Ltd., 42 McDougall Street, Milton, Queensland 4064, Australia
Wiley-VCH, Boschstrasse 12, D-69469 Weinheim, Germany

Library of Congress Cataloging-in-Publication Data
ISBN 978–0–470–82527–3 (Hardback)
ISBN 978–0–470–82704–8 (ePDF)
ISBN 978–0–470–82703–1 (Mobi)
ISBN 978–0–470–82705–5 (ePub)

Typeset in 10/12pt, New-BaskervilleRomanA by Thomson Digital, India
Printed in Singapore by Markono Print Media Pte. Ltd.
10 9 8 7 6 5 4 3 2 1

To Don, Jack, Charlie, and Theresa

Table of Contents

Foreword

Several years ago, I was asked to lead the transformation of an organization with a record of success that spanned a century. In an effort to continue and to grow that success, we embarked on a comprehensive program to transform some areas within the company. One of the most important was pricing. The leadership team knew we could improve our pricing, and that the value this would create was larger than any other improvement initiative we could undertake. As a result, I had the opportunity to work closely with several of the authors. I have personally applied what you are about to read, and can attest to the value it will create.

I have more than a passing familiarity with pricing, from both my academic background and my career in business management. There are literally dozens of books on pricing theory, and I have read a fair number of them. Most address specific aspects of pricing; while helpful in addressing specific challenges, they do not provide an integrated, holistic approach to setting and managing price. If we were truly going to transform our organization, we needed an approach that incorporated theory, but also gave us a pragmatic and realistic roadmap for applying advanced pricing capabilities as quickly and efficiently as possible. This approach also had to take into account that the business would not stop while we determined the future. We needed a roadmap that told us where to start, gave us the right tools and techniques needed to improve our performance, provided a sequencing that both built capabilities and delivered early results, and most importantly, told us how to do this in a way that the organization would accept and adopt as quickly as possible. We also needed to know the challenges we would face and how best to address those challenges, as well as how to manage expectations both internally and externally, with internal stakeholders as well as with our customers and competitors.

We knew when we started this program that we would be changing, in some cases radically, how pricing is executed, and who would set and execute price. Traditionally, pricing has been managed in pieces across various parts of the business, and this cross-functional integration is an ongoing challenge within any organization. With pricing, sales often sets base price and provides insights into customer behavior and competitive intelligence, marketing determines promotions, segmentation, channel, and brand positioning, operations determines cost, and supply chain drives cost-to-serve. Finally, finance sets hurdle rates, expected ROI and ROA, and holds the organization accountable for results. There are endless variations on the model I just described, depending on your specific circumstances. A key concept explored in this book is "how do these pieces all fit together? How should they fit together, and how do we align the organization to achieve and retain a high level of integration across pricing activities?" You will find the answers to these questions, and more, within this book.

When we started this journey, we were a relatively unsophisticated organization in terms of setting and managing price, especially in our field organization. Giving it tools that allowed them to understand and learn about the behavior/characteristics of its particular clients (willingness to pay), to understand the drivers of profitability (cost to serve), and to rank each different client (relative value) was especially valuable to us. I believe it attracts and identifies the "naturals" in the sales force that are at ease making analytically-based decisions, and also fosters the development of true business acumen in these same individuals. That by itself will be of significant benefit to the organization, and as the results become apparent, those talents become a core component of the organizational culture.

Another significant benefit comes with creating a framework and an environment where the organization can create experiments and learn. As an example, having an explicit methodology for testing various promotional and discount activities, and then using that information for developing better future pricing policies is a great way to get your people to think about what they are doing when they pull the various levers in sales and marketing, and how those actions can affect segmentation, willingness to pay, and so on. This is particularly valuable in exposing how apparently dissimilar, unrelated activities can and will affect other parts of the organization, and again, the customer in terms of driving behavior, both intended, and almost more importantly, the unintended consequences that often occur when potential pricing actions are not fully evaluated in terms of "what if" scenarios. The cultural impact of creating a "test and learn" environment should not be underestimated; removing the fear of failure will create a level of engagement and thinking that is not common in most organizations today.

Truly effective pricing requires a level of integration and analysis that has been and continues to be rare in most organizations. Driven by deep analytics, both from a price-setting and a price-execution perspective, companies now have access to information in a form and at a level of granularity that not only enables this integration, but demands it. This book is a practical guide, outlining why the integrated, holistic approach is essential, how to align disparate functions so that integration happens as planned, and most importantly, how to make that integration sustainable within your organization.

The benefits that will be achieved by the application of these concepts are significant. When we started our program, our expectations were high, but not unreasonable. In reality, we have achieved many, many times the benefits we initially expected, totaling literally hundreds of millions of dollars. In addition, these benefits are recurring, and there is a first-mover advantage from adopting the integrated approach outlined in these pages. Integrated price management capabilities are iterative; the more you do it, the better you become at it. Companies who adopt these capabilities before others in their industry will create a sustainable competitive advantage through their ability to manage price, even in the midst of continuing economic uncertainty, and the growing complexity of the global economy.

There are several things this book is not. This book is not a comprehensive guide to cost management. Cost management has been an established discipline for decades, and this book would need to be an order of magnitude longer to include even an overview of leading cost management techniques. While the authors go into great detail in understanding costs associated with specific transactions, the techniques required to manage cost effectively are not covered in detail. What is covered is the ability to determine what value a customer creates for you and how your costs in attracting, serving, and retaining that customer align with the value they create for you as a customer. This is not only the value of higher margins; business leaders today need timely information for making strategic tradeoffs. As an example, when should I place brand or marketplace considerations on par with economic value? What if market share is how the analysts evaluate us? What will that cost us, and what can we expect in terms of a payoff, again, not just in margin, but across strategic considerations?

This book is also not intended to explain the theory of economic value. Theory, while required as a base for charting your course, does not give you practical advice for dealing with hundreds of salespeople, thousands of customers, and hundreds of thousands of transactions. The challenge addressed by this book is not the development or further evolution of pricing theory, but the pragmatic translation of theory into tactics, in a way that drives results for both you and your customers. A consistent theme within this book is how to identify and quantify the value you create for the customer, the value specific customers create for you, and how to align your organization and capabilities so that every interaction you have with the customer creates value for both of you. At its best, the holistic, integrated approach to pricing will enable you to identify and implement pricing programs that drive value for everyone in your value chain, from you, through distributors and retailers, and on to end customers.

As I stated earlier, I have seen firsthand the value created through this approach. It is challenging, and will require your organization to change long-standing beliefs, roles, and operating models. While challenging, the value that will be created more than justifies the risks and effort required to make this real. Simply put, this works, works quickly, and creates tangible, measureable and significant improvements in both revenue and margin. Done well, it will also improve customer relations, and drive you and your customers into a much closer and mutually beneficial relationship.

Decades of research has shown that investing in improved pricing capabilities has a higher rate of return than any other improvement initiative you might launch within your organization. This book is a comprehensive guide to making that investment pay the highest possible rate of return as quickly as possible, while also giving you information you never previously had for making strategic decisions, and in time to make those decisions matter. You, your people, your customers, and your shareholders will all benefit. If you are responsible for the financial performance of your organization, it is imperative that you read this book.

Juan José Suárez Coppel
Chief Executive Officer,
Director General, Director and
Chairman of the Board
Pemex-Exploration & Production,
Petroleos Mexicanos

Acknowledgments

The authors would like to thank the following individuals for their contributions to this book:

Abhinav Agrawal
Louis Amoroso
Vlad Bolsakov
Matt Carpenter
Robert Ceccarelli
Leandro Dalle Mule
Joe Dworak
Rich Eagles
Susan Fitzgerald
Kim Frazier
Parvathy Hariharan
Maggie Laird
Alice LaPlante
Anthony Lazaro
Dave Pan
Nelson de Sa e Silva
Ranjit Singh
Rob Sproull
Brett Thompson
Steve Tom
Jeff Wannamaker
James Weaver

In particular, the authors would like to thank Elizabeth Whitehead for her tireless (but fruitless) efforts to make us better writers.

CHAPTER 1

Introduction to Pricing and Profitability Management

The moment you make a mistake in pricing, you're eating into your reputation or your profits.
— Katie Paine, founder and CEO of KDPaine & Partners

There is an old joke about a businessman who loses margin every time he sells his products. A customer asks, "How do you make money?" The businessman answers, "I make it up in volume."

A company that routinely sells products below its margins would hardly seem likely to remain in business for long. Nonetheless, many firms follow this approach today. In some cases, this approach is an unintentional move, which results in the company losing money on every transaction. In other cases, it reflects a carefully considered decision to maximize profitability across a portfolio of product offerings. However, in other instances, this approach is adopted by business leaders who simply misunderstand which of their products and customers are actually generating margin and the factors that truly determine their company's profitability.

The field of pricing management has been growing steadily in recent years. If you mention the subject in a group, many people will assume the ensuing discussion will be limited to price setting. But the discipline involves much more than just prices themselves. Pricing management is a strategic competency that involves people, processes, technology, and information. Its reach extends into virtually every corner of an organization (i.e., marketing, sales, IT, operations, finance, accounting, and executive leadership). Effective pricing management is capable of changing the way a company views and operates its entire business; it helps ensure the overall profitability of an enterprise and it can affect the bottom line profoundly. This book is intended to serve as a comprehensive introduction to the discipline and a reference work for business leaders, managers, and students who want to deepen their understanding of and sharpen their capabilities in this critical function.

Pricing: The Critical Lever for Raising Performance

Why make pricing improvement a focus for an organization? The answer is simple: the benefits are enormous. A study has shown that 90 percent of pricing investment meets or exceeds return on investment (ROI) expectations.[1] Put another way, *for any dollar invested in performance improvement, the greatest return comes when it is invested in pricing.*

Figure 1.1 reflects one version of an often-replicated analysis.[2] All versions lead to the same conclusion: pricing is the most powerful lever available to raise performance. Despite this, the evolution of pricing management has, until recently, been slow. Although it has long been recognized as one of the traditional *four Ps* of marketing, systemic and structural challenges prevented pricing management from achieving the same level of sophistication or having the same capacity to improve performance as it has now. In its early days, practitioners focused on revenue/yield management and operated almost exclusively in the airline and hospitality industries. But recent developments have led companies to appreciate the breadth and critical importance of the discipline. We discuss three of these developments briefly in the following.

The Search for Improved Data Management Solutions

The widespread adoption of enterprise resource planning (ERP), particularly over the past 10 years, has enabled firms to collect, process, and store

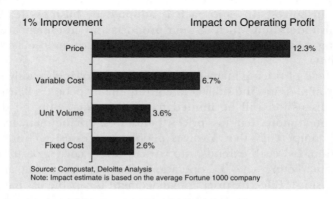

Source: Compustat, Deloitte Analysis
Note: Impact estimate is based on the average Fortune 1000 company

Figure 1.1   Profit Improvement Initiatives and ROI

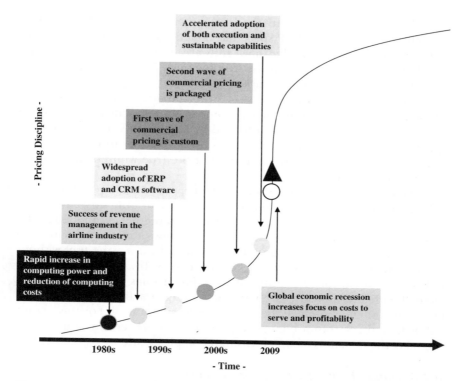

Figure 1.2 **Causes of Historical Growth of the Pricing Discipline**

more transaction-level data than ever before—a prerequisite for effective pricing management. However, management of this information has lagged behind. Data mining, transaction-level price analyses, demand-elasticity curves, price waterfalls, price-band analysis, customer segmentation, and transaction-level profitability measurement are all tools that require large amounts of clean, available data. Companies have aggressively sought new ways to manage this data, which, in turn, has led to an explosion in price optimization software (see Figure 1.2).

Traditionally, pricing software addressed demand curves, price optimization, and, at the highest level of sophistication, revenue/yield management. In the past five-to-seven years, however, the need for software to address price execution has been recognized and addressed. The software continues to evolve in response to market needs, as various packages leapfrog each other with improved capabilities. Overall, vendors have moved from offering purely custom solutions to providing true "off-the-shelf" functionality that can be implemented in months, not years. In addition, these vendors aggressively pursue the integration of stand-alone pricing software and core ERP systems.

The response to these software developments has been striking. Every single competitor in the ERP space has bought or built software, or partnered with other vendors that have software, to bring advanced pricing capabilities to the market. This is true for both the business-to-business and the business-to-consumer markets.

As this book was going to press in 2011, the pricing software industry was well into a consolidation phase. Some of the small niche players had gone out of business or been absorbed by larger firms that coveted the specific capabilities they could add to their existing application portfolio. A few key players had emerged, but the true winners had not yet achieved dominance.

However, despite its obvious importance, software alone will not provide a competitive price advantage; good data can only serve as a basis for developing an effective strategy. In fact, if software is positioned as the "silver bullet," it can actually decrease a company's ability to set and manage prices because sales personnel will likely resist using the tool without careful preparation. For example, an advanced software application can help calculate customer-specific pricing, but if sales incentives are not aligned with the new prices, then discounting practices may arise that undermine them and make the new price list suboptimal. For this reason and many others, software must be part of a comprehensive strategy that can meet the demands of an increasingly complex world.

The Growing Challenges of Global Markets

Globalization (and the expansion of cross-border arbitrage and gray market activity) has increased the need for multinational companies to create worldwide pricing strategies. If not addressed effectively, gray markets will cannibalize sales for manufacturers and jeopardize relationships with distributors who own contractual rights within a region. The need to address these issues strategically in international markets will continue to grow as companies realize that other profitability initiatives have ceased to work.

Reaching the Limits of Cost-Cutting

An organization can only undertake so many cost-reduction initiatives without diminishing its ability to serve its customers effectively. For example, a manufacturing company can consolidate plants to slash expenses only so long as its production capacity is still able to meet demand. Similarly, a retailer cannot continue eliminating sales personnel if this strategy interferes with the running of the store, causing revenue to drop. Companies can never "cut" their way to prosperity. Pricing, in contrast, is a constant means to profitable growth.

The emergence of these three trends—improved data management solutions, the challenges of global markets, and the limits of cost-cutting—

has helped companies see the tremendous opportunities that pricing management can produce. The benefits are both sizeable and quickly realized. (There is also a first-mover advantage: the earlier a firm addresses pricing, the further along its learning curve and ahead of the competition it will be.) Yet while companies have more and more tools available to help them develop an improved pricing capability, many still have failed to act. Why?

Common Obstacles to Pricing and Profitability Management

In a 2004 study, AMR Research found that fewer than 3 percent of companies effectively managed, communicated, and enforced prices.[3] Why? Because pricing, done correctly, is an extremely complex undertaking that requires a group of trained practitioners to view the business through a unique lens.

While executives may understand the benefits of improving their organizations' capabilities, the obstacles they face may seem insurmountable and can create institutional inertia. Many apparent barriers simply reflect the demands of pricing management itself. Other barriers reflect the natural confusion of an organization that lacks the structure and the personnel to handle the new strategic approach. A few of the common impediments follow.

Daunting Complexity

Pricing is an intricate and interdependent competency that affects all levels of an organization and the market it serves (including customers and competitors). At any given time, an organization must ask itself and address a multitude of questions:

- How can price be used as a competitive advantage, and how can we achieve results as quickly as possible?
- How do we position a price with our customers, and how do we differentiate our offering?
- What should our value propositions be for each customer segment?
- How does our product portfolio match the needs of our customers?
- What do we have to do to meet the promises made by our executives and our sales force, while still delivering the required margin?
- Can we use price to influence demand (and can we build that into our production and supply chain thinking)?
- What should our price be?
- Once we have the right price in place, how do we execute it effectively, and what will be the likely customer and competitor responses?

Internal Resistance

Pricing data collection and cleansing can be a challenging and time-consuming task that requires specialized technical skills and a cross-functional and multisystem understanding of the data. Winning cooperation between the different functional groups involved may prove difficult. Initial improvement efforts are often viewed skeptically by organizations simply because they reflect a new approach. In addition, individual units may rely on different data sets to form their assessments of the organization's needs and market position, which can lead to strategic disagreements. Thus, many pricing initiatives fail before they truly begin because managers find various reasons to resist changing the status quo and are unwilling to adopt a fresh, objective view of the business at a transaction level.

Fear of High Stakes

Besides being costly, pricing errors can produce long-term (if not permanent) consequences for an organization. Any organization that has engaged in a price war with a competitor can attest that the brand (and/or the price levels) never fully recovers. Many firms fear the negative consequences of poor decisions, and conclude that maintaining the status quo with acceptable margins is a safer path than trying to achieve better margins and risking a catastrophic mistake.

Unavailable, Inaccessible, or Unclean Data

If data are missing or otherwise unusable, then companies lack the basic information they need to formulate a plan. For example, a company will have trouble performing a profitability analysis by customer segment if it lacks organized transaction-level data and customer-level, cost-to-serve information. This problem will remain if effective modeling or sampling techniques cannot be developed to address the issues.

Human Resource Constraints

Engaging the right people for pricing improvement (i.e., those with the appropriate authority, political connections, and skills) can be challenging as many managers are already too busy executing their day-to-day activities to take on additional responsibilities. Many organizations struggle to dedicate the necessary personnel required to mount an initiative as ambitious as pricing improvement.

Hidden Problems

Many weaknesses in a company's existing pricing strategy can be masked or obscured by the complexities of overlapping functions. Uncovering the trouble spots can be a challenging exercise. Table 1.1 identifies some of the major pricing issues and their common indicators.

Table 1.1   Common Indicators of Major Pricing Issues

Symptom	Description of the Problem	Impact
Maverick Selling	• More than 30% of all deals are closed below the established discount guidelines or policies.	• Unwarranted discounts are issued.
Price Erosion	• Lack of visibility into historical pricing of comparable deals (or into historical trends) causes deeper than necessary discounting.	• Unwarranted discounts are issued.
Margin Erosion	• Below-the-line transactional expenses and incentives are not considered during deal negotiations or not recovered after deals close.	• Revenue leakage and lost profits.
Slow Response Time	• The time to respond to a customer's pricing request is relatively long.	• Deals are lost.
Unsegmented Pricing or Discounts	• Prices are not set at a level granular enough to capture the maximum profit from a transaction.	• Unwarranted discounts are issued to unprofitable customers. • There are revenue leakage and lost profits for price-insensitive customers.
Price Agreement Compliance	• A single customer has multiple agreements for the same product, but consistently makes purchases at the lowest price.	• Unwarranted discounts are issued.
Customer Volume Compliance	• Customers have an established agreement with volume commitments, but do not buy to their full potential.	• Unwarranted discounts are issued. • Revenue is not realized.
Less Productive Pricing Team	• The team does not have the ability to prioritize and analyze special pricing requests properly to have the maximum impact.	• Unwarranted discounts are issued.

Cross-Functional Chaos

"Pricing touches everything, and everything touches pricing." This simple truism is recognized by pricing professionals, but it is not often recognized across an organization. In a typical organization, Marketing sets list (or market) prices and gathers customer and competitive pricing information; Sales negotiates prices with customers; IT provides data and maintains the systems that support pricing decisions; Finance shares costs and "profitability" data; Operations offers input regarding capacity; Order Fulfillment determines how best to process purchase requests (and generates the costs that flow from these decisions); and Executive Leadership monitors pricing and profitability, while reporting key metrics to external stakeholders. Lack of coordination and conflict between these functions (which have different agendas) can make it nearly impossible to set up a dynamic, informed, and integrated pricing competency.

Organizations that lived through the wave of reengineering in the 1990s still bore the scars, more than a decade later, of attempting to manage processes across functional boundaries. The results were impossible to quantify and simply set various functional groups against each other. The good news is that pricing, unlike other options, drives immediate and recurring results and produces measurable improvements to the bottom line. Effective pricing gives a place at the table to all the internal groups affecting, or affected by, its policies. Unlike many cross-functional initiatives, pricing does not require one function to win and others to lose. In fact, the balancing of each group's' objectives creates a natural tension that, when used effectively, actually improves pricing performance by ensuring that the various functions' needs and goals are addressed.

Differing Organizational Pricing Perspectives

The internal debates on pricing are endless. The level of real insight into customer buying behavior is limited; value propositions are nonexistent (or worse, come from an internal perspective); and the real margins by customer, product, or salesperson are poorly understood and difficult, if not impossible, to calculate. Thus, there are several distinct perspectives, which generally follow functional lines:

- *It's all about the numbers.* According to this school of thought, deep analysis of the numbers (derived either algorithmically or by regression) will produce profound insights into customer behavior; the product or service value proposition; and, ultimately, what the optimal price offering should be.
- *The sales force should be given complete freedom.* Advocates of the sales team believe that the sales team, because of its daily interaction with buyers and direct insight into customer behavior, should be the sole determiner of price. One senior vice president once summed up this perspective nicely: "My sales force needs total flexibility at the point of

contact with the customer." Is this ever really true? And, if it is, at what cost? Getting pricing right inherently requires the ability to make fully informed tradeoffs.

- *Get your costs right, and price will take care of itself.* Seasoned managers who have built successful careers on cost management believe too much effort is spent on the "soft side" (i.e., attempting to understand customer behavior). The real answer to any pricing issue, they believe, is to move further down the cost-experience curve, using production efficiencies and statistical process controls to produce goods more cheaply than the competition. This group tends to favor a cost-plus pricing approach, which determines margin (and ultimately selling price) by taking the cost to produce and adding a "fair" or "reasonable" markup.
- *Customers will pay us a premium if we create a better product.* Little emphasis is placed on pricing during the new product development process; innovation for the sake of innovation is valued. Yet while many products are high function and top quality, manufacturers are generally unable to recoup a margin that warrants their investments in development.
- *Better information systems are the silver bullet.* The failure to meet pricing challenges is often framed as the result of a lack of relevant information. If the IT systems delivered the right information, advocates believe, then setting and negotiating price would be easy, and deals would almost close themselves. (Of course, good data can serve as only the basis for developing a strategy—this should not be confused with actually having a plan.)
- *The customer rules.* For some in the organization, the voice of the customer represents the final word on what prices should be. Little or no effort is made to evaluate the value a product creates for buyers, let alone to determine if the offered price takes into account the value the customers create for the organization. Focus groups, surveys, and, above all, anecdotal insights from the sales force are used as the basis for determining what to charge and what a customer is willing to pay.

Each of the perspectives listed above is a key indicator of a corporate culture dominated by a certain function: the first by finance; the second, sales; the third, manufacturing; the fourth, innovation or engineering; the fifth, IT; and the final, marketing. Each perspective can produce important insights but offers only a fragmentary view of pricing. In this case partial answers will yield only partial results. The more one view predominates, the less effective pricing will be.

Why is it that a book on pricing begins with a discussion of corporate culture? Because the human factors are so significant that they can make or break the entire process.

Understanding—and Leveraging—the Human Side of Pricing

Price lies at the heart of the buyer–seller interaction, and an inherent conflict exists between a company's desire for long-term customer relationships and its effort to get fair value for its products and services. Most organizations encourage their sales teams to build strong relationships and to know their customers on a personal as well as a professional basis. Unfortunately, these bonds often become ends unto themselves, obscuring their original purpose, which was to establish profitable, long-term customers. Companies must continually analyze customer interactions at the transaction level and determine the value to both them and their customers. By understanding the worth of a product to buyers, a manufacturer can better differentiate its offerings from the competition. Similarly, by quantifying the buyer's value to the company, the company can decide which relationships warrant investment and which should be treated as opportunistic transactions. Both analyses contribute to a balanced, healthy customer portfolio.

A key driver of the buyer–seller relationship is sales force compensation, because poorly aligned incentives result in weak margin performance.

Consider the experience of a medical device manufacturer that compensated its sales team by unit volume. The products were new and evolving rapidly, so the company pushed for high rates of market penetration. Competition was fierce, and, for the sales team, getting buying groups to choose the products carried nearly as much weight as physician preference. Critically, compensation was entirely volume driven with no cap placed on sales earnings. The more you sold, the more you earned. The results were predictable: the sales team constantly pushed for prices to be reduced to challenge the competition.

At one point, as prices continued to fall, senior management actually believed a competitor had discovered a cost or manufacturing advantage. In reality, the company (the marker leader) should have looked at the behavior of its sales team: it, not a competitor, was driving the perceived price war. Eventually, a careful analysis of the situation led to an important policy change. Margin was included, for the first time, as a key compensation metric. This single change quickly altered sales behavior, and the decline in price began to level off almost overnight. Unfortunately, two other consequences of the volume-driven compensation policies were not so easily remedied. First, customers, taking advantage of every new price discount, had purchased supplies to last for years. Future sales had been pulled forward, skewing demand elasticities. Worse, buyers had been conditioned to expect that every sales visit would result in fresh price reductions. The situation took years to reverse. New products were affected by the effects of the earlier price war, while the existing product set suffered from chronic low profitability. The unintended consequences of a misguided focus on volume were far reaching, long lasting, and severe.

Another human challenge for pricing involves countering the tactics customers use to drive down price. *Strategic sourcing* is a practice that has been in existence for decades. Today, every well-performing company follows this approach to achieve the best possible price when purchasing goods and services. If you are a manufacturer, it is likely your sales force has been subjected to painful interactions with procurement agents who know and have quantified every aspect of their relationship with you as a supplier. Consider how often a member of your team has been hit with a variation of the following comment: "I know we don't buy large volumes of this particular product, but our aggregated spend across your portfolio is well over $100 million. We therefore expect a 5 percent price reduction across the portfolio for this, and every subsequent, year. After all, our volume is helping you move down the cost-experience curve, and we should reap some of those benefits."

The flip side of strategic sourcing is understanding what drives profitability at the transaction level with a particular customer. Firms need to arm their sales force with the information that lets them counter the traditional procurement approach. In many cases, they may still be able to provide that 5 percent discount while actually improving margin performance.

In general, successful pricing management requires a company to build the right sales team and to provide it with the correct training and tools, while aligning compensation with the desired outcomes. Once again, the need to take an integrated approach to pricing is obvious. A company can create the best, most optimally priced offering in the world, but if its sales force cannot execute it (or worse, the company's compensation structure incentivizes its salespeople to negotiate outside established guidelines), then the company's investment in price-setting capabilities has been wasted.

An Integrated Approach to Pricing: The Six Core Competencies

To meet the pricing challenge, companies cannot rely on any single internal or external perspective. Rather, all views must be combined in a way to maximize each of their strengths and to minimize each of their weaknesses. The following six organizational competencies are needed to achieve this (see Figure 1.3).

1. Price Execution

Price Execution refers to all of the processes and policies by which a company delivers its prices to the marketplace. These include everything from sales policies and procedures—for example, guidelines on how big a discount a salesperson can offer without checking with a manager—to the way products are tagged for sale at a retail store. Execution is the ability to

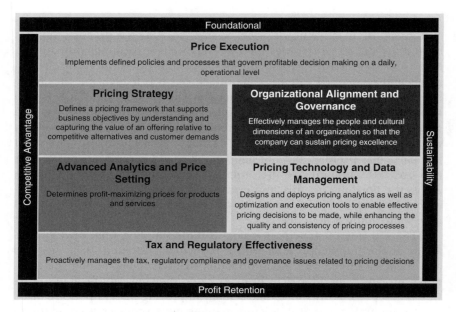

Figure 1.3   The Integrated Pricing and Profitability Management Model (The Six Core Competencies)

meet strategic goals efficiently, effectively, and consistently. If even one process operates poorly, then overall performance will suffer. An organization can have world-class capabilities in the remaining five competencies, but price and margin will be lost if execution fails (which is why Price Execution falls on the foundational axis of Figure 1.3). Put another way, the best salesperson can be armed with the optimal price derived from the best technology, but he or she still needs to get the price to the right customer at the right time with the right message about value to be successful. This is why firms should start by understanding, at the transaction level, what truly drives sales and profits. This understanding will enable them to develop the strategies they will need for their specific markets, products, and competitors (while improving other pricing capabilities).

2. Pricing Strategy

Pricing Strategy articulates the guiding principles behind a company's efforts to price its goods and services. At the highest level the strategy must be aligned with the overall business plan. Pricing leaders may assume, for instance, that prices should be set to maximize profitability when the company has, in fact, made increasing market share its priority. An effective strategy should be focused, nuanced, and dynamic. It should be regularly reviewed and revised, as needed, so it can meet evolving corporate goals.

More targeted pricing plans may focus on combinations of products, channels, customer segments, and geographies. These lower-level strategies typically focus on a well-defined goal, such as increasing market share for a certain type of product in a particular customer segment. These plans also address price positioning (setting prices for goods and services to reinforce a particular *price impression*; in other words, what a company wants to communicate about its brand, quality, and style) and pricing structure (how the company configures prices for its offerings). An effective structure allows elements of the product to be removed or added to meet the variations in value that different customers place on specific components relative to similar competitive offerings.

In general, the pricing strategy shows a company where it is headed, why it is going there, and what it can expect when it gets there. It should also provide actionable insights and expectations about markets, channels, products, competitors, and customers. Without an effective plan, an organization is governed by the pricing issue of the minute, losing sight of long-term goals.

3. Advanced Analytics and Price Setting

Advanced Analytics and Price Setting cover the use of data and specific analyses to view the business both retrospectively and proactively. Pricing analytics enables firms to review past transactions to understand profitability better. This historical analysis creates a unique pricing lens through which to view the business, and often redefines true profitability for a company. Data on product costs and prices paid (e.g., cost-to-serve elements, including sales expenses, product packaging costs, discounts, and off-invoice price adjustments) are collected and studied. Using this information, companies can develop profit-boosting strategies such as discontinuing unprofitable offerings or customer relationships and raising or lowering prices. *Optimization* refers to the use of mathematical models to determine the optimal price for a good or service calculated from historical information on customers, the marketplace, competitors, and a given set of constraints. A price optimization model can not only help management select an appropriate price, but also estimate the probable outcome of any changes.

Organizations must recognize and use the science of pricing. Transaction-level analyses, effective behavioral segmentation, and advanced logarithmic or regression-based price optimization all demand advanced skills. But data are blind; they should be combined with qualitative analyses to produce actionable insights. The effective use of pricing science does not mean the wisdom and experience of the sales force is devalued. Only the combination of analytic and qualitative perspectives will yield sound pricing actions that can work effectively in varying market and competitive environments.

Pricing Strategy and Advanced Analytics and Price Setting fall on the competitive advantage axis of our model because, when done well, they both enable companies to outperform market competitors.

4. Organizational Alignment and Governance

Organizational Alignment and Governance deal with the people and cultural factors that shape pricing behavior, including organizational structure, sales effectiveness, training, and talent management. It answers questions such as:

- How centralized or decentralized should the pricing process be?
- What are the roles and responsibilities, goals, and incentives for everyone who is involved in pricing, and are they aligned?
- How do we expect salespeople to spend their time, and do they have the right skills and tools to manage price effectively?
- Most important, are compensation metrics aligned with both our strategies and our execution capabilities?

Effective pricing management includes such tasks as enforcing sales policies and procedures, developing profitable sales compensation structures, and creating reporting relationships that help the company make and carry out pricing decisions. As discussed earlier in the chapter, pricing is inherently dominated by human interactions as it forms the basis for the buyer–seller relationship. Within a company, poor communication, an ill-conceived organizational structure, and inadequate skills or tools will undermine the value of improved price setting. Getting the people side right will help ensure effective execution.

5. Pricing Technology and Data Management

Pricing Technology and Data Management cover applications that can reveal customer, channel, and product profitability patterns across millions of transaction records, as well as provide the technical environment required for advanced price setting and optimization capabilities. This technology can help analysts to monitor and report on pricing performance continuously. It also provides salespeople with access to real-time customer and profitability information during negotiations, which enables them to calculate a deal's profitability using a variety of price and product combinations before closing a sale. To determine whether an organization needs advanced pricing technology, managers should ask (1) What software functionality will be important with respect to the organization's customers, products, and particular competitive landscape? and (2) How is technology used to improve price execution?

As with any emerging software, pricing technology is now being portrayed as the silver bullet that will slay a firm's pricing challenges. It is not.

However, it can be an invaluable tool to help a company maintain its strategy over the long term.

The Pricing Technology and Data Management and Organizational Alignment and Governance competencies appear on the sustainability axis of our model because they address incorporation of effective pricing management as a permanent improvement to an organization.

6. Tax and Regulatory Effectiveness

Tax and Regulatory Effectiveness enables a company to plan and execute more profitable pricing and, ultimately, to apply the benefits from these improvements to the bottom line. For example, profits can be directed to the most tax-friendly jurisdiction, thereby ensuring that they remain intact as they are converted from before-tax to after-tax income. This is not solely a transfer pricing issue. Where, when, how, and through whom a company makes pricing decisions can all impact tax calculations. Proactive planning should include analysis of income taxes that affect cash flow and, for multinational companies, their effective tax rate (ETR), a measurement often used by specialists to benchmark whether companies are best in class. Assessments should also be evaluated, such as value-added taxes that can quietly drain both cash flow and profits if not properly managed. In addition, pricing data should be studied to identify benefits in the form of tax incentives, credits, and deductions.

Regulatory mandates affecting pricing include antitrust legislation such as the Sherman Act of 1890, the Clayton Antitrust Act of 1914, and the Robinson-Patman Act of 1936 (which prohibits companies from selling the same product to competing customers at different prices). In addition, the Sarbanes-Oxley Act of 2002 requires companies to assess the adequacy of internal controls over financial reporting. This requirement can have significant implications for a company's pricing-related controls and documentation.

The Tax and Regulatory Effectiveness competency is on the profit retention axis of the model because proper planning can help companies keep a greater portion of the profit they generate.

Gestalt Pricing: The Value of an Integrated Approach

Each of the six pricing competencies (presented in Figure 1.4) delivers value in its own right. Unfortunately, there is a tendency to focus overly on one and to pay little or no attention to other competencies that can add significant value. This tendency is often driven by the culture of the corporation. In retail, for example, price setting and price optimization are widely recognized as the real drivers of value. Though they are critical, focusing on them, without a corresponding investment in other capabilities, can actually minimize their value.

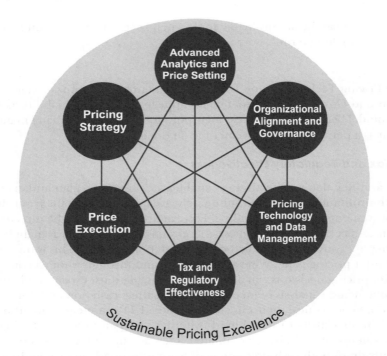

Figure 1.4   The Integrated Relationship of the Six Core Competencies of Effective Pricing and Profitability Management

Pricing can inspire a string of decisions leading to unintended consequences. Unless an integrated approach is taken, unilateral actions in one competency can lead to inadvertent problems in another. As a result, overall performance will suffer. One need not invest equally, however, in all pricing capabilities. The key is to understand the relative value of each pricing competency in terms of the target industry, customer, and product and then to invest accordingly. Firms should not pay for capabilities that do not add margin to the bottom line; obviously, over-investing in un-needed capabilities will simply drive down profitability.

Beginning the Journey: Key Questions to Ask

Given that pricing improvement initiatives can be so complex, emotional, interdependent, and impactful, organizations must prepare for an intense and a sometimes lengthy (often multiple year) effort. Here are some key questions management must ask itself:

- Where do we begin?
- How do we build our capabilities; understand our products, markets, and buyers; create effective value propositions; develop

One retailer learned this lesson as it attempted to master price optimization internally. Despite that added capability, margin performance actually declined. Why? A store-level analysis found that less than 50 percent of the items in stock had the right price labels attached to them. The tags often failed to arrive on time, and the stores did not have the staff in place to apply them to sales items efficiently. A constant stream of price promotions further confused staff. Clearly, the ability to execute was far below the company's ability to set an optimal price. The result? Unhappy customers who faced delays at the checkout as confused staff tried to confirm prices. Even worse, the customers, who suffered from the inconvenience and errors, began to doubt the value of their purchases when faced with shifting prices. The sales force was eventually given the latitude to set prices whenever confusion arose over what they should be. The negative impact on profitability was as predictable as it was profound.

Ironically, the retailer's price setting should have given it a competitive advantage, but poor execution negated that advantage and caused further price erosion and unnecessary added costs. Worse, the differences between advertised prices and the store tags led to charges being made against the retailer that it had engaged in misrepresentation and ''bait and switch'' tactics. It may have been unintentional, but the bad publicity was deadly to the company's reputation and brand.

and maintain effective segmentation models; and determine the right prices?
- How do we get the sales force (or whoever has the fundamental buyer–seller interaction) to manage its relationships so that it can execute prices in a way that meets or exceeds the required margin performance while at the same time satisfying the client?
- Just as important, how do we obtain and retain the attention of the organization? How do we quickly drive tangible value at a level that will demand continued executive attention and support?

There is no ideal time to address pricing improvement. The additional margin it can secure and the minimal time it can take to achieve means pricing improvement initiatives should be launched regardless of most external conditions. In a chaotic or recessionary economic environment, many companies mistakenly feel they cannot work on price performance. Money is tight, customers are extremely price sensitive, and the company may seem too stressed to take on a major cross-functional initiative. In reality, a market upheaval presents precisely the right circumstances to address pricing as a discipline. The turmoil helps set expectations among customers, competitors, and employees that change will happen, and is, in fact, essential to weather the storm. While difficult times do increase the stress level and drive resource challenges, they also open the door for change that would likely not be accepted, or be extremely difficult to implement, in less tumultuous conditions. Conversely, in times of economic growth, even greater opportunities can be found because companies tend to be more relaxed about policy enforcement or they prioritize capturing market share over quality of revenue.

Even small improvements in pricing capabilities will yield immediate results. In addition, initiatives can often be self-funding; programs can be started on a modest budget, and the almost immediate returns make the "there is no money" argument a non-issue. Many of the software firms and consultancies in the pricing space today are also willing to work on a contingency-fee basis. They get paid when a company makes money on its investment in pricing. The results are that tangible and predictable.

Conventional wisdom encourages companies to start with strategy and then work their way down through to execution. In an existing company, that is a flawed approach. Instead, a company should begin its efforts by developing a detailed understanding of the current pricing behavior existing internally (see Figure 1.5). Management should ask itself basic questions such as: What promotions, terms, discounts, rebates, samples, and incentives are currently being offered? How do payment terms affect transaction-level profitability?

A pricing strategy that is based in fact and on a rigorous analysis of the data is not only more likely to be successful, but also will be more widely embraced in the organization. A common excuse for not starting at this point is poor quality or inaccessible data. Many organizations invest heavily in ERP systems that capture tremendous volumes of information. The bottom line is that the necessary data exist, but generally not in the right form to be used immediately for transaction-level analysis. Accounting data have to be decomposed, verified, and rebuilt around specific transactions. In pricing, data aggregation is the enemy. Knowing exactly what drives or robs a firm of profitability at the transaction level is the antithesis of most accounting-driven reporting. Even activity-based costing (ABC) is suspicious. It is better to avoid allocations and allowances and to deal, instead, with the items in a transaction that can be influenced directly (see Figure 1.6).

Once a working model of transaction profitability has been built, it suddenly becomes easy to understand it by product, customer, geographic region, channel, and salesperson. Firms can build their revenue streams and operating margins one transaction at a time. Only by understanding what drives profitability at this level can it truly be managed. But once this granular insight has been developed, a firm can take the

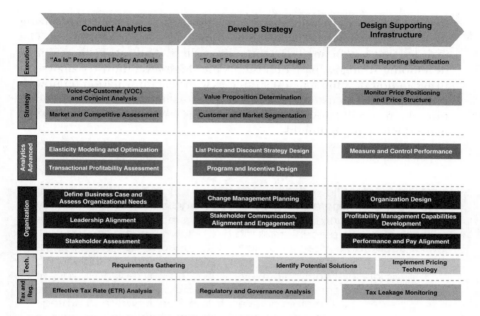

Figure 1.5   The Profitability Management Journey

necessary actions by purchaser, offering, market, channel, or the specific competitive situation to improve profitability. Critical questions should be asked: What are the real implications of channel discounts? Should we even be in that market? What holes do we have in our portfolio? Are

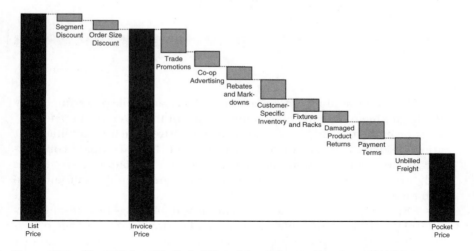

Figure 1.6   The Pricing Waterfall Provides Transaction-Level Insight Into True Profitability

new product introductions driving new business or are we cannibalizing high-margin sales, replacing them with low-margin contracts? The insights that can be made are literally endless. And rather than simply developing strategies based on theory and high-level industry analysis, a firm can now develop *and* test strategies with real information on how its prices, products, customers, and competitors actually behave. In addition, the firm will know *why* they behave this way, and those reasons will make the insights actionable.

Consider the Midwestern lawn care products manufacturer that launched an aggressive growth campaign on the West Coast. By the firm's accounting calculations, business in the target market was running at a 26 percent gross margin, below what the firm wanted, but acceptable when it considered the need to achieve penetration in a high-growth geographic segment. After completing a transaction-level analysis, however, the company realized it was not making 26 percent on average, but was actually losing an average of 6 percent gross margin on every transaction. It had set a strategy to target the West Coast, promised performance to its lenders and the capital markets, and made a significant public display of its intention to compete aggressively in the region. The firm had doubled its sales force over the past six months and was building a regional manufacturing and distribution structure to support the expected growth. By failing to understand its true margins, the firm literally risked growing itself into bankruptcy. Unfortunately, this manufacturer had made the cardinal error of developing and executing an expansion strategy that was based on faulty assumptions about its own business fundamentals.

The understanding of transaction-level margin, while powerful, is only the beginning of pricing improvement. Each of the six core competencies must be evaluated. Efforts should be made to strengthen capabilities that are underdeveloped and are of the greatest value to the company considering its particular situation. As the examples in this chapter have shown, only a truly integrated perspective will achieve the desired results and sustain them.

Effective price setting and execution will enable a firm to tailor its offerings to its most valuable customers and to stop margin leakage driven by overserving (or providing excessive discounts to) its most marginal buyers. If price setting and execution are used correctly, a firm may actually be able to improve margin *while* lowering price. The following chapters offer an in-depth look at the six competencies every company needs to use when embarking on the path to sustainable pricing and profitability management.

Endnotes

1. Yankee Group, "U.S. Price Management and Profit Optimization Survey" (Boston: Yankee Group, 2005).
2. Compustat, a Deloitte analytic tool. Note that the impact estimate is based on the average *Fortune* 1000 company.
3. Laura Preslan, "Price Management: Conventional Wisdom is Wrong," *AMR Research Outlook*, February 2, 2004, 1.

Conducting a Pricing and Profitability Diagnostic

Diagnosis is not the end, but the beginning of practice.
—Martin H. Fischer

Like many people, you have probably walked to your car one morning and found that it wouldn't start. After uttering a few choice words, you may have gone through a mental checklist: Has the battery died? Has the starter failed? Are there problems with my ignition switch or security system or something else? Finding no clear answers, you threw in the towel and had your car towed to a repair shop. Did the mechanic immediately start to replace random parts, or did he or she first do a diagnostic to determine the source of the problem? Likely the diagnostic was done. When the mechanic reported the findings to you, he or she would have described the problem, proposed a solution, and estimated the repair cost. Your mechanic may also have told you that a second worn part had been discovered that would be cheaper to fix now rather than later on when it had failed and potentially damaged your car.

This same process applies when an organization experiences problems with its pricing and profitability management. If the organization blindly begins to make changes without first carefully reviewing its processes, then it will likely produce an action plan as unfocused as it is ineffective. In this chapter, we will outline how an organization can carry out a well-designed diagnostic. These tactical recommendations will show how to assess internal capabilities, identify and prioritize functional gaps, and develop a targeted action plan for improvement.

The Case for a Diagnostic

Today's marketplace is flooded with advice on how an organization can improve its pricing capabilities: "fix processes"; "manage by pocket margin"; "buy pricing software"; "align sales force incentives to margin." Despite the plentiful generic recommendations, most organizations see their efforts flounder because they didn't start from the right point or didn't prioritize their efforts according to their own situation. To begin with, management should ask itself some basic questions:

- Where could our organization improve the most?
- Which capabilities are of the greatest importance?
- What is the best sequence for our improvement efforts?
- What can we do for ourselves, and with what do we need help?
- Where do we have a competitive advantage, and how can we sustain it?

A diagnostic can help provide the answers to these questions, while identifying and prioritizing improvement opportunities. Companies that skip this step and attempt to proceed in an unstructured manner will find pricing improvement a costly, and even destructive, exercise. For example, many companies limit their improvement efforts to simply standardizing their existing pricing and profitability management processes. But by doing this, all they typically accomplish is to reinforce and leverage their current, flawed approach—an exercise of questionable value. Though it is highly unlikely that any company using substandard processes could achieve a best-in-class pricing strategy (with top-notch supporting technologies), many companies apparently still believe this is possible.

In general, the complex, interdependent nature of pricing and profitability management requires that improvement initiatives be designed cross-functionally. This is necessary not only because a single capability is rarely the source of all problems, but also because adjustments in one area will inevitably impact other areas in an organization. A diagnostic can identify which capabilities need to be strengthened and in what order, while providing the overall roadmap for a planned pricing transformation. Following are some additional reasons why organizations should use a diagnostic—and the risks if they do not.

The Advantages of an Early Diagnostic

- *Quick turnaround.* Diagnostics can be scaled to the size and complexity of each organization. Even the largest organizations can complete an assessment in a reasonable amount of time (four-to-eight weeks is not unrealistic assuming availability of data and reasonable cooperation from internal stakeholders).

A top commercial food producer experienced multiple quarters of margin erosion. Management was convinced that misaligned market prices were causing the problem. The leadership team decided the company needed software to help calculate optimized list prices and so spent millions of dollars selecting and implementing a price optimization application. After nearly a year of effort, the team launched the new prices and eagerly awaited the reports that would show the margin improvement. Unfortunately, this did not happen; the margins stayed the same.

After many months of investigation, management discovered the true source of the company's problems: the sales representatives were adjusting prices regionally to sell more products to grocers. Because their compensation was based on volume, the representatives used low quotes from other regions as competitive benchmarks to justify price breaks and discounts in their own territories. The implementation of the new optimized prices actually exacerbated the problem because the sales representatives could draw on more price points to substantiate their assertions that the market could bear only lower prices. Ironically, the sophisticated models had actually made it harder for the company to identify and resolve its issue with its sales force. By the time management finally had addressed the problem, considerable time, resources, and money had been expended. It would be another year before the leadership team was willing to undertake another improvement initiative.

- *Cost-effectiveness.* A diagnostic requires far fewer resources than a full-blown improvement initiative—generally only a small team needs to be assembled to accomplish it.
- *Cascading benefits.* The diagnostic itself is not self-sustaining, but its results can be leveraged throughout the organization. Taking advantage of early improvement opportunities can yield financial benefits that will enable an organization to fund subsequent phases of the pricing improvement effort—a great advantage over other transformative initiatives.

The Consequences of Omitting a Diagnostic

- *Failure to win support.* Without a diagnostic to identify prospects for *quick wins*, a large—and expensive—pricing and profitability effort may fail to produce the immediate results that build confidence throughout an organization. Unfortunately, this lack of quick wins will arm naysayers with the ammunition they need to stop improvements in their tracks.

- *Resource overload.* Transformations that start before a comprehensive diagnostic has been conducted can end up spreading resources too thin. When management doesn't know which opportunities should be prioritized at the program level, it will often make the mistake of trying to tackle all problems at once.
- *Counterproductive initiatives.* The diagnostic often highlights the interconnectivity (and associated problems) of pricing capabilities. Failure to understand these relationships can produce suboptimal results and unintended consequences.

How to Execute a Diagnostic

A comprehensive diagnostic can be broken down into four basic phases:

- Scoping and planning
- Information gathering
- Consolidation of findings
- Opportunity definition.

Information gathering is by far the most time-consuming of these phases, though the other three also have labor-intensive elements. The tactical guidance that follows can be used to help conduct a successful diagnostic, while avoiding common pitfalls.

Scoping and Planning

When determining the proper scope for the initiative, firms will, of course, focus on the business units that are showing pricing or profitability problems. Obvious choices include Marketing, Sales, and Pricing (if the latter exists as a separate unit), but management should cast as wide a net as possible to create the most accurate picture of internal capabilities. Because pricing touches every element of a firm, all relevant functions should be considered—even those that appear to have elevated, or mature, capabilities. While adding top-performing groups may require incremental effort, it can also help leverage best practices and applicable tools to benefit the change management effort. Potential candidates for inclusion include the following:

- Marketing, which often sets prices and discount structures and knows both the competitive environment and the firm's pricing role in the industry (e.g., leader or follower)

- Sales, which communicates and negotiates price directly with the customer and has its compensation significantly affected by pricing decisions
- Customer Support, which must execute discounts, take orders, and, likely, receive pricing complaints
- Supply Chain or Manufacturing, whose actions and decisions have a direct impact on profitability and pricing-related decisions
- Finance, which often sets pricing and profitability goals and is often the only group that can actively track the effectiveness of pricing adjustments
- IT, which is able to describe the firm's technical capabilities and can extract critical data for pricing and profitability analysis.

Information Gathering

While numerous sources can be tapped for information, the four basic ones are (1) internal data, (2) surveys, (3) interviews, and (4) external benchmarks. A diagnostic can draw on some or all of these, depending on how much the organization can afford to spend on the effort. The advantages and disadvantages of each source are summarized in Table 2.1.

Internal Data Analysis. To identify potential areas for improvement, firms can examine internal data points to determine if they support the need for further investigation and investment. In reviewing top-level

Table 2.1   Advantages and Disadvantages of Information-Gathering Methods

Information Source	Advantages	Disadvantages
Internal data	Quantitative Will be accepted as indisputable	Often difficult to access
Surveys	Broad information base Efficient Inexpensive Can be anonymous	Survey design is complex Potential for self-selection bias Topics limited to predetermined questions
Interviews	Interactive discussion allows for additional questioning and richer insights	Time-intensive Qualitative
External benchmarks	Bring relativity to assessment	Can be difficult to identify and collect

business metrics, firms should look for both high and low performance as well as trends that can be discerned from a time plot. Potential data sources include the following:

Company-wide systems. (e.g., ERP systems). General business reporting systems should be used to identify metrics (good and bad) to complete the case for a pricing transformation. Invoice and transaction-level systems can be mined for simple variations in pricing or profitability (or other data points) to support interview or survey findings.

Employee computers. In many cases, the most detailed and helpful information is stored on individual employee computers. The location of these nice-to-have data points can be identified through interviews.

Creating and Executing a Survey.   A survey of pricing and profitability stakeholders can gather a variety of perspectives from across the organization in an efficient, timely manner. Because anonymity is guaranteed, the information is also likely to be unbiased and accurate. However, surveys are notoriously difficult to execute well. To achieve their important benefits, organizations must overcome the unique challenges surveys present—from development and distribution to collection and analysis.

Design.   Because the complexities of survey construction and design have given rise to an entire field of study, we will merely offer key insights here on how to avoid the most common pitfalls.

Know your audience

Pricing terminology varies across industries and between (and even within) companies. Thus, surveys should use language that will be easily understood by respondents. When in doubt, definitions should be provided to help ensure common interpretation and to add clarity. A pilot test can be run and the feedback used to tailor the survey for specific audiences, as needed.

Use modular answers where applicable

Modular responses allow survey participants to answer questions precisely. By decomposing a description into multiple parts, survey designers enable participants to select only those components that properly apply (see Figure 2.1). Instead, if too many elements are bundled together, respondents may be forced to pick an answer that in their view contains inaccurate information.

Customize where necessary to improve effectiveness

While more time-consuming to develop, tailored surveys serve two purposes. First, they allow people indirectly involved with pricing to address relevant portions of the questionnaire without wasting time on areas they know nothing about (if they were to complete areas they

---

Pricing Strategy: Price Planning

Select all that apply:

☐　Product price changes follow the market (i.e., the company is typically not the first mover).

☐　The financial impact of price increases or decreases is estimated before any changes are made.

☐　The volume impact of price increases or decreases is estimated before any changes are made.

☐　The price elasticity of products is known.

☐　Price planning is conducted at multiple levels (i.e., includes not only list price, but also discounted price, targeted invoice price, and so on).

Figure 2.1　Modular Survey Response Structure

nothing about, results could be skewed). Second, there could be differences in business models throughout an organization. A large conglomerate that encompasses vastly different enterprises may obtain meaningful insights only if it customizes its surveys to take these variations into account.

Beware of respondents anticipating the answers they perceive to be correct

Many internal surveys fail because they underestimate the tendency of participants to provide the responses that they think are right or desired by management. The choices should be phrased carefully to avoid signaling whether an answer should be positive or negative.

Pay attention to length

People are discouraged by long surveys, so surveys should be edited to include only the most relevant questions to test certain hypotheses and to generate the most appropriate insights. If the initial survey suggests deeper or broader problems in a particular area, then interviews are a good tool for following up the survey to make a more detailed assessment. While anonymity should be guaranteed to all survey participants, volunteers can be solicited to participate in interviews once aggregated results are in.

Provide a bailout

Include "I don't know," "Not applicable," or "Other" as appropriate; these options will allow the participant to move on when he or she cannot answer a question. And these responses may actually provide a company with some of its most meaningful feedback. Determining how many people in a company answered "I don't know" when asked to describe a firm's pricing strategy can be especially illuminating.

Survey Participant Selection.   A company must decide which business units (and employees) should be included on the distribution list for a survey. Sending out a survey is a fairly simple operation, so a company should make its list as inclusive as possible. The more varied the participating units, the easier it will be for the diagnostic team to compare and contrast responses across the organization.

Survey designers should next decide which levels of the employee hierarchy should be included. Ideally, this will be all levels if an organization hopes to gain an accurate understanding of the pricing and profitability management activities within it. Some of the most useful insights can be generated by comparing the responses from the leadership team with those from line or field personnel. Organizational misalignment can be a key driver of suboptimal price management, a problem that can be revealed when differences show up by level in survey results.

Distribution of the Survey and Collection of Results.   Having high-ranking executives send out questionnaires has become an effective practice to encourage people to participate and respond to them. Surveys should be emailed from a senior account or an announcement should be made by a top executive or local business leader, whoever the organization feels can drive the best response rate (this individual should *not* however be listed as the contact for troubleshooting or complaints!).

The work is not over when the questionnaires have been distributed. Respondent self-selection can bias the results. To combat unrepresentative (or merely slow) response rates, persistence is often critical. Firms need to send regular reminders to participants of the survey's importance. Aggressive solicitation of responses can be tried as long as it does not alienate or agitate participants.

Analyzing Survey Responses.   Some common patterns or techniques are helpful in assessing survey results. Listed below are a few of the most interesting and meaningful patterns.

Group comparisons

An analyst can determine the level of consensus and shared viewpoints across an organization by comparing selected data segments (e.g., staff level, business unit, and function). When two groups view the same process or capability very differently, this often indicates an unclear process, policy, or strategy. Figure 2.2 offers an example of how two groups—analysts and general managers—view the same process.

Consistently low responses

Participants tend to lean toward answering surveys positively, so a negative response from a large percentage of the group may suggest that a

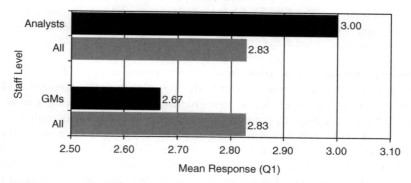

Figure 2.2   **Paired Comparison of Analysts and General Managers (GMs) for a Given Pricing Capability. Units are the Current Capabilities as Assessed by the Survey Respondents, on a Scale of 1 to 5**

capability is performing badly or is immature—or that a problem is even worse than reported.

Outliers

Isolated answers that diverge dramatically from the majority view generally indicate that a person didn't understand the question, wasn't paying attention, or is doing something drastically different (good or bad) from other people; the latter may provide a learning opportunity.

Survey fatigue

Evaluators must watch for a pattern of answers after which the responses are not meaningful (see Figure 2.3). A series of "I don't

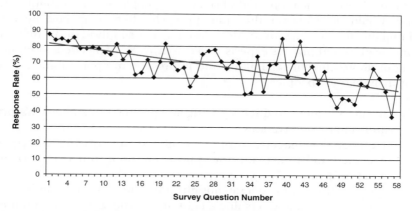

Figure 2.3   **Survey Fatigue Indicated by Declining Question Response Rates**

know" or "Not applicable" selections, particularly in the later sections of the survey, may indicate that the participant lost interest and was no longer providing accurate answers; suspect responses should be discarded.

Carrying Out Diagnostic Interviews.   Interviewing stakeholders requires significant time commitment from both interviewers and interviewees but yields some of the most valuable information. When questioning a participant about a pricing or profitability management process, an interviewer can assess both verbal and nonverbal (body language) cues to discern which answers are most accurate—or doubtful. To encourage candid responses, interviewers can offer to preserve anonymity by reporting results only in summary format so that a response cannot be attributed to a respondent.

Interview questions should be developed based on the need to do the following:

Investigate the business's current state. Employees should be asked about pricing processes and capabilities from strategy through execution. When issues are identified, firms need to have prepared probing follow-up questions to determine the root causes of problems.

Understand the desired future state of the process. Interviewees—particularly from the leadership team—should be invited to give their thoughts on how pricing and profitability could be improved. Employees might have great ideas, but they might not previously have had an opportunity to share them.

Interviewee Selection.   Interviewees can be selected either from a list of key stakeholders or by evaluating completed surveys to determine which topics merit further investigation (and who the best people to talk to about these topics would be). However, the latter approach is likely to extend the overall timeline for the diagnostic. Most design teams simply identify the functional leaders and process experts who can provide the needed additional insights about current capabilities and improvement opportunities. They may include these people:

- Business leaders, to discuss pricing and profitability strategy, history, and general observations
- Functional managers, to offer details on how pricing strategy is executed and to explain how reports are used to manage pricing and profitability
- Line employees, to generate insights into the most granular level of price execution and to shine a light on the root causes of identified problems. These are the people who can explain how pricing and profitability processes are actually carried out day to day.

- Pricing thought leaders, the people in the organization who tend to be on the progressive edge of pricing, but who, as noted above, (usually) have not been given the means to convert their insights into action.

Two interviewees should be used when probing important capabilities or functions: a lengthy interview with one participant can be followed by a shorter meeting with a second respondent who can validate—or refute—the former's answers.

When the process is complete, a consolidated summary of responses can be created, which categorizes answers into meaningful groupings such as business, function, and, most important, capability. Discrepancies in the results should be noted because both consistent and inconsistent answers can suggest opportunities for improvement. Follow-up emails or conversations with outliers may provide additional information that can add clarity to the summary document. Evaluators should also look for responses that can be validated or supported using quantitative data. For example, if an interviewee mentions that profitability is *always* lower in a specific area, then it may be appropriate to validate that point using internal data sources.

Identifying External Benchmarks.   Information about how other organizations perform in similar pricing environments can be helpful in assessing a firm's capabilities. The first step in benchmarking is to identify the relevant metrics. Superior or inferior pricing capabilities will be demonstrated by data points such as average price points, price variability, price change frequency, profitability (of public companies), and profitability trends.

The second step is to determine which external entities are appropriate for benchmarking. Direct industry competitors should be the starting point, but high performers in related industries can also be considered as they may provide creative ideas and best practices that may be applicable to the organization.

Benchmarks change constantly and are often a challenge to track. Sources that specialize in the collection and analysis of key benchmarks, such as professional service consultancies, trade publications, and industry associations, should therefore be made use of. Pricing-and-profitability-related industry conferences and publications also offer access to the latest processes, policies, and tools.

Finally, internal data analyses, survey results, and interview findings should be applied to compare the current state of the company's capabilities to the external benchmarks—particularly the company's position with respect to the competition. Benchmarks can also be used to generate ideas for potential capability improvement initiatives. To capture gaps and opportunities pictorially, simple graphics can be used, like the spider chart in Figure 2.4, which reflects the situation at one company as an example. In this company's case, the biggest gaps between current capabilities and

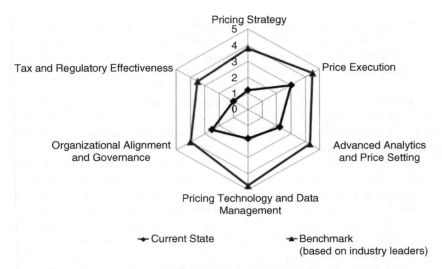

Pricing Strategy

Figure 2.4   Pricing Capability Benchmark Spider Chart

industry benchmarks are found in the pricing technology, tax and regulatory, and pricing strategy competencies.

Consolidating Findings and Identifying Opportunities to Improve Capabilities

The next step in a pricing diagnostic is to design the roadmap for organizational improvement. Management must first identify what its starting point is and then its goals for improving internal capabilities. Once the start and end points have been established, a strategy can be developed for moving forward. In the following, we show how a firm can mark out the path ahead.

Drawing a Picture of the Organization's Current State

All relevant data should be assembled and compared. In cases where the data points align, the pattern will be clear. But where variations or conflicts exist, additional work will need to be done to isolate the reasons and to determine which information source is the most reliable. The data should then be consolidated to paint as accurate a portrait of current capabilities as possible. Many teams fall into the traps of focusing on areas of personal interest or sheltering people (or groups) from less than favorable reviews. The value of the diagnostic is directly tied to the team's ability to provide an honest assessment. Any efforts to restrict the diagnostic—or the application of its findings—should be avoided.

When the combined findings from the data analyses, surveys, interviews, and benchmark investigations have been prepared, they can be put into a maturity framework (see Figure 2.5), which will illustrate the organization's current level of pricing maturity.

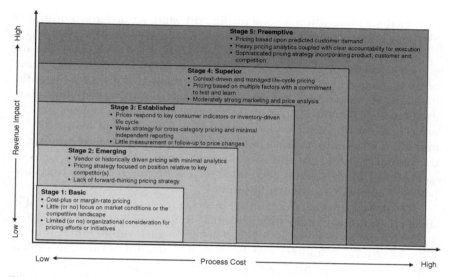

Figure 2.5   Pricing and Profitability Management Maturity Framework

Anecdotes and historical information often provide the *color commentary*, which can help reviewers understand why a business is performing the way it is. Illustrative examples should include both suboptimal and best practices. Figure 2.6 shows how an organization might capture the current state of each critical capability affecting pricing and profitability management. When the assessment is completed, it can suggest priorities for improvement and directly contribute to the transformation roadmap.

Determining the Optimal Future State

Though the vast majority of time a diagnostic takes will be spent on data collection and the current state assessment, a good diagnostic should

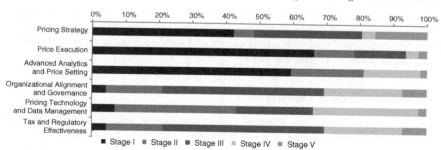

Figure 2.6   Pricing and Profitability Management Capabilities: Current State

further determine where problems lie and what actions are required to fix them.

The optimal future state of the organization is the state that yields the greatest benefit for an acceptable cost. During the data collection phase, best-in-class practices can be gathered and promoted as goals for the entire organization to strive for. External sources (e.g., books, trade publications, industry associations, professional service consultancies) can be used for reference. An organization must determine what level of maturity is required for it to compete and win in the marketplace. That level may not be the pinnacle of the maturity model—each organization should focus on establishing a target that is best suited for the timing, resources, and competitive needs of its particular business.

To seek an internal perspective, business leaders can be asked to offer their unique views. Those with genuinely innovative ideas can be particularly effective in developing a vision around which the organization can rally. Long-term employees may be extremely helpful as they can explain how the business has grown and progressed with respect to individual pricing capabilities, and they can also help avoid repeating mistakes as they will be aware of failed improvement efforts of the past. Not all management techniques apply equally well in all industries; sometimes only a seasoned veteran can explain why capabilities will—or won't—work.

Diagnosticians must be on the lookout for protectionist or "this is the way it's always been done" attitudes. Employees with extraordinarily long tenure in one company can be limited in their vision and feel a strong sense of ownership for the status quo because they may have helped develop current practices. Those with shorter tenure (but with experience from other companies or industries) can help balance a narrow, or myopic, point of view.

A *visioning session* is often an effective mechanism for gathering useful input. A skilled facilitator can lead a group to generate genuinely ambitious ideas on the future state of the organization. At the same time, the mix of the group with a representative mix of resources will help keep proposals grounded in reality as each member will naturally think of how various proposals might impact his or her particular area. Involving employees during these early stages of pricing improvement can also serve as an effective management tool: the participants will become change agents facilitating the adjustments that are sure to come.

Conducting a Gap Analysis

Once the desired future state of the organization has been identified, it should be compared to the existing state to identify capability gaps. The goal of this exercise is to create a comprehensive list of the pricing management competencies that will need to be strengthened to reach the desired levels. A sample gap analysis is provided in Figure 2.7.

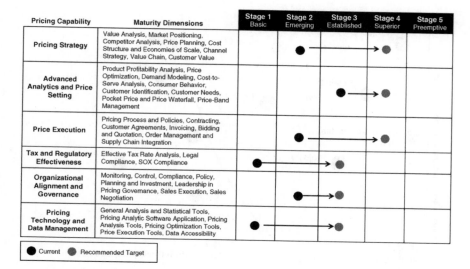

Pricing Capability	Maturity Dimensions	Stage 1 Basic	Stage 2 Emerging	Stage 3 Established	Stage 4 Superior	Stage 5 Preemptive
Pricing Strategy	Value Analysis, Market Positioning, Competitor Analysis, Price Planning, Cost Structure and Economies of Scale, Channel Strategy, Value Chain, Customer Value		●	→	●	
Advanced Analytics and Price Setting	Product Profitability Analysis, Price Optimization, Demand Modeling, Cost-to-Serve Analysis, Consumer Behavior, Customer Identification, Customer Needs, Pocket Price and Price Waterfall, Price-Band Management			●	→ ●	
Price Execution	Pricing Process and Policies, Contracting, Customer Agreements, Invoicing, Bidding and Quotation, Order Management and Supply Chain Integration		●	→	●	
Tax and Regulatory Effectiveness	Effective Tax Rate Analysis, Legal Compliance, SOX Compliance	●	→	●		
Organizational Alignment and Governance	Monitoring, Control, Compliance, Policy, Planning and Investment, Leadership in Pricing Governance, Sales Execution, Sales Negotiation	●	→●			
Pricing Technology and Data Management	General Analysis and Statistical Tools, Pricing Analytic Software Application, Pricing Analysis Tools, Pricing Optimization Tools, Price Execution Tools, Data Accessibility	●	→	●		

● Current   ● Recommended Target

Figure 2.7   Pricing and Profitability Management Gap Analysis

Building and Prioritizing the Opportunity List.   The opportunities to improve capabilities through a gap analysis tend to be numerous and of varying importance to business performance. How can the list of initiatives be rationalized and scheduled effectively? Consistency in language and prioritization metrics increases the probability of success if the pricing initiative is competing with other concurrent company programs. If a company does not have a standard framework for identifying and prioritizing proposed initiatives, then one should be created (see Figure 2.8) that weighs factors such as strategic alignment, duration, resource requirements, expected benefits, payback period, and dependencies (tasks that cannot be begun or completed until other steps are completed or certain conditions have been met). The following list discusses these factors in more detail:

- *Strategic alignment* can often be determined through workshops or facilitated sessions. A meeting with all relevant leadership stakeholders can provide the insights necessary to decide which opportunities are most closely aligned with long-term strategies.
- *Duration* and *resource requirements* are the cost side of a cost-benefit analysis. Outstanding project management and estimation skills are required to determine these important prioritization factors.
- *Expected benefits* and *payback period* can be estimated using industry benchmarks. The high-level metrics collected from internal data sources can also provide figures to estimate potential benefits.

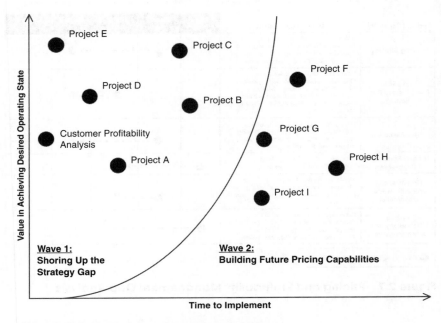

Figure 2.8   Initiative Prioritization Framework

- *Managing dependencies* requires project leaders to pay attention to opportunities that build on each other or that can be conducted more efficiently by using capabilities developed in related tasks.

Creating the Transformation Roadmap

A road map should be developed that details the path to the desired improved pricing and profitability management capabilities. It should explicitly lay out the sequence, duration, and dependencies of the individual initiatives so that stakeholders have a clear understanding of when and how their organization will be affected. The roadmap should be in a clear format that can be easily understood and distributed. A sample roadmap is shown in Figure 2.9.

Challenges and Considerations

Any organization can conduct a pricing diagnostic with some simple planning and by taking a structured approach. But here are some common roadblocks and challenges to keep in mind:

- *Concurrent initiatives and conflicting priorities.* Pricing and profitability transformations require greater focus than many other initiatives. This is primarily because pricing is an often contentious topic that

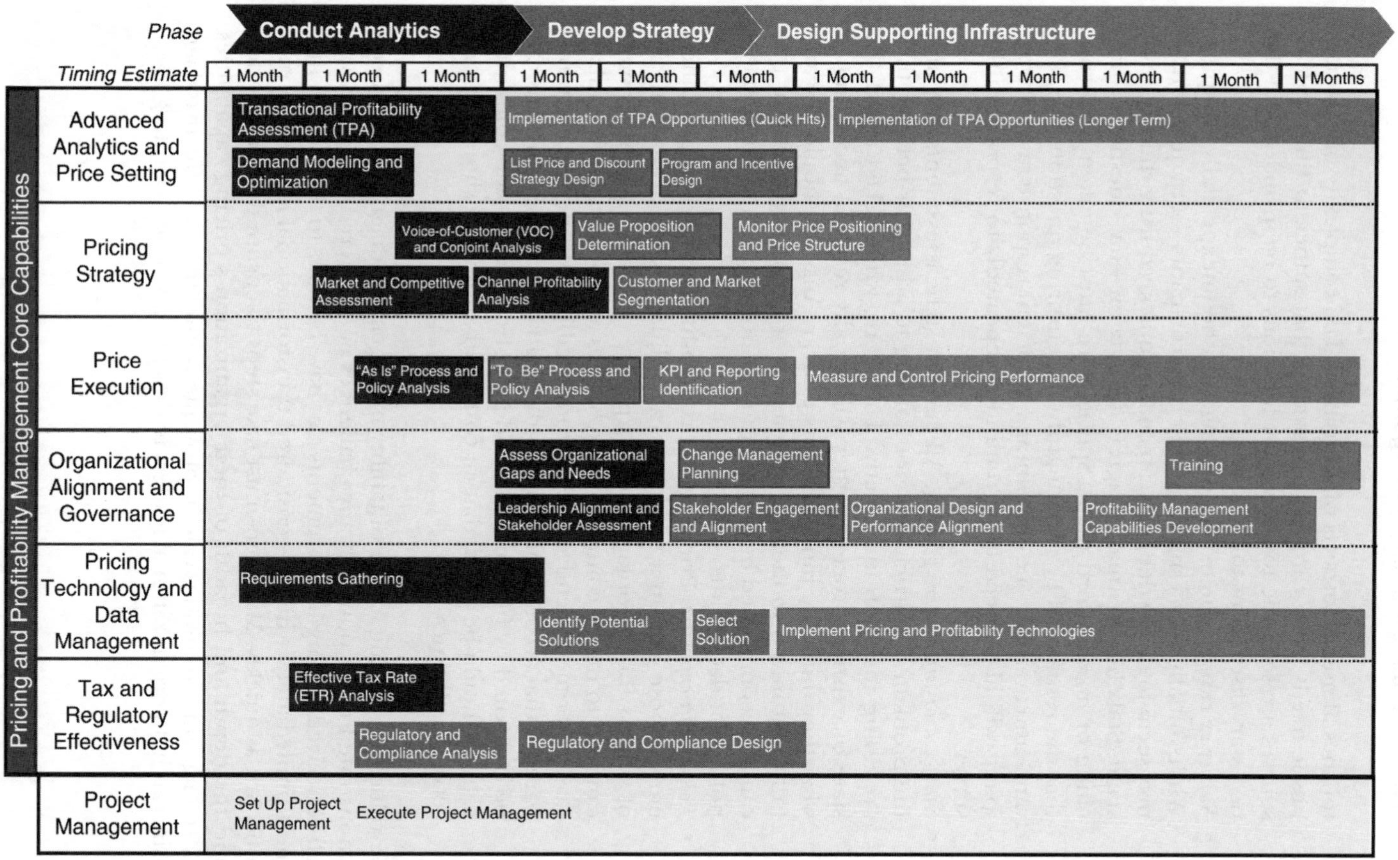

Figure 2.9 Pricing and Profitability Management Transformation Road Map

touches almost all aspects of a business. The complexity of the diagnostic needs to be carefully assessed so that sufficient time and resources are set aside to allow most functions to be included and the necessary discussions to be held.

- *Survey execution.* The execution stage can be unexpectedly complex. While initially only a small number of participants—and questions— may seem to be needed, this can change quickly during the planning stage. Stakeholders may disagree strongly on what questions to include or how to word them. Special care must be taken to ensure that the results will be meaningful (i.e., ensuring questions are relevant) and available (i.e., obtaining a sufficient response rate). Participants will likely need to be reminded repeatedly to respond to the survey.
- *Survey and interviewee gaming.* All current state assessments run into the problem of participants not wanting to admit (or believe) they are doing their job incorrectly. Therefore, when asked about the state of existing processes, they will usually respond according to what they think the inquirer wants to hear. Answers should be carefully scrutinized to identify misleading or errant information: this can be accomplished by triangulating responses from multiple stakeholders or data points.
- *Leadership exposure.* Pricing and profitability transformations inherently expose gaps in a business's capabilities. As the primary metric of success for any organization, exposure of profit mismanagement can lead to highly contentious exchanges and be potentially embarrassing. Some executives are uncomfortable with the level of transparency that accompanies this kind of initiative. These emotions can be combated by fully briefing leaders upfront. Blind-side communications should be avoided at all costs, and anonymity should be preserved at all times.

The value of a pricing and profitability management diagnostic has been demonstrated to far outweigh any challenges encountered along the way. Well-conceived pricing improvements can have benefits to the bottom line almost immediately, while ill-considered transformational efforts can ruin profits just as quickly. Managers must take steps to ensure that they understand the depth and breadth of their organization's pricing capabilities before engaging in a wide-scale improvement initiative. An effective diagnostic can help organizational leaders to develop that understanding.

3

Developing an Effective Pricing Strategy

What is a cynic? A man who knows the price of everything and the value of nothing.

—Oscar Wilde

Many organizations run into trouble when they try to develop a pricing strategy. An effective strategy should, of course, project the fair value of a company's products or services. However, it should also serve, among other functions, as a competitive signaling mechanism, a tool for managing capacity, an indicator of quality, and a means to drive customer behavior.

Unfortunately, many organizations fail to understand the importance and utility of a comprehensive, well-designed strategy. Instead, they allow pricing to proceed as a series of decisions, some reactionary (such as matching existing competitors' prices) and some overly simplistic (such as adding a margin to the variable cost of production). These tactical rather than strategic actions rarely extract the true market value of a product or service. In following this approach, companies unnecessarily limit their profit potential.

What Comprises a Successful Pricing Strategy?

An effective strategy should reflect an integrated pricing framework that supports business objectives by capturing the value of an offering relative to its rivals and customer demand. The strategy should guide an

A consumer durable goods manufacturer had grown significantly over the years, largely through acquisitions. Though it had absorbed different businesses, it had never developed a unified pricing strategy or a centralized pricing organization. Now, however, the company found itself facing fierce competition and considerable external pricing pressures (e.g., declines in the housing market and volatile oil costs). The sales force did not trust the outdated corporate price lists and did its best to set prices under a cost-plus model. However, without a cohesive strategy and policies to enforce it, there were extreme disparities in prices. The abuse of overrides put the majority of the manufacturer's realized prices well under the corporate minimums.

The company had been able to overcome these problems while the economy was good, but when it took a turn for the worse in late 2008, the company's margins declined sharply. Management needed to change its approach to pricing—and fast. The company assembled swat teams and conducted grueling workshops with employees from all levels of the organization to discuss the pricing strategy. Within six months, the firm had codified new pricing policies, revised specific practices that had been draining margin, created a sophisticated customer segmentation scheme, and revamped the corporate price list process. The result? In less than a year the manufacturer found it had *gained* an additional $12 million in profit.

organization's internal behavior as well as its external communications to the market for all pricing-related actions. A pricing strategy must be:

- grounded in data and fact rather than in anecdote and conjecture;
- aligned with overall corporate objectives as well as other functional strategies (e.g., marketing and sales); and
- flexible, adaptive, responsive, and monitored.

Grounding a Plan in Data and Fact

Many organizations believe a pricing improvement initiative should first define the overarching strategy, and then design the processes and analytics, which must conform to the strategy. However, a plan that is based solely on hearsay from the field or theoretical concepts of value is doomed to fail, regardless of how meticulous or accurate the subsequent pricing analytics prove to be. An effective strategy must start with a rigorous analysis of the relevant facts, including data about customers, competitors, market dynamics, and historical transactions. When all the information has been gathered and understood, it can be assembled into an insightful, cohesive, and operationally effective framework that will guide pricing decisions.

Because it can be tested and refined against a company's competitive and market landscape, a fact-based pricing plan is far more likely to yield the desired results than a plan based solely on theory or conceptual models. A company should incorporate a number of elements when developing its strategy including the following:

- market and competitive analyses to understand industry and market forces that affect demand, competition, and potential profits
- customer and product value analyses to assess how buyers perceive the value of a good or service
- customer and product segmentation to develop prices that are specific to buyers and products
- multichannel pricing management to reduce channel and distribution conflict
- a pricing structure that reinforces price positioning and reflects the variations in value that different customers place on a company's offerings relative to those of its competitors.

In addition, a fact-based strategy allows companies to run *what-if analyses* to identify key risk areas and important issues that might develop during implementation of improvement initiatives. Tactics can then be developed to deal with them. These analyses address questions such as:

- What if competitors decide to take advantage of our pricing actions to capture market share?
- What if raw material costs increase unexpectedly?
- What if a competitor opens a new plant, resulting in significant supply increases?
- What if imports enter the market and put pressure on prices?
- What if we decide to implement the pricing actions in only a few segments?
- What if we delay the pricing actions for a few quarters?
- What if our contracts do not allow us to apply pricing actions to all customers or channels?

Without compelling, quantifiable facts, firms often hesitate to change what they perceive as a winning pricing strategy. And, even if they have the necessary pricing data, many firms lack the tools or analytics to exploit it effectively. Thus, strategic pricing decisions become haphazard or reflect reactionary, short-term choices that are detrimental to the overall organization.

By taking a fact-based approach, companies can not only better align their pricing and overall business strategies, but also address a broad range of common pricing-related problems. Analyses of historic transaction data, marketplace and competitor information, customer profiles, and other information can alert pricing executives to critical issues and their potential impact on strategic goals (which may focus on revenue, profitability, market share, or other objectives). Management can then assess the probable effect of corrective actions before actually implementing them. Later in this chapter we will outline the types of analyses that can be used to help companies develop robust pricing strategies.

Ensuring Alignment of the Pricing Strategy with Overall Corporate Objectives and Functional Strategies

Every organization needs to develop a tailored pricing plan that reflects not only its unique competitive position, but also its overall business strategy. An organization's stated goals may be to maximize revenue, to improve profitability, to increase market share, or some combination of the three. The pricing strategy, then, should be clearly aligned with these objectives. It may seem obvious, but if both the pricing plan and the overall business strategy are not documented and communicated, then conflicts may easily arise in daily decision making when the plan and strategy become operational.

Managers may assume, for instance, that prices should be set to maximize profitability when in fact the company's higher priority is to increase market share. Even if the market-share goals are short term (due to, for example, a product launch or a specific competitive threat), the pricing leaders must still be aware of them so that processes, guidelines, and metrics can be adjusted to support the overall business objectives. For this reason, companies should generally include senior corporate executives when developing the pricing strategy, which should be regularly evaluated and revised to reflect evolving corporate goals.

The plan must also be aligned with the objectives and strategic plans of specific functions. For example, Marketing's projected spending and campaign activity should support the revenue, profit, and volume goals of the pricing strategy. Similarly, Sales' incentives and planning should be aligned with the overall pricing objectives, so that sales representatives can reinforce these goals with every deal.

Misalignment of corporate objectives and functional strategies most often occurs as corporate goals evolve.

Creating a Plan that is Flexible, Adaptive, Responsive, and Monitored

Pricing issues manifest themselves in countless ways. Potential resolutions may have far-reaching consequences, so a company's pricing strategy must take into account the dynamic competitive environment and changing organizational priorities. For example, a new rival may enter the market or an existing one may initiate a pricing action that requires a response; the company's performance may alter enough that shareholder expectations are affected; the industry as a whole may shift due to a new technology or political administration; or the global economy may falter to such a

For example, take the hypothetical beverage company, Big Fizz, which wanted to change its strategic objective from increasing market share to maximizing profit. Historically, the company's sales team had been rewarded on volume and so utilized heavy discounting to close deals. But when Big Fizz switched to a profit-centered strategy, it increased prices and asked Sales to lower discounts. However, in a critical oversight, management failed to align incentives for the sales team with the new corporate goals. Thus, the sales representatives did not merely continue their traditional discounting practices, they actually *increased* them as prices rose. As a result, Big Fizz never achieved its profit goals and continued to operate with low margins.

degree that a worldwide recession becomes imminent. All of these scenarios (and others) may impact pricing decisions, so the overall framework supporting them must be able to adapt accordingly.

To be implemented properly, a pricing plan must be carefully monitored. Thus, the people tasked with executing the strategy need to understand current pricing performance at all times. Alerts should be put in place to signal when the strategy no longer supports the overall revenue, margin, or market-share goals and therefore needs to be adjusted. For example, if a revenue trend lags significantly behind that of the prior year, if planned volume growth is not materializing, or if margins are declining, then pricing managers should be alerted early so they can modify the strategy. An effective plan includes a set of metrics that can act as early indicators of trouble, so that minor course corrections or major overhauls can be carried out as needed.

Most pricing problems are open-ended and require unique solutions. A well-conceived plan provides the means to solve problems in a consistent, predictable manner. A plan that is flexible, responsive, and monitored supports timely, realistic, and profitable decision making.

How to Make Value Your Focus—and Why

As Warren Buffett said, "Price is what you pay. Value is what you get." *Value* refers to the importance or usefulness of a product or service to a specific customer or group of customers. *Price*, on the other hand, is the way to capture the value of a product or service offering in the market through the mechanism of exchange. Understanding these two separate, but related, concepts is critical to creating a strong pricing strategy.

Let's look at value more closely. Generally speaking, it correlates closely with the various benefits a buyer receives from a specific offering and its features. In some cases, though, value can reflect an emotional or irrational response to an intangible element, such as a brand name that has a special cachet. For example, the value of a handbag for many people lies in its utility; it allows its owner to carry many necessary items easily throughout the day. Ordinary handbags differ by size, color, and quality of construction and material, but they don't vary much in their overall utility. Luxury handbags, however, can distinguish themselves further with a segment of customers that believes style, design, or the elite status conveyed by a high-end brand name offer added value. And these buyers are willing to pay for the added value. While consumers may typically spend $20 to $100 on a standard handbag, a luxury one can sell for thousands or even tens of thousands of dollars.

Perceived value can be influenced by a host of factors beyond the obvious benefits of the product or service, including a company's reputation, competitive offerings, technological characteristics, customer service, and advertising. Value is also affected by individual assessments, such as the emotional, mental, physical, social, and cultural gains identified with the product or service. For these reasons, value can be difficult to measure and quantify.

While value represents an *analysis* of the market, the customers, and the offering itself, pricing requires firms to make tactical and strategic *decisions* based on measured value and their overall business objectives. Each product price should reflect a conscious decision by the seller either to realize all of the value or to leave some of it on the table in pursuit of another goal. For example, a company could charge minimally for razors—thereby sacrificing margin—to lock in customers, market share, and the promise of future revenue from its higher-margin razor blades.

In general, a pricing strategy based on the value of a product or service has the potential to achieve more revenue and higher margins than other strategies. In Figure 3.1, two products are shown. Customers' perceived value of Product A is higher than the price at which it is offered to the market: the difference between these two figures is the unrealized value that the company has failed to capture from buyers. Product B, on the other hand, has a lower perceived value than its price. Customers presumably would not purchase the product at the offered price, resulting in missed sales opportunities. Clearly, if prices were to be aligned more closely with the perceived value of each product, then Product A would achieve higher margins and Product B would gain additional revenue.

A value-based pricing strategy differs from other common pricing strategies in its focus on what a customer or group of customers is buying rather than on alternative factors (see Table 3.1). Under cost-plus pricing, for example, a company determines its costs in providing a product or service and then applies a desired profit margin to calculate a price. While this is certainly a simple approach to pricing, it doesn't capture the potential (available) revenue or margin for the offering from each

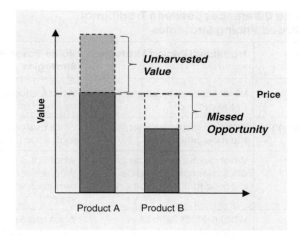

Figure 3.1   Value versus Price

Table 3.1   The Advantages and Disadvantages of Different Pricing Strategies

Pricing Strategy	Advantages	Disadvantages
Cost oriented	• Simplest to calculate and administer • Provides a profit on each sale	• Costs are very sensitive to volume • Does not account for market influences
Competition oriented	• Least risky approach for new products • Does not risk consumer sticker shock over price	• Requires consumers to perceive product as being truly similar to existing products • Does not allow firm to benefit fully from truly differentiating characteristics
Context oriented	• Provides a great degree of control over the price charged to customers • Allows for fine-tuning of embedded incentive schemes in pricing • Acts as a launching point for revenue management	• Puts a significant strain on many legacy transaction systems • Change management for price administrators can be significant • Potential to over-tweak prices
Value oriented or Performance based	• Provides the greatest revenue and margin potential	• Requires analytic effort to understand the market • Can induce customer resentment if product is Insufficiently differentiated

Table 3.2   The Differences Between Traditional and Value-Based Pricing Strategies

Focus Area	Traditional Pricing Strategies	Value-Based Pricing Strategies
Features	What features should be part of the product?	What features create value for the customer?
Customer segments	What customer segments are the most attractive?	What customer segments realize the most value?
Pricing structure	What product structure and offer variations should be created for the customers?	What value proposition structure and offer variations best track with differences in value?
Metrics	What metrics (units of measure) should be used in charging for the offerings?	What metrics (units of measures) best align the price with the value created?
Price levels	What price level is consistent with the customer's willingness to pay?	What price levels best reflect the differential value provided to various customer segments?
Training and tools	What training will the sales force need to explain the product?	What tools and training will allow the sales force to sell the value effectively?

customer or customer segment. In addition, it can be fraught with errors. In many industries, calculating unit costs accurately can be difficult because they can change based on volume. With a value-based pricing strategy, on the other hand, a company begins by understanding how each customer segment values its offering and then calculates a price aimed at capturing that value (both tangible and intangible). Table 3.2 lists the differences between traditional and value-based pricing strategies for key focus areas.

Formulating a Value-Based Pricing Strategy

To develop a value-based pricing strategy, a company must first determine the value of its offerings. This can be challenging given the number and variety of factors that must be considered. As discussed earlier in the chapter, customers perceive value through logical, practical, and rational criteria as well as through emotional (e.g., a teenager placing high value on an acne medication), psychological (e.g., a parent valuing a fire alarm system that gives peace of mind at night), and irrational criteria (e.g., a strong aversion to the color blue), which are all are extremely difficult to identify and measure.

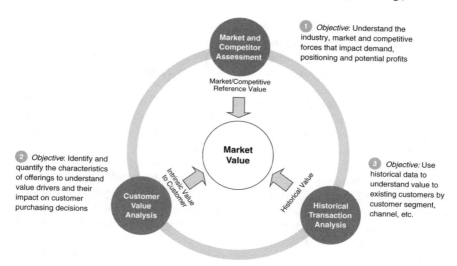

Figure 3.2   Three Approaches for Estimating Market Value

Three types of analyses can help calculate or approximate the market value of a product or service (see Figure 3.2). Each analysis can individually provide a helpful assessment, but the analyses should be combined to provide the most accurate estimate of value. The types of analyses are:

- *Market and competitor assessment*: identifying the industry forces and competitive behaviors that impact the seller's pricing ability
- *Customer value analysis*: understanding what product characteristics customers will pay for
- *Historical transaction analysis*: assessing the willingness to pay and price elasticity of existing customers and offerings.

Each of these three approaches on its own is not sufficient for developing a pricing strategy. For example, a customer value analysis that researches what consumers are willing to pay for is meaningful only if the pricing team also fully understands the product's position in the marketplace and competitors' prices. Used together, the three approaches can generate powerful insights. They provide a more complete picture of market value, and they can also validate the findings of and build confidence in the individual analysis areas.

Customer Value Analysis

Companies can make more profitable pricing decisions by:

- quantifying the value that customers and market segments place on their offerings

- identifying and prioritizing product or service features that influence customer perceptions
- setting prices based on the value buyers receive rather than on internally generated cost calculations or markup formulas.

The information gained through this type of value analysis can also help firms develop segment-specific value propositions, better competitive positioning, improved product or service development, stronger marketing communications, and more effective selling tactics.

In essence, this kind of value analysis pays homage to the business adage "Give customers what they want." It requires understanding what product characteristics buyers value and how these impact purchasing decisions. No single standard methodology exists for assessing customer value. Companies approach the task from many different angles, depending on how distanced they are from customers, how much time they have to make pricing decisions, and how much their organizations already understand about customer tradeoffs. Three typical tools are:

- voice-about-customer analysis
- voice-of-customer analysis
- conjoint analysis.

Marketers often make the mistake of concentrating more on a product's specific characteristics rather than on how consumers weigh the individual elements against each other. Thus, when readying a product for launch, firms may find it difficult to determine a price that captures how customers prioritize a product's features. Using these standard tools can help—as can effective segmentation, which we will discuss in the following.

Voice-About-Customer Analysis.   Voice-about-customer (VAC) is a qualitative approach for assessing customer value. Interviews and surveys are used to gather information from key stakeholders in Sales and Marketing, including field representatives who interact with customers on a regular basis. VAC is the easiest form of customer value analysis to execute because data can generally be collected and analyzed faster when from internal sources. Also, as this approach doesn't require any interaction with customers, no new communication channels need be developed. However, VAC also produces the most uncertain results of the three approaches because the analysis depends heavily on internal perspectives, which may not always represent the true nature of the market and can reflect personal biases or long-standing beliefs.

To limit the shortcomings of the VAC approach, companies must choose the right internal personnel to consult and use a hypothesis-driven interview approach. A VAC effort should target the individuals who interact the most with customers and, if they are available, those who conduct market research. A direct sales force can provide valuable insights if it has an ongoing relationship with clients and it can provide specific examples of the value trade-offs customers make. Companies can leverage the current market research they already possess to help design and validate interview and survey questions.

VAC should be conducted in two steps, which will help distill the results into key themes rather than producing unrelated findings that make it difficult to generate general insights.

1. *Build a list of value drivers* reflecting which characteristics of the product or service customers value. This will help the company to form hypotheses on their respective weights in purchasing decisions. The drivers can be determined after conducting a few introductory interviews and drawing on existing market research. The more a firm already knows about the tradeoffs made by customers when making purchasing decisions, the more relevant the hypotheses.
2. *Evaluate and assess* the information to validate hypotheses and determine how influential each driver is in relation to the others.

A note of caution: when conducting VAC surveys and interviews, management should take into account how personal biases or underlying motives may distort findings. For example, a senior sales executive might exaggerate the impact that his sales representatives have on customers to argue for an increased budget or an expanded organization.

Voice-of-Customer Analysis. Getting feedback from past, current, and potential future customers on products is critical. Voice-of-customer (VOC) research provides a tool for doing this. It is usually conducted through a variety of channels, including interviews, surveys, and focus groups. In contrast to VAC analysis, which offers more freedom to follow leads and develop hypotheses, the VOC approach is highly structured and tends to be more time-intensive. Data collection vehicles must be designed and adequate time allowed for a sufficient number of responses to be gathered to draw meaningful conclusions. Then, of course, the results must be analyzed. Often, a VOC analysis follows a VAC analysis to confirm or deny the hypotheses internal personnel have made regarding customer value drivers and tradeoffs.

Companies should assemble a list of customer preferences in advance of conducting a VOC analysis; otherwise, it may include haphazard or arbitrary questions that will not produce actionable conclusions. The entire VOC effort could, in fact, be wasted if a key attribute is overlooked in the rush to move toward data collection. Like VAC analysis, it has two key steps:

1. *Identify the audience.* The group must be diverse enough to represent the different segments the product might appeal to and large enough to produce adequate response rates (i.e., a statistically significant sample size). Research participants should be customers who have had a fair amount of exposure to the market in general; that is, they should know both the target product and its competitors. This will enable them to provide a more seasoned perspective on the importance of different product or service attributes as value drivers. Both preferred *and* difficult customers should be included. VOC analyses that focus only on the buyers who provide favorable feedback will result in greatly skewed, and therefore invalid, findings.

2. *Design the data collection vehicle.* Surveys are the most typical format for data collection because they can reach the broadest audience and gather data on a wide variety of topics. However, survey fatigue is a real phenomenon that not only affects the accuracy of the results, but also can alienate customers. Firms should consider the tolerance levels of survey participants when assembling the questions. Simple analyses should be run on the number of "I don't know" or "Not applicable" responses in the later sections of the survey to determine if the results are skewed by fatigue.

Other data collection formats include interviews and focus groups, both of which limit the number of customers who can be reached due to time and budget constraints. However, these formats do allow questions to be adapted in real-time based on participant responses. Often companies opt for a combined approach: surveys to a broad audience followed by interviews or focus groups with a select subset of participants to gain additional insight into key customer segments.

One significant way that the VAC approach differs from the VOC is in the number of discrete versus open-ended questions that are asked. By using a defined set of criteria, one can determine how purchasing decisions vary between the different customer groups surveyed. In the example provided in Figure 3.3, the criteria on the left and the adjacent colored bars show how three segments might differ.

VOC analysis is an effective way of identifying the tradeoffs and understanding the value of each offering's features relative to each other. The analysis can provide adequate insights into setting the pricing strategy.

Conjoint Analysis.   To move a step beyond the relative, qualitative insights of VOC analysis, companies can use conjoint (*considered jointly*) analysis. This market research technique requires significant time and effort, but yields the most in-depth information of the three value analysis tools to

Relative Importance of Attributes

Service Attributes			
Technical/Hotline Service	71%	22%	7%
Brand/Reputation	63%	26%	11%
Vendor/Sales Relationship	42%	47%	11%
Field Service	37%	40%	23%
Total Cost of Ownership	22%	38%	40%
Reliability	13%	49%	38%
Quality/Accuracy	22%	37%	41%
Breadth of Tests	16%	21%	63%
Price	13%	21%	66%

Figure 3.3   Voice-About-Customer (VAC) Analysis by Customer Group

companies preparing to craft pricing strategies. Considering the investment needed, it should generally be used only if it can generate major insights; that is, when market trends and customer preferences are not well known, or when VOC research fails to validate management's current perspective.

Conjoint analysis forces customers to make tradeoffs when choosing between hypothetical offerings. In theory, buyers find it easier to consider attributes jointly (as part of a product or service profile) than evaluating them in isolation. In a conjoint study, a survey will present respondents with profiles and ask them to either choose one profile from a list containing two or three or state the likelihood of their purchasing a particular profile. Conjoint analysis asks questions that are more tangible for customers because it simulates decisions that buyers confront in the real world. Figure 3.4 shows a summary of the conjoint analysis process, which is described in detail in the following.

1. Define Offering Attributes and Levels. A conjoint analysis is begun by defining the number of attributes and levels, or range of options, available within the analysis. Prior VAC and VOC efforts should have identified features that can be integrated into the conjoint offerings presented to

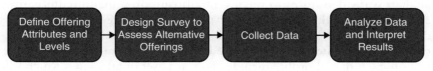

Figure 3.4   The Process of Conjoint Analysis

research participants. However, this integration must be done carefully. While more attributes and levels can generate greater insights and specificity in understanding the relative value of a good or service, too many combinations can cause the number of questions to rise exponentially and try the patience of participants. Too few attributes and levels, on the other hand, can limit both the survey design and the complexity of the responses.

Once determined, the most important attributes and level characteristics should be designated according to the principles that follow to obtain the best results from the conjoint analysis.

- *Objective attributes.* The buyer's preferences are not defined by emotional or aesthetic elements.
- *Multilevel attributes.* These can be qualitative (e.g., "car manufacturer" could be the attribute, and Ford, Toyota, and Fiat could be the levels) or quantitative (e.g., "number of minutes included in the monthly cell phone plan" could be the attribute and 400, 1,000, or unlimited could be the levels).
- *Attributes with mutually exclusive levels.* In this case, a survey might have an attribute such as "nights and weekend hours" and deliberately exclude overlapping levels such as weekends and Saturdays.
- *Attributes with unambiguous level definitions.* The survey can be very specific in its choices of levels; for example, $300 as opposed to $250–$350 or very expensive.
- *Independent levels across attributes.* To capture correlations such as price and brand, single attributes may be offered for some products but not others because the levels may differ between the products. For example, one attribute could be "mobile phone model" (and the levels could include iPhone or Blackberry), but a second attribute such as "keyboard" might be excluded because the levels are not consistent between the phones (i.e., Blackberrys have physical keyboards and iPhones only have digital ones).
- *Equal number of levels across attributes.* So as not to complicate the analysis and interpretation, each attribute should have the same number of levels. For example, the survey should not offer two options for "length of contract" and ten options for "number of free minutes."

2. Design Survey to Assess Alternative Offerings.   This next stage of conjoint analysis is divided into two phases: identifying presentation alternatives and establishing the sample size for the conjoint survey. The former are determined through the use of full or partial profiles. A full profile includes all attributes to be measured and keeps them the same across responses. A partial profile includes only a subset of attributes, which will vary across responses.

Sample size depends on a number of factors, such as the following:

- number of responses required from each participant
- number of alternative offerings per task excluding "None of the above"
- maximum number of levels per attribute
- desired confidence interval
- the expected degree that individuals may differ in their preferences and utilities (i.e., the value someone gets out of a good, or individual preference; e.g., Jack may get five units of utility out of a blender, but Susan only four)
- whether the objective of the project is to understand overall preferences or to quantify utilities
- whether the analysis is being conducted in aggregate or by segment
- the budget for the project
- the total available population that can be considered.

3. Collect Data.   A company should carefully consider which medium to use for conjoint analysis. Will participants prefer to be queried in person, by telephone, by online survey, or by paper survey? Participants should not only comprise existing customers, as they may reflect a bias that could lock the company into an existing paradigm and limit its growth. Former and potential new customers should be included.

Two types of conjoint analysis are used predominantly today: choice-based (discrete) and adaptive. Choice-based conjoint studies are accurate and easy to deploy in multiple formats (such as by telephone or in-person interviews). Choice-based surveys often include the option "None of the above," increasing the reliability of the study because a respondent is not forced to choose an unwanted option (erroneously suggesting a purchase choice that would not be made in real life). This survey format has its drawbacks, too. There are only so many levels and attributes one can test if survey length is a constraint, so tradeoffs will have to be made. In addition, because the questions or combinations of attributes cannot be changed mid-survey (in response to unexpected responses), the various alternatives offered to respondents should be realistic. They should reflect actual differences in product and not be included solely to identify extreme options that might change customer behavior.

The second type of conjoint study is adaptive. Adaptive studies are software based and therefore must be conducted online. Based on the respondent's initial answers, the software adapts and focuses on the subject matter most valued by him or her. This eliminates unnecessary questions that could be burdensome to the respondent and shortens the time he or she must spend on the survey. An adaptive approach can help to increase the number of people who complete a survey. The main drawback to this method is that the survey must be completed online.

Although computers seem to be ubiquitous, large multinational companies understand that many of their customers do not have them or prefer to interact with individuals for survey purposes. That said, an adaptive study can produce statistically significant results with lower demands on survey respondents.

4. Analyze Data and Interpret Results.   Interpreting the results of a conjoint analysis can be as difficult as it is important. Two major elements must be considered: attribute importance (the absolute ranking respondents place on the individual product attributes tested in the study) and utility score. Each attribute has different levels that receive a utility score, representing the importance users place on the individual levels relative to each other. While intuitively it may seem appropriate to make comparisons across attributes, the utility score acts as only a relative marker within the attribute itself and is not a measure of absolute degree.

Figure 3.5 presents an example involving medical devices in low-volume and high-volume hospitals (where volume refers to the number of patients and therefore the number of times the device is used). The choices in uptime (i.e., the percentage of time the device is functioning appropriately and not shut down for maintenance or repair) and price are fairly concentrated and tend to reflect the competitive landscape for these devices, but service response times tend to vary more among competitors.

Of the three customer value analysis methods, conjoint analysis provides the most explicit insights into the customer purchase decision-making process. It is, however, the longest and most costly to execute. In addition, it may not always yield dramatically different results from a well-executed VOC analysis (depending on the amount of market knowledge already possessed by the organization and the likelihood of conditions to remain stable).

Customer Segmentation.   Before taking the next step in formulating a value-based pricing strategy, a company should segment its customers, generally with the help of market research. Differentiating services and products for customers enables a company to create multiple price points and to increase market share (see Figure 3.6). Segments can be refined based on criteria such as value to customer and value to business. Once groups or *clusters* of similar customers have been identified and the purchasing behavior of the clusters understood, a company can prioritize sales and marketing efforts and develop pricing plans to extract the desired value from each.

Put simply, customer segmentation means customizing offerings, product attributes, and pricing for different buyer groups. This essential task enables a company to develop product and price offerings that will maximize profitability and minimize customer conflict or cannibalization.

Customer Segmentation Methods.   The four general methods of segmentation range from simple (based on buyer characteristics) to complex

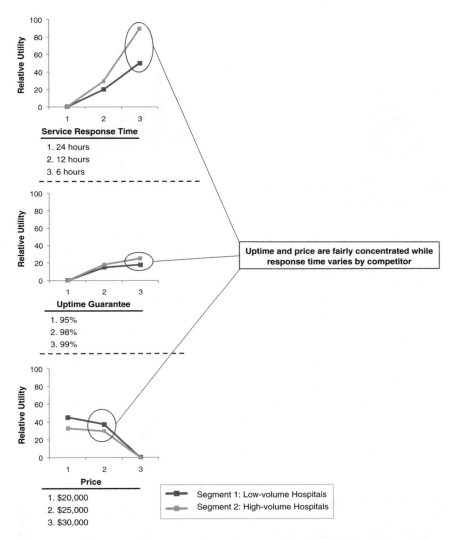

Figure 3.5   A Low-Volume versus High-Volume Hospital Conjoint Analysis for Hospital Devices

(attitudinal). They can be plotted along a maturity curve (see Figure 3.7) according to their level of complexity and the benefits realized by them. The four methods of segmentation are described below.

1. Customer characteristics segmentation

The simplest form of segmentation relies on customer characteristics or on the basic demographics that can be derived from sales data.

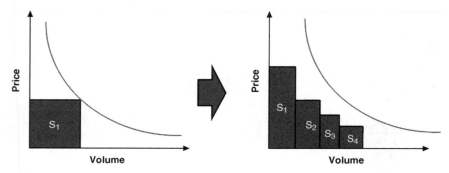

Figure 3.6   Effective Segmentation Can Increase Revenue and Market Share

Identifiers such as geographic region, the size of the client's annual business, and the types of products the client purchases can be used. An example of this kind of segmentation is presented in Chapter 5, "Advanced Analytics and Price Setting" (see the section "Conducting Transactional Profitability Assessments"). In that example, four simple segments are identified based on profitability and total volume of business. Also often referred to as *size-based segmentation*, this approach allows for rapid development of basic clusters in the existing customer base, but it doesn't reflect how customers value the offering.

2. Behavioral segmentation

More complex than customer characteristics segmentation, behavioral segmentation offers greater benefits. This method is based on how customers use a product or service as well as on how often and when they make a purchase. This information helps organizations understand customer behavioral patterns enabling them to design special

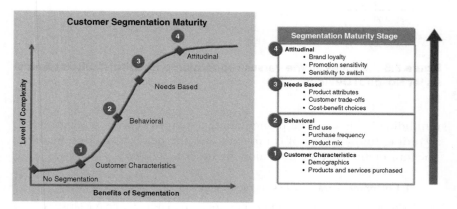

Figure 3.7   The Stages of Customer Segmentation Maturity

programs during slow sales periods or to provide incentives to encourage more frequent purchasing from a low-volume segment. Behavioral segmentation provides organizations with a deeper understanding of how customers vary in their habits and consumption of products.

3. Needs-based segmentation

Rather than focusing on the product, this approach targets the consumer. More advanced than the first two segmentation methods (because it is more outwardly focused and does not align directly with products), needs-based segmentation more effectively identifies buyer preferences, while addressing the preferences that will likely drive future purchasing behavior. Though it does focus more on customers, it does not match the needs of buyers with their perceptions of products.

4. Attitudinal segmentation

This is the richest of the segmentation methods as it provides information on how products perform in the marketplace, how much customers are willing to pay for offerings, and how they use them. The most granular approach, attitudinal segmentation cross-references products with customer needs and behavior. It also provides organizations with a powerful tool for understanding how perceptions of products and buyer needs impact purchasing decisions.

Pricing structures (along with individual price points) must reflect the differences of each customer segment to capture the greatest value. For example, if one segment prefers a more menu-based approach to purchasing (i.e., cherry-picking the most appealing services and components from an offer), and another segment prefers a premium, one-stop shopping experience with an all-inclusive price, then the pricing structure for each segment should be different.

Cluster Analysis.   One technique a company can use to move to a more sophisticated segmentation model is cluster analysis. Its goal is simple: to identify and classify customers according to the similarity of the characteristics they possess. Ultimately, the resulting segments are expected to minimize the variation within a cluster (i.e., so that the customers within a cluster are highly similar) and maximize the variation across clusters (i.e., so that customers across clusters are highly dissimilar to each other). When completed successfully, future customers, products, or services can be easily moved into mutually exclusive clusters reflecting very distinctive differences.

The best groups use a wide range of variables that require advanced statistical techniques to identify clusters. Note that the attributes or variables used to segment customers are often of differing forms. Some are binary (e.g., governmental or commercial), others represent an ordered scale (e.g., discount level), and yet others are data-centric (e.g., revenue in the past year). Analyzing all of these variables in combination can be a highly complex task.

There are two major methods of cluster analysis. The first is *hierarchical* clustering, which is often represented by a dendrogram (tree diagram). In essence, attributes are grouped in order of importance by category, and either a bottom-up (agglomerative) or a top-down (divisive) approach is used to create appropriate segments. The end result is a series of clusters based on the attribute similarity and dissimilarity among groups of customers. This is very useful when clustering products into categories or grouping customers based on their inherent similarities.

Figure 3.8 shows a dendrogram reflecting an agglomerative approach. In this cluster technique, nearest pairs, which are generally determined using a Euclidean distance method, are combined with the next layer or segment. This iterative approach can take a significant amount of time if there are a large number of seed elements (customers, products, or services).

To be truly useful, the segment outputs must be sliced at a meaningful level; that is, the level at which the business is managed. The number of segments helps determine how they will be handled. For instance, it could be that the dendrogram is sliced to create four clusters of customers according to certain attributes. These clusters then provide a basis for differentiating services and ultimately producing four separate prices. The prices could be associated with the costs-to-serve for the custome groups based on their attributes (e.g., customers who primarily order over the Internet versus those who primarily order through a customer-service agent).

The second method of cluster analysis is *non-hierarchical* clustering, which is built on a foundation of data and uses complex algorithms (see Figure 3.9 for an example). The most common non-hierarchical clustering technique is known as k-means analysis (or *MacQueen's algorithm*), and it seeks to combine data randomly into k clusters, moving customers from one group to another based on their nearness to the mean of the group. Each iteration results in a new cluster mean and, if sufficiently accurate seed data are used, the groups will almost certainly form again with the same key attributes, statistical outcomes, and cluster participants. The k-means analysis is not without its challenges, but the fact that it can be run across large data sets quickly, and the fact that it mirrors in many ways the agglomerative hierarchical approach, can make its results very powerful.

With both hierarchical and non-hierarchical clustering, as much art as science needs to be applied to interpret and apply the results effectively. Any theoretical algorithm can produce clusters meeting certain mathematical criteria, but the clusters won't necessarily be useful until practical knowledge of the business is applied. For example, if several new customer groups are identified, then Sales might note that two of them tend to buy-in the same way. As a result, the company might consider combining them

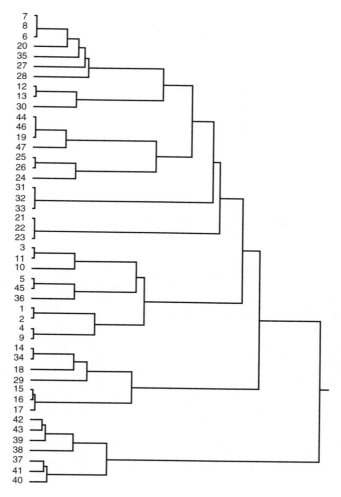

**Figure 3.8   Agglomerative Hierarchical Cluster
(Where Numbers Shown Represent Attributes)**

into a cluster. Ultimately, the combination of analytic capabilities and business knowledge should produce a series of clusters that provide meaningful insights into customers, products, or services.

Market and Competitor Assessment

Customers are only one group of influencers of pricing strategies. The overall market environment and the nature of competitor behavior are equally important in the process. Market and competitor analyses can help a company understand the forces at work in its industry, and the ways it might use

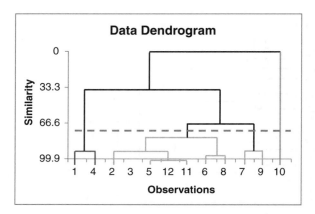

Figure 3.9   Non-Hierarchical Dendrogram

Consumer electronics retailers must cope with constantly changing products, many of which lack historical price references. High definition televisions come from a variety of manufacturers and have significantly different specifications, from screen size to contrast ratio. In this complex scenario, when a new product is introduced, what comparative offerings might represent the price profiles for retailers to draw on? The answer might be to conduct a statistical analysis of various attributes to produce a series of appropriate clusters. This exercise should make it possible to say *this* new product should be in the price category of 1,080 pixels, 10,000–25,000: 1 contrast ratio, 150–180° viewing angle, 60–120 Hz, LCD televisions. These ranges, developed statistically, are much more valid (and valuable to the business) than selecting groups by visual means or guesswork.

pricing to take advantage of these dynamics. These assessments evaluate overall market characteristics and look at how they impact a company's ability to succeed. Evaluation includes recognizing the power struggle between different actors—suppliers, buyers, competitors, and customers—to exert influence on one another. Competitor assessment can help companies understand where their products and services are positioned relative to the competition, on both a product feature and a pricing basis.

Three types of market and competitor analyses are discussed in this section:

- Porter's Five Forces analysis
- Competitor positioning assessment
- Economic value analysis.

These three tools (combined with customer value analysis) can help organizations begin to determine which pricing strategies might be more effective than others. Consider a competitive positioning assessment that leads executives to conclude that little difference exists between the brand perception of their product and that of a higher-priced competitor product with the same features. If a customer value analysis also suggests that price is the number one decision factor, then the organization might pursue a penetration strategy to expand market share and to build its credibility with customers.

Porter's Five Forces Analysis.   One framework for analyzing an industry is Porter's Five Forces.[1] Porter's analytical model takes a snapshot of the current environment and measures the influences of four dimensions on it: threat of new entrants, threat of substitution, buyer power, and supplier power. These dimensions drive competitive rivalry between the different players. A summary of the model and some example considerations are included in Figure 3.10.

Porter's Five Forces is a topic covered extensively in many business publications. This book will cover only a few key questions, as follows, for each dimension of the framework as it affects pricing strategy.

Threat of New Entrants

- Can new entrants provide lower-priced products with competitive margins to challenge incumbents' market share?
- Can the market be expanded into new segments with different pricing structures or lower introductory prices?
- How have competitors used pricing in the past to react to new entrants?

Threat of Substitution

- Are alternatives outside the industry priced in such a way that they encourage trial use and switching from the current sector's products?
- Do customers perceive adequate value from existing offerings in the marketplace or are there unmet needs that could be filled by other products?

Buyer Power

- How easy is it for customers to search and compare product features and prices across the industry? Is there a standard set of criteria customers use to evaluate products?
- What intangible features valued by buyers are included in the price?

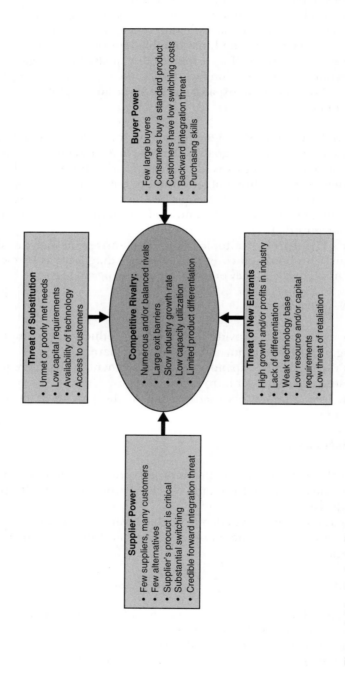

Threat of Substitution
• Unmet or poorly met needs
• Low capital requirements
• Availability of technology
• Access to customers

Supplier Power
• Few suppliers, many customers
• Few alternatives
• Supplier's procuct is critical
• Substantial switching
• Credible forward integration threat

Competitive Rivalry:
• Numerous and/or balanced rivals
• Large exit barriers
• Slow industry growth rate
• Low capacity utilization
• Limited product differentiation

Buyer Power
• Few large buyers
• Consumers buy a standard product
• Customers have low switching costs
• Backward integration threat
• Purchasing skills

Threat of New Entrants
• High growth and/or profits in industry
• Lack of differentiation
• Weak technology base
• Low resource and/or capital requirements
• Low threat of retaliation

Figure 3.10 Porter's Five Forces Analysis

- What is the concentration of buyers? Are any customers large enough to negotiate prices or to threaten suppliers?

Supplier Power

- How fragmented are suppliers? Do they engage in price wars with each other?
- What portion of a supplier's business does an individual company's purchase volume constitute?

Competitive Rivalry

- How have competitors behaved in price wars in the past?
- How critical are specific products in the market to competitors' financial performance?
- How adept have competitors been at capturing the perceived value of products from customers?

Competitor Positioning Assessment.   A competitor positioning assessment can help an organization grade its products' strengths and weaknesses versus competing offerings. Market position is a strong determinant of where price can be set. Assessing position requires a review not only of features, but also of more subjective areas such as the power of the brand and the perceived social status it confers. To complete a competitor positioning assessment, an organization must select the product attributes to compare (which can be determined through a customer value assessment, such as a VOC analysis), define the competitive set, and then score the gap between the organization's product and that of its rival offerings.

A competitor positioning assessment should be distinguished from a customer value assessment, which measures the perceived value of an attribute to the buyer, but not how competitors perform along those same attributes. In theory, one can analyze an endless number of product attributes, but firms should limit themselves to the ones that have customer value. For example, if packaging is not a value driver in any segment, then its value in a competitor assessment is extremely low.

The product's competitive set in the market should be defined next. Major rivals should be compared, of course, but new entrants and other companies that offer close substitutes outside the marketplace should also be included. Finally, for each attribute, the firm must assess the competitors' advantage or disadvantage in relation to its product.

In the example competitor positioning assessment shown in Figure 3.11, the degree to which the circle is filled indicates the level of advantage for the competitor. A fully filled or three-quarter-filled circle indicates a strong advantage; a half-filled circle indicates that the advantage

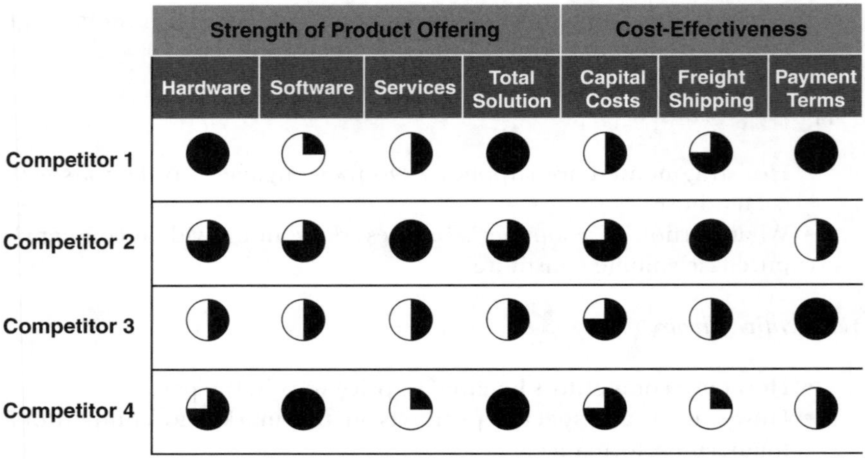

	Strength of Product Offering				Cost-Effectiveness		
	Hardware	Software	Services	Total Solution	Capital Costs	Freight Shipping	Payment Terms
Competitor 1	●	◔	◐	●	◐	◕	●
Competitor 2	◕	◕	●	◕	◕	●	◑
Competitor 3	◐	◐	◑	◐	◕	◐	●
Competitor 4	◕	●	◔	●	◕	◔	◑

Figure 3.11   Competitor Positioning Assessment

is about even; and a one-quarter filled or empty circle indicates that the organization's product has an advantage over its competitors. Executives can take many pricing cues from this analysis. For example, if a product is positioned above all of its rivals, then a premium or prestige pricing strategy might be appropriate.

Competitor positioning assessments can help organizations formulate an attribute-by-attribute comparison of products across multiple competitors. However, when the comparisons can be quantified, and customers primarily base their choices on measurable value, organizations should employ a more exacting assessment method.

Economic Value Analysis.   Companies can derive a specific value for a product or service based on its measured positive and negative differentiation against a competitor's offering. Known as economic value analysis,[2] this method combines a positioning assessment with a competitive price comparison. This method is best utilized when the benefits of a product can be quantified well. For example, if a company sells a cleaning product that lasts 30 percent longer than rival products, then customers will have to make fewer purchases of the product and therefore save money over the course of a year. In general, the more subjective the attribute benefits, the more difficult they are to measure; but this challenge can be offset by a supporting conjoint analysis.

To complete an economic value analysis, two steps are required: (1) determining the price baseline or competitor reference values and (2) assessing differentiation to ascertain the relative economic value. To form a price baseline, the analyst can draw on publicly available information about competitors' price points for their comparable products. In a business-to-business setting, where actual prices tend to be more difficult

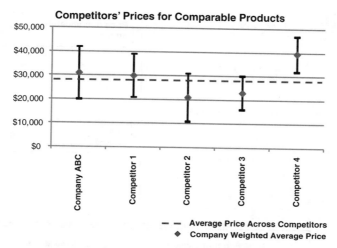

Figure 3.12   Competitive Pricing Landscape Analysis

to determine, data can be gathered from trusted customers, industry associations, and independent research firms.

Figure 3.12 provides an overview of the pricing landscape. The minimum, maximum, and average prices are plotted for each competitor. The red dashed line indicates the weighted average price across all competitors. Though difficult to obtain, firms should use volumes, if possible, to derive greater insights. The average price observed for each competitor can then be weighted by volume and flagged or color coded to indicate the high-volume price points.

The next step is to use value analysis to compare the reference prices for rival products. First, the reference value for each competitor is set (which is usually the average price observed). Then, product attributes that drive customer value are listed, and the benefit differential between the two competing offerings is calculated. In Figure 3.13, one example of a positive differential is the labor savings of $10 per machine. Attributes that detract from the offering's position relative to its competitors, of course, lessen the product's economic value.

By using economic value analysis, an organization can better understand its ability to price and capture value when comparing its products to its competitors' products. Economic value analysis requires the most effort and resources of the market and competitor assessments, but it pays off by quantifying both the value of the product in the existing market and its overall competitive position.

Historical Transaction Analysis

To determine market value, we have been focusing on forward-looking external analyses to assess the competition and customers. But when

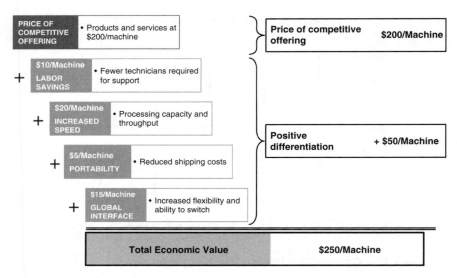

Figure 3.13   Economic Value Analysis

developing a pricing strategy, we must also look through the rear view mirror for another critical perspective. Historical transaction analyses utilize companies' existing sales data to gauge the tradeoffs between price and volume made by existing customers as well as the opportunities to refine pricing structures to increase profits across different customer segments. These analyses help companies refine their strategy by identifying which pricing actions have been successful, the degree of price elasticity, and the continuing appropriateness of existing segments.

In Chapter 5, "Advanced Analytics and Price Setting," we will discuss which historical analyses best inform strategic pricing decisions, including price-band analysis, price waterfall analysis, demand analysis, and segment performance analysis.

Designing and Integrating an Effective Pricing Structure

Companies use pricing structures to configure prices for their offerings. When used effectively, these structures allow different components of a product to be removed or added depending on how various customers value them relative to the competing choices available to them. The pricing structure also affects *price positioning*—the way in which organizations seek to reinforce a *price impression* with consumers. Proper positioning is critical because it reflects what a company wants price to communicate about the brand, quality, and style of its goods and services. It also helps a company to support its goals, with respect to not only revenue and margin, but also brand communication, customer segmentation and targeting, and channel management. Thus, companies must ensure that their pricing structure reinforces the desired positioning.

An effective pricing structure, working in concert with a modular product, is essential when establishing a pricing strategy that elicits the maximum value from each customer and market segment. As with prestige pricing (which we will discuss later in this chapter), even the cents portion of the pricing structure affects how buyers perceive value. Five variations of pricing structure are discussed in the following:

- list prices and discounting
- price bundling
- price fencing
- price menus
- price metrics.

Each of these structures can support the implementation of a pricing strategy. For example, if a company decides to use skim pricing (an explanation of which is provided later in this chapter) after an initial high-price launch, it can either use discounts to lower the cost to the consumer (while maintaining the list price) or adjust the list price down. The two options have different goals: the first is a targeted, short-term decrease to produce in buyers the perception that they got a deal, while the second is a long-term adjustment to encourage broader adoption.

List Prices and Discounting

Companies have long attempted to influence perceptions of value and quality (while maintaining price integrity) by setting a manufacturer's suggested retail price (MSRP) or a list price. Equally important, though, is the discounting scheme used to encourage purchases.

For example, by discounting the price of a different brand of potato chips to $1.99 nearly every week in a local grocery store (which will likely stimulate sales), manufacturers and retailers are signaling to customers that MSRPs are not the true price they should form attitudes about. The rotating discounting behavior conditions the customer to wait for, and value the product at, the familiar promotional price. This can be effective for highly commoditized products because customers will consistently look for the best price—they know that just because a bag of chips has a $3.99 label doesn't necessarily mean it is of a higher quality than a bag tagged at $3.49.

Although the list price may often be artificially high, sellers must weigh the risk of potentially undermining loyalty to their brand with overly aggressive discounts, which may encourage customers to price shop among rival offerings.

The reverse approach can be seen with luxury goods, where retailers rarely deviate from list prices. By not discounting, the retailer projects confidence that its product is worth the price. In other words, the retailer is communicating that it would rather sell to a customer who recognizes value than to one who is merely looking for a discount. A stable list price removes timing from customers' consideration because they have little incentive to wait to purchase the product. However, this approach may limit customers' trialing the product if they deem the price too high when compared to its perceived benefits.

Many organizations attempt to compromise between the two extremes, favoring price integrity for the list price, but also using some measure of selective discounting to stimulate demand when needed. Rather than make wholesale price changes, they use coupons, limited-time promotions, and loyalty incentives to target discounting to specific customer segments. These steps can help minimize the loss of price credibility because the discounting is neither widespread nor available to all customers.

Price Bundling

Price bundling involves combining multiple products into a single offering to deliver value beyond what the individual products could provide to the consumer.

> For example, over the past few years, cable television providers have begun to offer high-speed internet access and digital telephone services among other offerings. However, as they have expanded their services, the cable providers have found themselves facing new competition from satellite television, long-distance phone, and internet access providers. Competing on three different fronts is a complex proposition, so cable companies are increasingly bundling their services into *triple plays* to create new value. These multiproduct packages offer consumers the convenience of one-stop shopping and a single bill each month. They also simplify consumers' purchasing decisions and reduce the hassle of dealing with multiple vendors. Originally, the bundles even became differentiators themselves, while competitors struggled to close the gap.

Price bundling can be an ineffective strategy if an organization tries to buttress the margins of a weak product by pairing it with a high-value one. The overall value of the combined offering must be enhanced to entice consumers.

Price Fencing

Price fencing uses restrictions and behavior-based rules to force consumers to reveal which segment they most closely identify with. Price fencing is the art of capturing the varying perceptions of value among segments. In general, rules should be tied to buyer behavior and the attributes that buyers value.

Airlines, for example, use the Saturday Night Stay restriction as a price fence. Hotels have also engaged recently in price fencing, offering lower rates for full payment far in advance of the reservation date, while maintaining higher charges for flexible cancellation policies and rooms booked with shorter notice. Business customers who require cancellation options and immediate reservations are generally more accepting of higher rates. Many companies now create tiered pricing structures, limiting which prices customers can access by their purchasing habits.

A note of caution: price fencing can encourage buyers to look for alternatives. In fact, a buyer may masquerade as a member of another segment to take advantage of lower price points. A company using the price fencing approach should identify the key differences in needs between segments. It should then design the simplest price restrictions possible to capture these differences rather than creating a litany of rules that become difficult to interpret and ultimately frustrate and discourage customers.

Price Menus

Companies can offer customers the added advantages of choice and customization with price menus. These provide companies with a mechanism that allows them to compete in several customer segments at once. The menus decouple product offerings and enable companies to price each attribute separately, reflecting the direct correlation between its value and price. More creatively, a company might price the commoditized product elements aggressively to beat back the competition, but differentiated attributes might still be sold at a premium. This approach allows the company to attract both price-conscious customer segments and premium buyers.

Price menus do present bigger management challenges because firms have to oversee a list of priced components rather than one comprehensive offering. For example, national home builders offer a few basic housing models but then use extensive lists to maintain pricing for the hundreds, or even thousands, of available options and customizations. While price menus are effective when value is tied to physical products or services performed, they may not capture intangible value, such as brand perception. Some organizations attempt to capture these intangibles in the base price, but they also need to take them into account when pricing the menu options as well.

Price Metrics

The price metrics approach redefines how customers perceive value from a particular service or product.

> For example, enterprise software companies have, in the past, used per-seat licensing to determine prices. Customers asked themselves how many people would be accessing the system and then purchased the number of seats necessary to support the user base. In time, though, customers became wary of this structure. If some users only use the system sparsely, then why pay full fees for these seats? Emerging players in the enterprise software industry approached the issue by offering new price metrics. Rather than licensing by seat, the revised structure focused on overall software usage, tracking the number of times users accessed the system. The new approach transformed how customers perceived the value of the offering.

In general, by shifting price metrics, a company can differentiate a pricing plan and align the pricing structure more closely with customer value perceptions.

Identifying and Using the Principal Pricing Archetypes

Increasingly, companies have come to rely on several archetypes to address common pricing situations over a product's entire lifecycle. These archetypes can serve either as blueprints for an overall pricing strategy or as components of a plan. Pricing archetypes are not mutually exclusive and may be used individually, in combination, or interchanged throughout a product's lifecycle. All of the archetypes may be in use simultaneously at a large company that has many different products and products lines at various stages of their lifecycles.

While not an exhaustive list, the classic models to be discussed in this chapter are characteristic of typical pricing strategies used in the marketplace today:

- *skim pricing:* extracting the most value from the product adoption curve
- *penetration pricing:* aggressively entering and defending markets
- *revenue management or elasticity pricing:* changing the price based on the unit response and limited inventory

- *performance pricing:* deriving value from a product's benefits
- *prestige pricing:* conveying status, exclusivity
- *phase-out pricing:* discontinuing a product.

Skim Pricing

This strategy aims to maximize the value captured from customers at each point in the product adoption curve.

> For example, in early 2007, Apple was preparing to unleash its latest technological innovation, the iPhone. The company had used a savvy marketing campaign to generate high consumer demand before launch, and reviewers had applauded the device's capabilities and revolutionary user interface. However, the iPhone's pricing caused some consternation among analysts and potential users. Though innovative, was the new smartphone, priced at $599, worth hundreds of dollars more than most of its competitors?
>
> Within months, Apple had dropped the price to a more palatable $399.[3] And just two years after its launch, the iPhone could be purchased for less than $100.[4] Although the device itself was original, the skim pricing strategy Apple had used (and which drew so much attention) had actually been a mainstay of the technology industry for decades.

Skimming strategies are almost exclusively used in new product introductions when prices are initially set intentionally high. Early adopters, desiring to be on the leading edge of technology, have a higher willingness to pay. They are attracted by the satisfaction of being the first to have a desirable new item. In the case of the iPhone, the early adopters lined up at stores days in advance.

The graph in Figure 3.14 illustrates a skim pricing strategy during the introduction and growth stages of a product's maturity life cycle, when sales volume is low.

With new product launches, setting a high initial price can be a maneuver to obtain maximum profitability, but that same price can double as an attribute that reinforces the perception of quality. Skim pricing borrows the prestige pricing concept temporarily. Prices can remain high in the absence of competition until the demand from the early adopter segment is exhausted. This strategy can also be used to manage supply and capacity actively.

While many think of skim pricing as optimizing the price-demand function, it offers additional benefits. When companies launch new products, their manufacturing capabilities and customer support functions

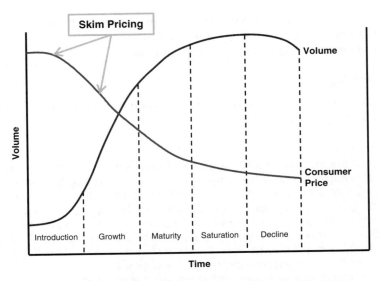

Figure 3.14   Skim Pricing Within the Product Maturity Lifecycle

may still be in their infancy. The higher price allows a company to manage the supply and grow the supporting operations. In addition, in the technology space, components are more expensive in the beginning, so the variable costs to produce the product decline steadily following the initial launch. While managing cost is not the primary driver for using skim pricing, it complements the strategy effectively.

Over time, companies decrease prices to encourage additional demand and adoption from a broader audience until the market is saturated. But this approach generally poses a sophisticated problem: When is the best time to *slide down* prices to lower levels to stimulate demand? Apple waited approximately three months before reducing the price of its phone. Was that the right time? Some in the media suspected that the price drop was a response to slowing sales of the device after its launch.[5] To determine the optimal time to reduce prices, managers need to adopt a highly data-driven approach. From market research and forecasts, companies can develop an understanding of the potential market size and the likely rate of uptake. Assumptions should be based on comparable products or similarly sized leaps of innovation from other industries. Both the market and the product demand should be closely monitored. Some factors can prove decisive: market trends seem favorable, production capacity is ready, or a competitor is preparing to launch a rival offering. Each of these situations may allow a company to trigger a fresh wave of consumer buying. The follow-on price is designed to stimulate new demand, as shown in Figure 3.15.

As prices drop, consumers may begin to believe that they are getting a deal or discount, as their only point of comparison is the original product

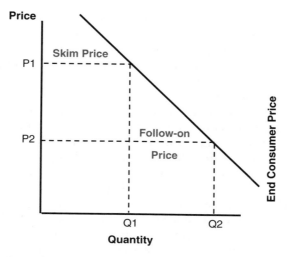

Figure 3.15   Skim Pricing Supply Versus Demand

introduction price. However, skim pricing requires careful execution. When Apple dropped the price on its iPhone, it experienced a backlash from early adopters who were angered that they had paid 50 percent more only months earlier.[6] Reducing the price gradually or issuing coupons and promotions without blatantly changing the original price should be strongly considered. Alternatively, a new model could be introduced which would help discourage purchasers from comparing prices directly.

Skim pricing strategies are strong *value capture* vehicles and work best in new product introductions. Mature products and most "me too" offerings are not good candidates for skim pricing as they boast little competitive differentiation. These products and services may be more effectively priced using the strategy described next.

Penetration Pricing

Vizio was launched as a two-person startup with less than $1 million in capital and became, in five short years, the top manufacturer of high-definition televisions in the U.S. market.[7] Management knew that, without a brand reputation or flashy ads to promote it, the company needed another attention-getter. Quality would also be a difficult attribute to tout when competing with traditional industry powerhouses like Sony, Samsung, and Panasonic. Soon though, skeptical customers were won over by the 40–50 percent price advantage of Vizio's products. Basically, the company used a penetration pricing strategy to take market share, establish itself as a major player, and build a brand reputation.[8]

Penetration pricing, also known as a low-price strategy, undercuts competitors and resets customer expectations over what products are worth. Useful in mature markets where competitive differentiation is difficult to achieve, price can substantially influence the purchase process. Southwest Airlines is another company that has employed this approach, much to the dismay of incumbents in the industry.[9]

Maintaining a penetration pricing strategy can be risky if a business does not understand its financial position relative to its rivals. It must have a strong grasp of each competitor's margins, financial health, and competitive psyche. Are competitors likely to match the low prices or to surrender that part of the market? How critical are those products to the financial wellbeing of the competitors? Answering these questions will provide some insight into the expected reaction.

A company must also understand its own financial state. Can it outlast a competitor in a price war? How does its margin compare to competitors' margins at different price points? At Vizio, sales overhead comprised less than 1 percent of sales, while in most consumer electronics companies it comprised closer to 10 percent.[10] Borrowing from the Dell model of buying components just in time, Vizio pays the lowest prices possible for components at the moment when a television is assembled.[11]

A common misperception is that penetration pricing requires a company to have the lowest costs. That's not true. It's helpful, but not entirely necessary to succeed. The ability to prevail with higher costs depends on the size of the warchest a company can draw on when taking on the competition. Deep pockets can help a company subsidize lower-margin sales, but only for a period.

Unlike skim pricing, where a high price reflects a certain quality, penetration pricing runs the risk of communicating low value to the consumer. To reduce the potential that low price and low quality become inseparable in the consumer's mind, firms can utilize an important tactic. A higher list price can be set to signal better quality, but then limited-time promotions and coupons or first-time buyer incentives can be used to reduce the actual cost. This approach also offers firms an indirect way of applying penetration pricing practices when challenging established players in the market.

Vizio effectively used penetration pricing to become a major player in the consumer electronics space. As demand increased, the company benefited from scale economies and increased brand awareness to drive profits higher as prices fell and a new consumer segment emerged, one that could afford high-definition televisions.[12] Penetration pricing worked well for Vizio, but the next archetype offers an entirely different path to increasing profits: raising prices with demand.

Revenue Management Pricing

As highways become increasingly congested with commuters, and as government funding has evaporated, states have struggled to find ways to fund new road projects. In the Washington, D.C., area, local governments are considering leveraging a lesson learned from the airline industry: revenue management pricing. This strategy, also known as elasticity pricing and better known as revenue management, is being used to ease traffic jams during rush hours and to raise funds for future construction of express lanes.[13] By turning certain thruways into toll roads, governments can discourage motorists from driving altogether during peak periods. As traffic increases, so do the tolls. Thus, commuters are encouraged to shift to off-peak driving times. Those who wish to drive on express lanes during peak periods pay extra for the privilege of a speedier commute home.

While companies implement complex revenue management systems built on mathematical demand algorithms, the underlying concept is simple: prices remain low while demand is limited but as demand increases, so do prices. The goal is to extract as much revenue from different demand segments as possible. In the toll example, the price for use of the express lanes at 6:00 A.M., while traffic is still relatively light, might be $1. A motorist might save five minutes on his or her commute. At 8:00 A.M., with traffic volumes peaking, the toll might be many times more, perhaps between $6 and $8. The same commuter, at this hour, could save 15 minutes. The key advantage of the revenue management strategy is its ability to extract the highest willingness to pay of a customer at any given time and to change prices continuously based on demand.

The critical distinction between a revenue management strategy and other pricing archetypes is that it involves elements that are fixed and perishable in nature. Airplanes have only so many seats; hotels can reserve only so many rooms; and roads can carry only so many cars before a traffic jam occurs. Special pricing software can help companies keep control of pricing in real time. This is particularly important in sectors where delayed adjustments can result in business being permanently lost. For example, on a particular highway at 8:00 A.M., a toll price may be set overly high at $20. The result? Most drivers avoid the express lane, and valuable revenue is lost. The window for an adjustment may be only half an hour, when traffic naturally begins to lighten again at 8:30 A.M. Thus, managers need to have the right pricing software in place to make adjustments in real time to maximize revenues before the opportunity disappears.

While the product in most revenue management scenarios is homogeneous, the customer base is likely heterogeneous. For example, different customers will generally value the same airplane seat differently. Revenue management is generally most effective in direct sales relationships, where price can be centrally controlled. As one can imagine, coordinating real-time price changes to meet changing demand in a chain of distributors, retail stores, and wholesalers is extremely difficult. Adjusting a price on a website, reservation system, or highway billboard is far easier.

While maximizing revenue in real time obviously benefits sellers, the downside is that it can condition customers to expect price fluctuations, which can undermine price credibility. In such an environment, customers may feel incentivized to shop around for alternatives or to delay the timing of their purchases. As suggested earlier, the creation of a toll road might incentivize drivers to change their commuting patterns. And though companies can gain a competitive edge by adjusting prices rapidly, the actions of a competitor might interfere with even the best-designed revenue management strategy. For example, if a rival airline decides to lower price irrationally in a market, management must decide whether to match that price or cede the demand to the competitor.

A variant of this archetype is *flexible pricing*, in which price varies according to demand, but is not associated with a limited capacity. For example, an internet provider may vary what it charges based on its current inventory and the demand for an item, but it can always request additional stock. Like revenue management, flexible pricing works best when the relationship between the business and the customer is direct. Another example of it occurs when a price is linked to an index, such as for fuel or raw materials, to ensure that a company maintains its margins. The flexible components in the prices usually manifest themselves as surcharges.

In revenue management models, the product exchanged for the price is fairly homogeneous and quantified. But what happens if the outcome is not as tangible? In these cases, companies have increasingly turned to another archetype.

Performance Pricing

On April 29, 2007, a tanker containing more than 8,000 gallons of gasoline overturned at a critical highway interchange in San Francisco. The resulting fire and intense heat caused the interchange to collapse.[14] This artery was vital to the city and economically important to the region, so pressure mounted on government officials to devise an immediate solution. The state of California contracted C. C. Myers, a company known for completing large-scale projects quickly, to rebuild the highway section. The arrangement stipulated that if the highway was completed before June 27, then the state would pay the company an additional $200,000 for each day saved.[15]

Buyers and sellers who enter into performance pricing arrangements share risk. If the product or service doesn't perform as advertised, or the quality of the materials is less than expected, then the buyer is protected and will pay a reduced price. Conversely, a seller earns more if the product performs as expected or better. Chemical manufacturers and parts suppliers sometimes employ these arrangements, earning higher prices for a lower defect rate, stronger chemical concentrations, or better capabilities.

Performance pricing also works well when the seller faces a situation where a buyer can't easily quantify, is skeptical of, or isn't willing to pay for the benefits a product or service generates without seeing the actual results. This is an excellent pricing mechanism for introducing value to customers. A company can invite the buyer to enter into a relationship, and the two parties then share any future success.

While it may sound like a straightforward sales tool to win over risk-averse customers, the challenges of performance pricing lie in determining under which circumstances and timelines prices will be set and invoices paid. These agreements require the same scrutiny as any legal contract. One must specify precisely what performance means, how the two parties will measure and agree on results, and what recourse both sides have to resolve issues. Why all of the focus on legal issues? In many instances, a performance pricing agreement takes place between parties that are unfamiliar with each other, resulting in some degree of skepticism. Protecting the interests of both sides should be a priority when entering into a contract, and the expectations of each should be laid out in detail.

Performance pricing also raises important financial issues that must be carefully considered. Because products and services will not be paid for upfront (thus delaying cash flow), a company will face the challenge of having to forecast and accrue for the most likely end result of the agreement. If the sales portfolio contains many performance pricing arrangements, then making accurate financial predictions can be challenging. In addition, while a sales executive may be confident in his or her product's abilities, the customer may use it inefficiently or not apply it properly. In these cases, a company typically establishes a base price to mitigate risk somewhat, while still providing a substantial upfront discount to the client. C. C. Myers used this strategy in winning its contract from the State of California. Its bid of $870,000 was far below those of other competitors.[16]

The benefits of performance pricing to companies that understand the value of their products or services might seem limitless. If the seller engages the buyer in the process and structures an agreement with a low initial price, then as the benefits accumulate the business will earn generous profits along the way—the rewards of taking a risk. But sellers have to take care not to jeopardize a fragile relationship with buyers. A skeptical customer likely will not enter into an arrangement that might require payments far above the reference price it initially envisioned. To address this concern, many firms cap prices and total revenue in these performance pricing deals. C. C. Myers followed this strategy, agreeing to a $5 million maximum fee with the state government.[17]

Performance pricing can overcome risk aversion, establish value, and align incentives for both buyers and sellers. C. C. Myers worked nonstop, completing the highway well ahead of schedule, earning the company the full $5 million fee. As a result, residents were able to use the interchange just one month after the tanker accident.[18] When executed correctly, performance pricing can greatly benefit both the buyer and the seller. However, in situations where value is well established and recognized, performance pricing yields to another time-tested strategy.

Prestige Pricing

Since 1853, Steinway & Sons has been handcrafting high-quality pianos that are a favored choice of concert halls, theaters, and schools around the world. Though it commands 98 percent of the concert venue market, this market segment does not drive Steinway's business results; only 15 percent of sales are to such institutions. Rather, the majority of sales are to individuals and musicians. These customers aspire to emulate the sound, but more importantly the status and exclusivity, of concert halls in their own homes and music studios. To enhance its image, Steinway sets price points very high, with buyers paying in many instances more to buy a piano than a luxury automobile.[19,20]

A prestige pricing strategy seeks to reinforce customer opinions of a product's exclusivity and quality. The price point itself becomes a lever to influence perceptions. Luxury fashion brands such as Louis Vuitton and Versace are other examples of prestige pricing. While these companies generally sell products that cost marginally more to produce than rival offerings, the primary driver of pricing is not the margin, but rather what customers are willing to pay.

Prestige pricing supports a luxury product's aura of exclusivity. Steinway pianos can be purchased at only a small number of preapproved dealers who meet authorization criteria set by the company. The dealers are restricted in what discounting behavior they can engage in and so closely adhere to the manufacturer's suggested retail price. The company produces a mere 5,000 pianos annually, keeping inventory scarce, while other manufacturers produce 20 times that figure.[21] Prestige pricing complements the status that owning a product conveys to the customer. With some pianos priced at nearly $60,000, purchasers of Steinways believe they are also buying exclusivity, as relatively few individuals and musicians can afford to invest so much in a musical instrument.

Similar to skim pricing, the high price used with prestige pricing can convey quality. However, unlike skim pricing, where price drops can occasionally be used to make the customer believe he or she is getting a deal on a top-quality product, prestige prices generally remain high. This strategy is more easily accomplished when customers cannot easily compare value or product features. Are the wealthy customers' ears so well tuned that they can discern the difference between the sound of a Steinway piano and that of a competitor piano? In fact, no definitive authority or accepted mechanism exists for measuring piano quality, and there are no widely known resources for understanding the specific features and characteristics of each instrument on the market. Therefore, customers use other more subjective cues, such as what influencers are using, the reputation of the product, and the price, to determine the value of their prospective purchase.

But a prestige price cannot only be reflective of a sales transaction. Customers expect a high degree of service and support, and companies need to factor this additional cost into their pricing. Quality must be maintained as the feeling of exclusivity and prestige will quickly dissipate if buyers feel they were cheated. Customers also expect sellers to maintain the aura of exclusivity. This somewhat limits the levers a company can pull. For example, Steinway cannot simply decide to lower the price dramatically in an economic recession to drive volume. The ripple effect of a perceived loss of exclusivity would likely affect the brand and future pricing for years to come. For this reason, prestige pricing rarely works well for companies with fixed capacity or with the need to drive economies of scale. With this strategy prices must remain relatively high regardless of slowing demand.

Another intriguing aspect of the prestige pricing approach is how the price itself is presented. Some research suggests that the cents portion of a price can drive different impressions. Robert Schindler wrote in the *Journal of Retailing*: "Despite often being considered similar to the 99 ending, the 95 ending was found . . . to be not correlated with low price appeals."[22] A prestige price will typically not include any trailing digits beyond the decimal, using whole-number prices alone. This tends to perpetuate the perception of high value and premium quality.

Steinway & Sons remains one of the world's most revered piano manufacturers and continues to charge premium prices for its products.[23] Pianos tend to retain their value (and usefulness) for a considerable period of time, and models don't differ dramatically from one year to the next. But other products may not endure so well or they may simply run their course in the market. The final pricing archetype discussed in this chapter will highlight a strategy that companies can use for products approaching the end of their shelf life.

Phase-Out Pricing

As advances in refrigerants technology make cooling houses and cars more environmentally friendly, government legislation has mandated that manufacturers of older coolants, like R-22, phase out production and eventually stop offering these products entirely. While new R-134a systems are constructed with less costly technology, owners of older houses and cars find themselves subject to rising prices and an increasingly scarce supply.

Many of these owners must consider a tradeoff: whether to migrate to the new standard or pay a higher price to service their existing cooling equipment.

Phase-out pricing encourages customers to switch to a new product or standard at the conclusion of an existing product's lifecycle. This typically occurs at a point when a company updates its offering to be more profitable or to include new features, but also happens (as in the case above) when government regulations or evolving industry standards necessitate product changes.

In general, higher prices should be used when demand is likely to decline gradually and sizable manufacturing capacity is still needed. By taking this approach in the case of R-22, the growing cost of operating increasingly underutilized production facilities will be offset as demand dwindles. The steeper prices will also encourage adoption of the new standard as customers weigh maintaining outdated equipment against purchasing newer, better technology.

Phase-outs don't always take the shape of a price hike. Low phase-out pricing is effective in the reverse scenario, where manufacturing capacity is nearly exhausted and customer demand is likely to decline more rapidly. With no need to offset manufacturing costs, the key objective becomes reducing the remaining inventory. For example, when the longstanding battle over which media would become the high-definition standard was decided in favor of Blu-Ray, retailers raced to phase out HD-DVD media and players at firesale prices.

Careful coordination is clearly critical when one offering is being phased out in favor of another that is entering the market. If skim pricing is used for the new offering's launch, then the phase-out strategy for the old offering should mirror the price changes of the new one. R-22 will continue to increase in price until its manufacture is no longer permitted in 2020, but by then the government hopes that the vast majority of refrigerants equipment will be serviced with the newer R-134a compound.

One drawback with phase-out pricing is that it can alienate customers or cause them to search for alternatives. A decision to stick with a particular manufacturer, which may once have been automatic for a customer, may now be questioned—even if the replacement product has a higher value with better features than the original. To mitigate this risk, firms can provide incentives for a customer to purchase the new product while phasing out the old one. Loyalty discounts on new cars are a prime example of this practice. Another option involves attaching promotional coupons to an old product to incentivize buyers to try the new one.

Critical Challenges Faced by Pricing Strategists

Most efforts to develop winning pricing strategies begin with admirable goals, but run aground during the implementation stage. Myriad problems crop up, from the availability of relevant market research data to the functionality of existing technology systems. This section highlights typical challenges confronting organizations and the actions that should be considered to mitigate them.

Challenge: Market Research Is Expensive or Unavailable

Interviewing customers and stakeholders directly can be costly in time and money. Companies launching new products often face this problem because extensive market research is required. In some cases, a product is so revolutionary that secondary research options (e.g., industry reports, news articles, or customer Internet forums) don't yet exist. For these situations, a proxy product launch can be used to shed light on how customers might react. For example, if a company is releasing a new trend-setting phone, then the pricing strategy, market conditions, and customer preferences revealed in the earlier launch of another breakthrough handheld device may prove relevant. Industry influencers can also be instrumental in understanding and predicting customer needs.

Challenge: Competitors Behave Irrationally

Some rivals understand the marketplace, their financial levers, and customer needs better than others. Smart sellers make shrewd pricing decisions to advance their strategies, while irrational players use price as an emergency lever to drive volume without considering the impact on the market. For instance, a rival company might notice that its year-to-date volume is trailing the previous year's numbers. As its financial health worsens, the company might rashly announce a blanket price decrease. Your company should consider establishing a pattern of response to this irrational competitor. Every time it reduces its price, you could match the cut, or even exceed it a little. Though it will take time, as these scenarios play out, the competitor will begin to realize its actions have consequences.

Challenge: Intangibles Prove Difficult to Measure

In measuring customer value, intangibles are often difficult to quantify. How much is a brand worth? What is the value of having a product be a limited-edition run? To better estimate value, firms can use *aware* and *unaware* lines of questioning in customer value research. For example, participants may be first asked to indicate what they would pay for a certain set of features plus the brand, and then they could be asked the same question again, only this time with a *white label* (a non-branded label). Or two similar offerings may be compared and customers asked whether they would be willing to pay $0, $5, or $10 more for the branded product. While no perfect measure exists for calculating intangible value, asking comparative questions in a customer value analysis can provide an approximate figure.

Challenge: The Sales Force Needs Convincing

Persuading the sales force to adopt new pricing strategies can be difficult, particularly in a sales-driven culture. Nonetheless, it is of paramount importance. A sales team that has been accustomed to selling under a certain set of rules and guidelines (or worse, under no rules or guidelines) will likely be skeptical of anything but the status quo. To address this challenge, companies should consider aligning incentives with the objectives of the new pricing strategy. For example, if a mature product will be phased out, then salespeople should receive a special incentive each time a customer purchases the replacement product, but a reduced commission for the sale of a discontinued item. Additional techniques for aligning an organization can be found in Chapter 6, "Achieving Effective Organizational Alignment and Governance."

Challenge: Customers Balk at Changing Price Structures

When organizations introduce new, unfamiliar pricing structures, existing customers can have a skeptical, suspicious reaction. In this situation, an effective response is to consider communicating the reasons for the change, the benefits it will bring to the customers, and the new prices customers will see for products they typically purchase. These messages should be shared before the new structure is implemented as customers tend to be far less forgiving when surprised. Organizations should identify, in advance, the groups that will be most impacted as they pose a high risk of defection. The sales force can be an important ally in this effort and can help to prioritize conversations with those customers. In a business-to-consumer environment, an appropriate campaign can be designed (e.g., using advertising or social media) to get the word out early.

Challenge: Customer Segmentation Is Outdated or Invalid

Organizations sometimes attempt to leverage an existing customer segmentation model when devising a new pricing strategy. While this can work in stable markets, taking this approach in a more volatile selling environment can lead to misaligned pricing strategies. To test whether a new segmentation is needed, organizations should assess whether the competitive landscape has changed, whether customers use the product the same as they have in the past, and whether buyer characteristics have altered. When updating a segmentation scheme, organizations should not force customers into the existing definitions. If new or different segments emerge, they should be accepted. In addition, further research should be conducted to generate the needed customer value insights. Ultimately, the pricing strategy will be undermined if it is not drawing on timely and relevant segmentation models.

Challenge: The Pricing Plan Must Work for Multiple Channels

Developing a strategy that spans multiple channels, while still recognizing the intricacies of each, requires a balancing act (particularly in retail). In some channels—such as the internet or direct mail—retailers have direct price control, whereas in the retail distribution channel, final pricing authority might rest with the channel partner. While companies may be tempted to vary price based on the differing costs of doing business, they should also consider which customer segments purchase in which channels and the specialized needs being served. For example, if a store can offer a more consultative sell and help customers get acquainted with their purchases, then product pricing can be higher than for the Internet channel, where the transaction is more impersonal. Alternatively, a service such as renewing a driver's license might be more convenient to purchase over the Internet than in a physical location, thereby meeting the needs of a harried segment and justifying a premium price for the time saved. Companies should align the discounting, incentives, costs, and margins for each channel to elicit the desired behavior from their partners.

Despite these complexities, multi-channel pricing strategies offer organizations the opportunity to be more surgical in their approach, creating localized plans to address competition in different regions or to direct low-margin products into more cost-effective channels. Executing this kind of plan requires close cooperation between an organization and its channel partners. For example, if an organization is implementing a prestige pricing strategy, then channel partners and the organization must agree to sell at a suggested retail price—with no deviation—to preserve the integrity of the product and price offering. An integrated pricing strategy can support profitable growth across all channels, while reducing channel and distribution conflict.

Tips for Moving Forward

Collecting all of the data and conducting all of the analyses described in this chapter can be a herculean task. It may seem even more challenging to synthesize these findings into a workable strategy, which must then be regularly updated to keep pace with market and organizational changes. Most daunting of all can be the task of convincing people to execute the strategy the way they are supposed to—bringing the sales, marketing, procurement and fulfillment, and other stakeholders into line with the company's agreed-upon pricing practices. Following are some tips that have proven helpful to companies in overcoming these challenges.

- *Understand where you are before deciding where you want to go.* Successful pricing projects generally begin with an insider's assessment of the organization's current pricing initiatives. This assessment includes analyzing qualitative as well as quantitative input from the internal stakeholders who are closest to existing pricing policies and practices. With this information in hand, the organization can then focus its efforts on improving those areas that have the potential to yield the most significant returns.

- *Strengthen processes and information tools to enable rapid, fact-based decisions.* Does the company have the systems and software needed to gather, store, analyze, and report on historical transaction data? Does it have the necessary competitor and market research and analysis tools? Are there well-defined processes for getting the right information to the right people? Has the company clearly marked out roles and responsibilities for determining who makes which decisions? If not, then getting these tools and processes in place is a crucial first step to developing a fact-based pricing strategy.

- *Obtain—and retain—executive buy-in.* No major strategic initiative can make much headway unless top-level executives support it. Leaders across all the functions who are involved in pricing (including Sales, Marketing, Finance, and Operations) must not only agree to a single strategy, but also agree to provide support for major components of the pricing program, including establishing discount and negotiation discipline for key customers and segments.

- *Identify key risk areas and the red flags that trigger pre-defined response plans and actions.* A what-if analysis can help management evaluate the risks of a new pricing strategy and create contingency plans. Red flags (e.g., margins or volume dropping below certain thresholds, increasing salesperson turnover, and new competitors entering the market) can alert management to a new risk that requires corrective action. Organizations should plan how they will react to potential threats (which *will* arise) in advance. The understood responses should be executed with calm, cool actions.

- *Translate the pricing strategy into tangible actions to be executed at the operational level.* It should not be assumed that pricing analysts, salespeople, marketing professionals, and others involved in price setting and execution will figure out what they need to do on their own. Policies and procedures to guide all stakeholders' day-to-day actions should be developed and communicated.

- *Incentivize your team to promote compliance.* There is nothing like pay and performance measurements to motivate people to do what is expected of them. Companies must align compensation and performance metrics carefully with their pricing strategy. If they do, then they will elicit the desired results.

Endnotes

1. M. E. Porter, "How Competitive Forces Shape Strategy," *Harvard Business Review*, March/April, 1979.

2. Thomas Nagle and John Hogan, *The Strategy and Tactics of Pricing*, 3rd edn., (Englewood Cliffs: Prentice-Hall, 2005), 76–80.

3. Jefferson Graham, "Apple Slices $200 Off iPhone, Rolls Out New iPods," *USA Today*, September 5, 2007.

4. As of February 2010 at the Apple Store (http://store.apple.com/us).

5. Connie Guglielmo, "Apple's Jobs Cuts iPhone Price by $200, Updates iPods," *Bloomberg*, September 5, 2007.

6. Michael Santo, "Apple Offers $100 iPology after Angry Messages Flood iPhone Forums," *RealTechNews*, September 7, 2007.

7. William Wang, "How I Did It: William Wang, CEO, Vizio," Inc., June 1, 2007, http://www.inc.com/magazine/20070601/hidi-wang_pagen_2.html.

8. Alex Pham and *Los Angeles Times*, "Vizio Founder Follows His TV Vision; Low Prices, Thin Margins Spur Growth," *Los Angeles Times*, October 22, 2007, http://www.bizplanhacks.com/offsite.php/http%253A%252F%25 2Fwww.chicagotribune.com%252Fbusiness%252Fchi-mon_plasma_1022oct 22%252C0%252C4117363.story&src=http%253A%252F%252F www.bizplan-hacks.com%252F50226711%252Fthe_vizio_story.php.

9. Jim Ritchie, "The Southwest Effect," *The Pittsburgh Tribune Review*, 17 April, 2005.

10. As told to Mark Lacter in Wang, "How I Did It."

11. Pham and the *Los Angeles Times*, "Vizio Founder Follows His TV Vision."

12. Pham and the *Los Angeles Times*, "Vizio Founder Follows His TV Vision."

13. Eric Weiss, "HOT Lane Plan Comes With Promises," *The Washington Post*, April 18, 2007.

14. Heather Ishimaru, "580 Connector Ramp to Re-open Friday Morning,"ABC7 KGO-TV/DT (San Francisco), May 21, 2007, http://abclocal.go.com/kgo/story?section=news/local&id=5324143.

15. Ishimaru, "508 Connector Ramp."

16. Ishimaru, "508 Connector Ramp."

17. Ishimaru, "508 Connector Ramp."

18. Ishimaru, "508 Connector Ramp."

19. Benjamin Ivry, "A Truly Grand Monopoly: How Steinway Calls the Tune," *The New York Observer*, June 30, 2006.

20. *Entrepreneur Magazine*, "Steinway Dealers Report New Records at Annual Sales Meeting," March 2001, http://www.entrepreneur.com/tradejournals/article/72613046.html.

21. David J. Glenn, "High Percentage of Sales Brings Steinway to Westport," *Fairfield County Business Journal*, October 6, 2003, http://www.allbusiness.com/north-america/united-states-connecticut/1036883-1.html.

22. Robert M. Schindler, "The 99 Price Ending as a Signal of a Low-Price Appeal," *Journal of Retailing*, 82 (2006): 71–77, doi:10.1016/j.jretai.2005.11.001.

23. Ivry, "A Truly Grand Monopoly."

CHAPTER

Price Execution

Strategy gets you on the playing field, but execution pays the bills.
—Gordon Eubanks

A team from ManuCorp[1] completed a project to refine the company's pricing strategy. Part of its mission was to calculate list prices that would maximize profits based on current competitive dynamics and the products' core benefits and value propositions. Though the exercise had proved challenging and required a lot of resources, the leaders at ManuCorp were sure the investment would pay off once the new prices were realized in the market. After receiving the required approvals from Finance, the team sent its final price recommendations to the Sales Operations department to distribute to its field representatives.

When the new fiscal year began, the project team was called into the CEO's office for a meeting. The agenda was to discuss the recent decline in profitability of ManuCorp's products. The team was shocked. How could the firm have lost margin after implementing its carefully crafted new pricing strategy? With no recent changes in external factors (competition and costs), what could have prevented the new, scientifically derived prices from achieving their planned performance?

After some investigation, the CEO determined that several flawed internal processes and policies had contributed to the failure:

- *Price distribution and communication was poor.* When Sales Operations received the new list prices from the project team, it should have entered them into the forms used by the sales team during deal negotiations. Much of the information was entered incorrectly, resulting in inaccurate pricing reaching the field.

(continued)

(*continued*)

- Sales policies were inadequate. The company's existing guide-lines for prices (+10 percent (ceiling) and −10 percent (floor)) were neither considered in the price-setting process nor amended afterwards. In most competitive bid situations, the sales team would quickly go to the floor, and sometimes below, because no guidelines had been established to manage price exceptions.
- *Promotions management was kept in the dark.* No one had informed Marketing, whose promotional calendar was set months in advance, of the new prices. This was a problem because Marketing was already running deep-volume discounts and rebates on many of the top-moving products.
- *Customer agreements were not audited.* On top of the current promotions, many customers with existing yearly contracts were receiving additional discounts off the negotiated price based on volume commitments. Yet no process had been put in place to audit their purchases once the fiscal year ended. Many customers did not fulfill their requirements and received unwarranted discounts.

In sum, the CEO learned that the company's profitability declined because of a failure to execute.

What Is Price Execution?

The policies and processes that govern profitable decision making on a daily operational level are combined in price execution. In business-to-consumer pricing, execution more narrowly refers to the process of getting product prices to the shelves in the stores. In this chapter, however, we will address the broader definition.

Effective execution brings discipline to pricing and profitability management. It requires hundreds—or thousands—of small actions, dispersed across various functions and levels, to be done correctly. Proper execution can help ensure these actions consistently work in concert by using well-defined processes and clear policies to help define how prices are communicated, executed, measured, analyzed, and adjusted by every element of the organization involved in pricing management.

Execution extends from price setting and customer negotiation to performance monitoring and compliance. It should be considered *foundational* because all other pricing management competencies are built upon it. As ManuCorp's CEO discovered, a company can have world-class capabilities in all other major areas, but if it falters in execution, the other capabilities may not matter. The latest software and most advanced mathematical tools may be used to calculate optimal prices, but if these prices do not reach the market quickly or accurately, then the projected benefits will not be realized and the company could lose money on every transaction.

Establishing Price Execution Guidelines

For all the reasons just mentioned, organizations should make the effort to improve their execution capabilities, whether this involves a major overhaul or a simple fine-tuning of existing procedures. Generally, to achieve target margin, the implementation sequence should be (1) price execution, (2) price enforcement, and (3) price optimization.[2] Solidifying execution capabilities early means an organization will be better positioned to reap the benefits that come from improving other pricing competencies. These positive returns can be far-reaching for both the organization and its customers. For example, efficiently communicating and distributing prices or managing exceptions effectively are advantages shared with an organization's customers.

In contrast, poor execution affects the entire business, presenting many issues and obstacles to improvement, such as:

- Low compliance rates with profitability guidelines set for deal negotiations
- Slow delivery of price quotes when responding to customer opportunities
- Inaccurate quotations provided by field sales representatives
- Failure to manage price exceptions promptly and efficiently
- Increased time and costs devoted to price administration
- Creating a history of unsustainable price increases
- Tight control over list price, but no control over pocket price
- Unclear authority and accountability for pricing decisions
- No process for gathering and monitoring competitive actions in the marketplace
- Manual, rather than automated, pricing processes, which can result in increased costs, understaffing for the volume of manual actions, and a high error rate.

The good news is that flawed price execution can be addressed by taking some basic, often simple, steps to improve processes, policies, and performance monitoring.

Using the Best-Practice Pricing Process Framework

Effective pricing management is founded on clearly defined and documented processes. The simple act of documentation often reveals inefficiencies, poor handoffs (when the owner of one activity completes that activity and the owner of the next activity in the process flow starts his or her activity), lack of ownership, and other process problems. Careful process mapping can help:

- Improve standardization across locations
- Identify gaps between existing and best practice processes
- Better define roles and responsibilities
- Identify training needs
- Define performance metrics
- Pinpoint IT development needs
- Establish refined policies
- Identify necessary sales tools.

When designing new pricing processes, organizations must be prepared to do the following.

- *Standardize, then deviate when necessary* to strike the right balance between supporting the uniformity of processes an organization should strive for and meeting the unique needs of different business units and regions.
- *Specify roles and responsibilities.* Determining which personnel need to be assigned to what roles is a separate step, but should be driven by process documentation.
- *Incorporate feedback mechanisms* into the process design from the start.
- *Conduct periodic reviews.* to update processes to reflect changes in customer expectations, competitor behavior, and market conditions.
- *Align different organizational calendars with internal processes* so that pricing gives and receives the right input at the right time. For example, the segment price and discount structure for a product should be developed in conjunction with the volume and profitability targets set by Marketing. Similarly, a sales manager should have information about customer programs, promotions, and profitability for his or her annual account planning meeting with sales representatives.
- *Design with regulatory compliance in mind.* Ensuring pricing complies with all laws can be burdensome and time-consuming; but, with proper planning, it can become a normal part of doing business. Thoroughly understanding antitrust legislation such as the Robinson-Patman, Sherman, and Clayton Acts, and financial and accounting requirements under the Sarbanes-Oxley Act, will enable an organization to incorporate appropriate documentation and control points from the start.

Pricing processes have to be customized to meet the unique needs of every business. However, many pricing elements and principles transcend organizational idiosyncrasies. These critical features are assembled in the Best Practice Framework (see Figure 4.1), which shows the structure and

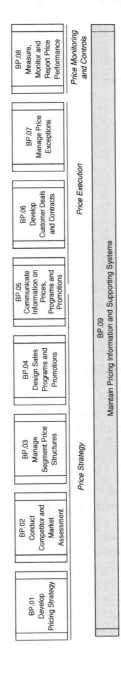

Figure 4.1 End-to-End Best Practice (BP) Framework for Pricing Processes

Item	Level	Purpose
Pricing Framework 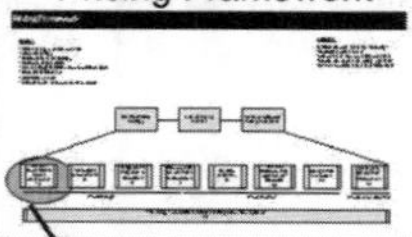	Level 0	Standardized process framework/overview
Pricing Processes 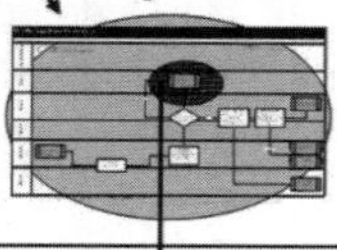	Level 1	Set of flows and procedures that provide a standard view of comprehensive future pricing processes
Pricing Subprocesses 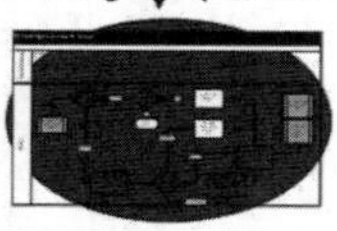	Level 2	Set of flows and procedures at a greater level of detail than Level 1
Activity Flows 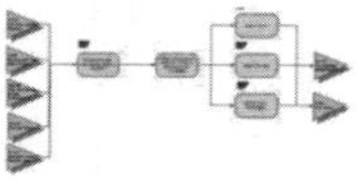	Level 3	A pictorial representation of the flow of activities in the future, used in training materials, communications documents, and as the definitive source of process information
Tasks/Transactions 	Level 4	Flows, procedures, and instructions that include specific components of the pricing process and will be used as the basis for training during the implementation phase

Figure 4.2   The Pricing Process Hierarchy

general sequencing of the processes, subprocesses, and activities that are essential for effective pricing and profitability management. This high-level, visual framework not only serves as a documentation and training tool, but also provides a roadmap for making improvements throughout the organization.

The business processes of the Best Practice Framework can be decomposed further in a hierarchy (see Figure 4.2), as follows:

1. *Process:* A series of complex, systematic actions required to manage and run an organization at the highest level.
2. *Subprocess:* A logical grouping of activities resulting in a workflow with multiple inputs and outputs, which often involves various people and departments. These sequential activities support and contribute to the accomplishment of a process.
3. *Activity flow:* A discrete action, or set of actions, required to produce a particular result or outcome in support of a subprocess. Activities can require one or multiple individuals to complete.

4. *Task/transaction:* A single step or action performed by an individual or a small team. A task typically has a specific input and output, which can be performed in a short period.

The best practice pricing processes discussed below are at Level 1 (the lowest at which they can be abstracted). Adding more detail requires company-specific information, such as industry practices, organizational culture and capabilities, customer preferences and habits, and competitor strengths and weaknesses. Note that the roles have generic labels so that they can be applied to any organization with some mapping or translation. For example, sales supervisor can reflect any position that oversees the sales team. It can be a regional sales manager, a product sales manager, or the vice president of Sales, depending on the size and structure of the organization.

Developing Pricing Strategy

Obviously, no firm can move forward without a clearly defined vision and a road map to achieve it. See Chapter 3, "Developing an Effective Pricing Strategy," for a detailed description of how a pricing strategy can be developed.

Conducting Competitor and Market Assessments

Chapter 3, "Developing an Effective Pricing Strategy," and Chapter 5, "Advanced Analytics and Price Setting," discuss different techniques companies can use to assess their market needs and the competition. We focus here on how processes and people should be organized to gather, share, and capitalize on critical information to improve price execution. The process (depicted in Figure 4.3) involves the following steps:

1. Conduct competitor analyses to evaluate competitors' marketing and sales strategies as well as market profitability.
2. Gather and document field intelligence on competitors from public and non-public sources.
3. Analyze field intelligence to identify the most critical insights.
4. Compile and review competitor, customer, and marketing data to better understand trends that impact pricing.
5. Conduct competitor and market assessments to identify issues and opportunities impacting Pricing, Marketing, and Sales.
6. Distribute competitor and market assessment reports to decision makers in Pricing, Marketing, and Sales.
7. Develop coordinated, proactive strategies and tactics to respond to competitors' tactics and customer demand.

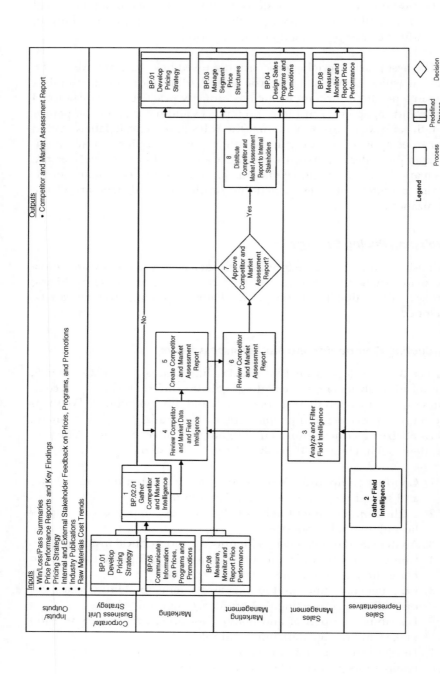

Inputs
• Win/Loss/Pass Summaries
• Price Performance Reports and Key Findings
• Pricing Strategy
• Internal and External Stakeholder Feedback on Prices, Programs, and Promotions
• Industry Publications
• Raw Materials Cost Trends

Outputs
• Competitor and Market Assessment Report

| Inputs/Outputs | Corporate/Business Unit Strategy | Marketing | Marketing Management | Sales Management | Sales Representatives |

Corporate/Business Unit Strategy

BP.01 Develop Pricing Strategy

1
BP.02.01 Gather Competitor and Market Intelligence

BP.05 Communicate Information on Prices, Programs and Promotions

BP.08 Measure, Monitor and Report Price Performance

4
Review Competitor and Market Data and Field Intelligence

5
Create Competitor and Market Assessment Report

6
Review Competitor and Market Assessment Report

7
Approve Competitor and Market Assessment Report?

No

Yes

8
Distribute Competitor and Market Assessment Report to Internal Stakeholders

3
Analyze and Filter Field Intelligence

2
Gather Field Intelligence

BP.01 Develop Pricing Strategy

BP.03 Manage Segment Price Structures

BP.04 Design Sales Programs and Promotions

BP.08 Measure Monitor and Report Price Performance

Legend

Process

Predefined Process

Decision

Figure 4.3 Competitor and Market Assessment (Best Practice Framework, Level 1)

The following roles and responsibilities are defined for this process:

Role	Responsibilities
Analyst	Conduct competitor and market analyses
	Compile and review field intelligence
	Create and distribute to business leadership competitor and market assessment reports
	Develop proactive marketing and pricing strategies and tactics
Analyst supervisor	Conduct competitor and market analyses
	Create and distribute to business leadership competitor and market assessment reports
	Develop proactive marketing and pricing strategies and tactics
Sales representative	Gather and document customer, competitor, and market intelligence
	Review field intelligence
	Develop proactive sales strategies and tactics
Sales supervisor	Gather and document competitor and market intelligence
	Review field intelligence
	Develop proactive sales strategies and tactics

A company must perform a competitor and market assessment to help ensure that pricing decisions are effectively informed. A good assessment outlines the forces at work in an industry, and the ways a company can use pricing strategies to capitalize on market trends. The first step in any assessment is creating a clearly defined scope and time frame to gather information. The scope provides parameters for research and answers questions such as the following:

- What is the market and geographical area to be included?
- What brands, product categories, and product lines will be analyzed?
- Who are the competitors?
- Which customers and stakeholders will be impacted by this pricing strategy?

Effective organizations establish recurring processes to gather and incorporate essential information into pricing practices and marketing strategies. This data can be collected in various ways:

- Marketing may create periodic sector reviews as part of ongoing planning processes.
- Organizations may use their sales team to collect intelligence on market prices from competitive bid situations.
- Organizations may purchase reports from third parties that detail both the current state and the future trends of particular industries.

The combination of market analyses and field intelligence can help companies identify critical issues and opportunities in Pricing, Marketing, and Sales. Companies should note the key value drivers, trends, and growth rates of their target industries, as well as the overall strategies and business capabilities of their competitors. Marketing is usually the function that will lead these assessments. They typically examine or include the following:

- *Competitor benchmarking* to measure the company's market share, pricing performance, financial performance, and so forth against its rivals.
- *Growth or decline in target markets* to determine the profitability trends of current and prospective customer and market segments.
- *Market economics* to identify how product supply and demand impacts segment profitability, growth, cost to serve, supplier costs, and prices.
- *Emerging products and services* to identify cutting-edge technologies or trends that affect the market.

Companies should collect intelligence in the field to identify the value drivers for their buyers and the selling strategies of their competitors. While Marketing and the Sales leadership team can identify high-level trends, customers and sales representatives can provide insight into local market conditions and the actual value proposition of every transaction. Though companies often hesitate to bother their customers or don't have the resources to do it, pricing strategies simply cannot, and should not, be developed without obtaining direct and meaningful input from them.

In general, sales force intelligence, while potentially biased, is much easier to obtain than customer feedback and can provide insight into the marketplace, the competition, and the effectiveness of different tactics. Sales intelligence will not only provide a ground-floor view of the market, but will also help build buy-in for any new pricing processes. This is critical as ultimate success will largely depend on the sales force, which will likely have to execute a large part of the new processes. Sales representatives can typically provide and document the following information:

- competitor products and services
- customer-based market demand (improvements and additions to products and services requested by customers)
- win/loss summaries (by competitor and based on quotes, bids, reverse auctions, and so on)
- competitor value proposition for specific customers or products (e.g., competitor always has lowest price)
- competitor price points (quote or bid prices)
- competitor sales strategies, trends, and customer relationships.

Companies can use the data collected in the field to conduct robust analyses of the competitive landscape. For example, analyses like VOC (described in Chapter 3, "Developing an Effective Pricing Strategy") allow companies to perform an economic value assessment in which products or services are measured based on their differentiators (positive and negative) against competitors' products or services. Other more qualitative and subjective analyses, such as an assessment of a brand's ability to confer social status, are far more valuable when they include insights from the customer and the sales team. Thus, even though field-level data may be more difficult to obtain and must be filtered and analyzed, it will ultimately yield important insights into the ways pricing may be used to capitalize on market conditions. A cautionary note: companies should never gather information merely to have it—they should assemble only enough to make good pricing decisions.[3] Losing focus during research wastes time and leads to less accurate findings as messages can become blurred.

After compiling and reviewing competitor, market, and field intelligence data, an analyst (usually in Marketing) develops a detailed report, which should identify issues and opportunities that may impact the pricing, marketing, or sales strategy (e.g., direct competitive threats and sector opportunities). The assessment should be distributed to the appropriate decision makers to develop coordinated strategies and tactics to respond. The entire process can help build consensus within the organization, and also establish a running history of the competitive environment. While changing market forces will require adjusting the structure or using different analyses over time, the framework should remain consistent and repeatable.

Managing Segment Price Structures

A global specialty chemicals company segmented customers by revenue rather than profitability. As a result, though 21 percent of the company's customers was actually unprofitable, these customers were treated the same as profitable ones. This situation was remedied through an improved process that segmented and managed price structures (the way a product or service price is constructed and presented to the market) to deliver appropriate pocket margins (see Figure 4.4). The process involves the following steps:

1. Conduct price analytics to understand price, cost, and market information as preparation for setting and adjusting base prices.
2. Set and adjust base prices based on reviewed analytics.
3. Develop discount and premium structure.
4. Carry out scenario tests of base price and discount and premium structure to evaluate their impact on national and local market sales volume and profitability.
5. Get base price and discount and premium structure approved by the appropriate authority.
6. Update pricing system to include final base price and changes in discount and premium structure.

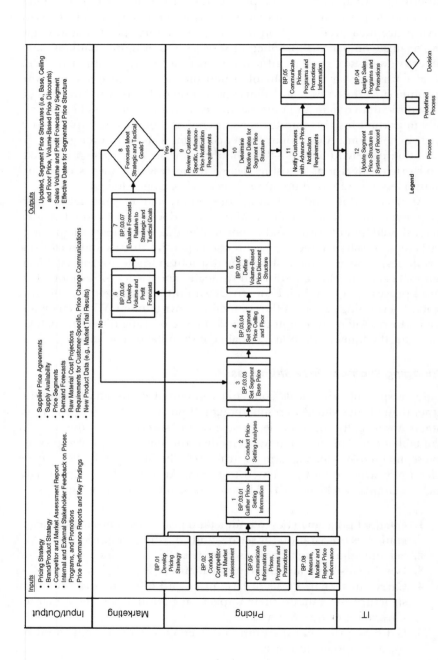

Figure 4.4 Management of Segment Price Structures (Best Practice Framework, Level 1)

Inputs
- Pricing Strategy
- Brand/Product Strategy
- Competitor and Market Assessment Report
- Internal and External Stakeholder Feedback on Prices, Programs, and Promotions
- Price Performance Reports and Key Findings
- Supplier Price Agreements
- Supply Availability
- Price Segments
- Demand Forecasts
- Raw Material Cost Projections
- Requirements for Customer-Specific, Price Change Communications
- New Product Data (e.g., Market Trial Results)

Outputs
- Updated, Segment Price Structures (i.e., Base, Ceiling and Floor Price, Volume-Based Price Discounts)
- Sales Volume and Profit Forecast by Segment
- Effective Dates for Segmented Price Structure

Input/Output

Marketing

Pricing

IT

BP.01 Develop Pricing Strategy

BP.02 Conduct Competitor and Market Assessment

BP.05 Communicate Information on Prices, Programs and Promotions

BP.08 Measure, Monitor and Report Price Performance

1 BP.03.01 Gather Price-Setting Information

2 Conduct Price-Setting Analyses

3 BP.03.03 Set Segment Base Price

4 BP.03.04 Set Segment Price Ceiling and Floor

5 BP.03.05 Define Volume-Based Price Discount Structure

6 BP.03.06 Develop Volume and Profit Forecasts

7 BP.03.07 Evaluate Forecasts Relative to Strategic and Tactical Goals

8 Forecasts Meet Strategic and Tactical Goals?

No

Yes

9 Review Customer-Specific, Advance-Price Notification Requirements

10 Determine Effective Dates for Segment Price Structure

11 Notify Customers with Advance-Price Notification Requirements

12 Update Segment Price Structure in System of Record

BP.05 Communicate Prices, Programs and Promotions Information

BP.04 Design Sales Programs and Promotions

Legend

Process

Predefined Process

Decision

100

The following roles and responsibilities are defined for this process:

Role	Responsibilities
Base price determination coordinator	Understand price-setting analytics Set base prices for products and services Conduct a scenario analysis to evaluate how changes in price impact national and local market conditions
Discount and premium coordinator	Understand price-setting analytics Develop discount and premium structure for products and services Conduct a scenario analysis to evaluate how changes in price affect national and local market conditions
Base price approver	Understand price-setting analytics Validate final base prices and discount and premium structure for products and services
Pricing data entry coordinator	Update base price and discount and premium structure in the pricing system

Effective price and discount structures allow companies to develop targeted strategies for their customers and products, enabling them to capture previously unharvested margin and missed sales opportunities. As discussed in Chapter 3, "Developing an Effective Pricing Strategy," the structure can also influence how customers perceive products. Typically, a base price (the segment-specific price for a product before any adjustments are applied) will be adjusted according to various factors, including customer purchasing behavior, internal revenue and margin targets, and product features or delivery terms. Here are some other business issues (and information) that should be considered to help inform the decision:

- historical data by product and customer reflecting sales, profit trends, price points, pricing performance, and so forth
- internal financial budgets and sales goals that provide the key parameters for base price and discount and premium structures when conducting scenario analyses
- marketing and sales forecasts to understand future customer demand for products and services
- data to understand raw material and product cost trends
- price promotions, coupons, rebates, and price supports to assess impact on profitability (information can be drawn from historical marketing and sales data)
- value proposition of the product for customers (when measured against competitors), which can suggest the potential price point

- competitors' marketing and sales strategies to assess impact on product and pricing by customer segment
- product and customer elasticity to understand product and customer sensitivity to price changes by segment.

Setting Base Prices by Customer Segment.   When segmenting price levels, companies must quantify the value customers place on a given offering and identify the specific characteristics that influence customer perceptions. Various methods such as price optimization (see Chapter 5, "Advanced Analytics and Price Setting") and economic value analysis can help quantify the dollar value of a brand, product, or service and should be performed to establish price levels for each customer segment. This will enable companies to capitalize on previously missed sales opportunities (see Figure 4.5) and to capture value from the market.

Prices across segments must have a logical structure, align with customer perceptions, and illustrate a clear value proposition for the difference in price. If there is no rationale, then buyers may deem prices unfair and take their business elsewhere. One useful way to approach this dilemma is to use a matrix that lists the economic value (or price) for a given product and all of its variations across all customer segments (see Table 4.1).

One challenge when establishing different price levels is to determine how to create fixed boundaries to prevent customer cross over. To address this issue, companies can tailor strategic pricing structures (such as bundling, menus, and so on) for specific segments and then integrate them into their marketing campaigns. After establishing the base prices, a company will still need to create guidelines to ensure effective execution. A structured price range should accommodate the economic value proposition for each customer, while improving the overall profitability of the business.

When setting a price range, companies should establish the ceiling and floor first (see Figure 4.6) with different discount levels in between

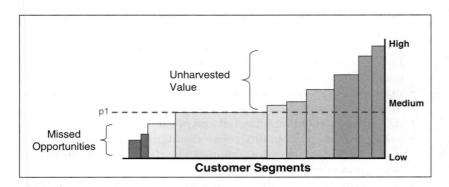

Figure 4.5   Value-Based Segmentation

Table 4.1 Segment-Based Price Structures

		Segment 1	Segment 2	Segment 3
	Basic	$3,000	$4,000	$5,000
	Plus A	$3,090	$4,120	$5,150
Product	**Plus B**	$3,183	$4,244	$5,305
	Plus C	$3,278	$4,371	$5,464
	Plus D	$3,377	$4,502	$5,628

(most often set by volume). Within each segment, the range of possible prices for a particular product is called the *deal envelope*, and is defined by business policy and legal requirements. Each price also represents differences in competitive situation or costs to serve. The deal envelope should be used to identify pricing transactions outside of the range.

- *Ceiling price.* The highest price within a segment that the business can charge based on all applicable cost-to-serve elements. Prices above the base price and at, or below, the ceiling price reflect the business's need to charge for additional cost-to-serve elements and require appropriate justification. Ceilings prevent excessively high prices from being charged (which can damage customer perceptions).
- *Floor price.* The lowest, acceptable price within a segment that the business will tolerate according to a minimum margin threshold it establishes. Prices below the base price and at, or above, the floor price represent the business's need to meet a competitive price and require justification. Floor prices let the sales team know what the lowest possible selling price is. The floor should be calculated based on its relationship to—or impact on—pocket margin.

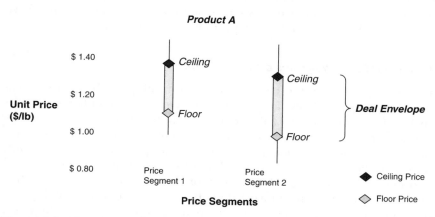

Figure 4.6 Deal Envelopes

Once the base prices, discount and premium structures, and deal envelopes are created, they should be tested. Modeling several scenarios can help evaluate how the first two affect national and local market sales volume and profitability targets. A segment's base price should achieve a balance between value to the customer and to the company. At a corporate level, base prices should reflect customer perceptions of the product or brand, while meeting the overall strategic objectives of the company in terms of share, revenue, and profit. If the price structure does not allow a company to achieve its target goals, then the base prices or the discount and premium structure, or both, must be modified.

In addition to establishing ceiling and floor prices, companies need to create multiple levels of authority in the sales process for the escalation of negotiations as important deals are brokered or additional customer concessions are made. For example, companies can establish multiple price floors and align them with different levels of authority for approval or denial of bigger discounts. Similarly, companies can mandate that only senior sales personnel negotiate with larger clients. These guidelines ensure that concessions will be made only at the appropriate level of authority.

Two potential problems can be eliminated by effective pricing guidelines. First, cumbersome, demanding negotiations, which can anger both the customer and the sales team, while tarnishing a company's reputation. Second, if concessions are not properly tracked, then they will likely lead to excessive margin leakage, hurt price perceptions, and undermine overall profitability. Ease of implementation and traceability are critical in the system. By implementing clear guidelines, a company can streamline the negotiating path for sales representatives and customers, while also ensuring that pricing anomalies are picked up and key insights into consumer behavior are recorded.

Finally, firms need to develop different price-setting scenarios for changing market conditions. If competitors lower prices, new regulations are passed, the economy enters a recession, or other events occur, these scenarios will allow a firm to react promptly and effectively.

Designing Sales Programs and Promotions

Loyalty programs reward customers for continuing to choose one company over another. They can provide, for example, accumulating benefits such as free products (e.g., airline miles or hotel nights) or access to discounts for retail store members. These programs may or may not have time limits, which can affect price and customer profitability. Promotions, on the other hand, are always timebound (i.e., they have a specific start and end date) offerings of discounts or product giveaways (e.g., "Buy One, Get One Free" incentives) that affect pricing and profitability, but do not typically target specific customers or customer segments. An effective pricing program and promotion process (see Figure 4.7) includes the

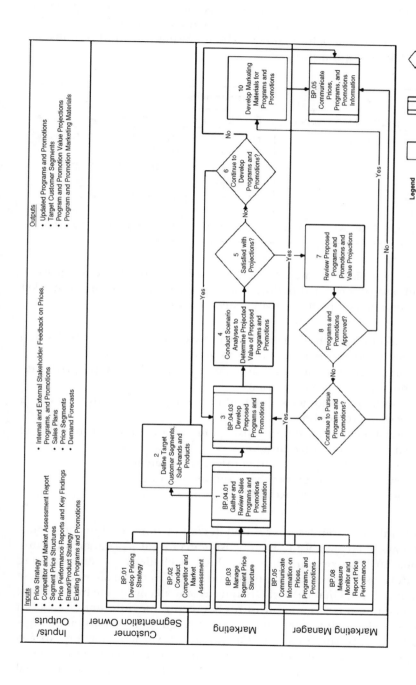

Figure 4.7 Design of Pricing Programs and Promotions (Best Practice Framework, Level 1)

105

evaluation of existing information (such as current promotions, price and promotion historical performance, and marketing materials) as well as current market data before launch. The following roles and responsibilities are defined for this process:

Role	Responsibilities
Customer segmentation owner	Develops and updates list of target customers
Programs and promotions developer	Evaluates existing promotional programs and information on promotions
	Develops new, targeted programs and promotions
Programs and promotions approver	Approves programs and promotions
Promotional materials developer	Develops promotional marketing materials

Various tools and materials may be used to research and evaluate existing and past promotional performance as well as to assess current market conditions and competitor activity. These include:

- marketing promotions and price break structure to help develop new, competitive promotional programs
- current promotions from suppliers to help establish appropriate customer promotional programs
- reports on customer segmentation strategy to assist in developing focused promotions
- assessments of customer satisfaction and of overall profitability of existing promotional programs
- updates or changes to market prices and strategies
- identification of competitive promotional programs
- cost calculations of past and current promotions.

All of these resources can be used in conjunction with historical transaction data to create a list of target customers for sales programs and promotions. In large organizations, the biggest challenge when designing new offerings is the coordination required across departments. Because Marketing, Sales, Finance, and Operations may all contribute information, finding common terms and measures between these different groups can prove difficult, but it is a necessary task. For promotions in particular, organizations must be sure to involve Operations heavily in managing capacity and optimizing promotion timing. In addition, many details must be collectively agreed upon, including eligibility rules and the promotional calendar.

Communicating Information on Prices, Programs, and Promotions

> Oil prices have fallen lately. We include this news for the benefit of
> gas stations, which otherwise wouldn't learn of it for six months.
> *Bill Tameus in Toronto's* National Newspaper, *1991*

This wry statement reflects an imaginary oil company's desire to capture
more value from the market by simply delaying its pricing communications. While ironic, it nonetheless underscores the importance of effective,
timely, and accurate communications, both internally and externally.
Some motorists may tolerate the delay because of the convenience of a
particular gas station (or the lack of competitive alternatives); but in most
markets, customers will seize the opportunity to buy gas elsewhere, and
competitors will try to differentiate their offering based on price.

The pricing communication process shown in Figure 4.8 outlines the
necessary steps for sharing prices and promotions with both the sales team
(particularly in a business-to-business environment) and customers. These
steps include the evaluation of communications requirements, development of contingency plans for at-risk customers, and distribution of pricing announcements. The following roles and responsibilities are defined
for this process:

Role	Responsibilities
Internal price change communicator	Evaluates communications materials
	Assesses need for formal pricing communications to customers
	Communicates prices internally to the sales representatives
Sales representative	Identifies at-risk customers
	Develops contingency plans
Customer relationship owner	Approves contingency plans
External price change coordinator	Distributes communications materials on pricing

As base prices are developed or modified, and programs and promotions are created, organizations must evaluate how, when, and what to
communicate, and to who. When evaluating the need to make a pricing
communication, the following should be considered:

- format and mode of communication agreed upon with customers
- requirements for advance notice and price protection as established
  in buyer contracts and agreements

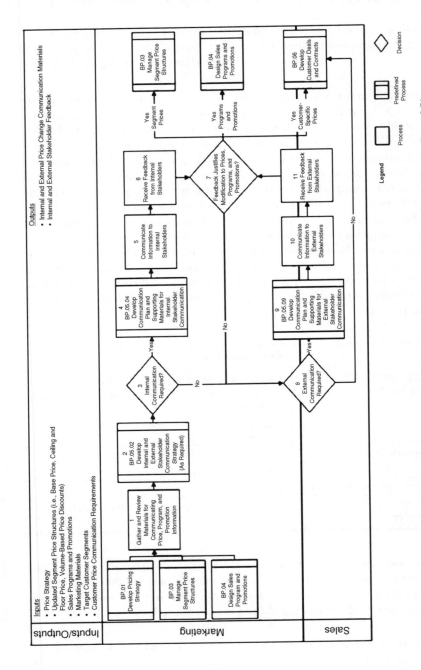

Figure 4.8 Communication of Pricing Programs and Promotions (Best Practice Framework, Level 1)

Table 4.2   Types of Internal and External Pricing Communications

	Prices	Promotions	Programs
Internal	• Pricing strategy • Price lists • Price guidelines and procedures • Approvals	• Promotional calendar • Customer eligibility	• Loyalty programs • Other incentives
External	• Price lists • Price changes	• Current promotions	• Loyalty programs

- what should be shared with the sales organization and the customers (see Table 4.2 for a list of typical internal and external pricing-related communications)
- the most effective method to use with established promotional plans.

Many of the decisions depend on standard industry practices, the customers, the culture and capabilities of the organization, and the content of the message itself. Can sales representatives be most efficiently notified of price changes and new deal envelopes by email, or is there a company-wide computer system with alert functionality? Do customers need to hear about price changes through a corporate announcement or individually through their account managers? Are there any customers who require a unique message regarding prices or promotions?

Customer contracts often require that formal communications are made when any changes affect price. There may also be stipulations regarding timing; for example, the total number of allowable changes per year or an advance warning period for changes. Agreements may also spell out the format the communications must take. Of course, all of these requirements must be adhered to so that you can avoid legal penalties and unhappy customers. Clients who have a significant impact on profitability may resist or reject price changes. Organizations must be able to identify these at-risk clients and develop a customer-specific communications plan, including scenarios and contingencies.

If an organization has a centralized system that makes automatic price adjustments, then either the system or designated team members must be able to accommodate the various communications requirements. All announcements should be made in a timely, accurate, and tailored manner to ensure optimal price execution and customer goodwill.

Developing Customer Deals and Contracts

While executives may formulate detailed marketing and pricing strategies, the sales team has the most control over who the customers are, what products are sold, and how profitable the transaction is going to be. Misguidance anywhere in the sales process can have a severe impact on the bottom line, and the repercussions can last months, if not years (especially in long-term contract negotiations). To achieve profitable price execution, companies need to establish a formal process to target customers and to develop deals and finalize contracts with them. While terms and tactics may vary, all negotiations must follow a similar process (see Figure 4.9). The following roles and responsibilities are defined for this process:

Role	Responsibilities
Credit processor	Establishes and extends customer credit
	Confirms that updated credit is sufficient
	Determines if management override will be granted
Contract or agreement developer	Confirms that updated credit is sufficient
	Determines if management override will be granted
	Develops and updates quote or contract or agreement in the system
	Determines if quote or approval is a formal contract
	Documents required information to justify price exceptions
	Verifies that final agreement has been reached on the contract
	Verifies that contract or agreement is within accepted parameters
	Confirms contract is within legal guidelines
	Files the legal contract, as required
	Communicates to all parties
Data entry coordinator	Enters quote or contract or agreement data into the system
Business approver	Confirms the contract has received required approval
Legal approver	Alters contract to adhere to legal guidelines

Targeting the Customer.   While many customers fall within a target segment, not all present a company with an attractive value proposition. For this reason, before entering into a negotiation, a company needs to assess the attractiveness of a given opportunity. Evaluating criteria such as opportunity size, customer financial history, product offering, service requirements, and plant capacity can help a company identify potential customers. However, more qualitative and subjective characteristics that give a customer strategic value should also be considered as there can be special circumstances that justify pursuing the opportunity. For example, a company may choose to build a relationship with a particular client if that client has a great sphere of influence over a given market. This type of strategic tradeoff often occurs when companies enter new markets or introduce new products. The targeted customers or segments should align with the sales plan for that region or product.

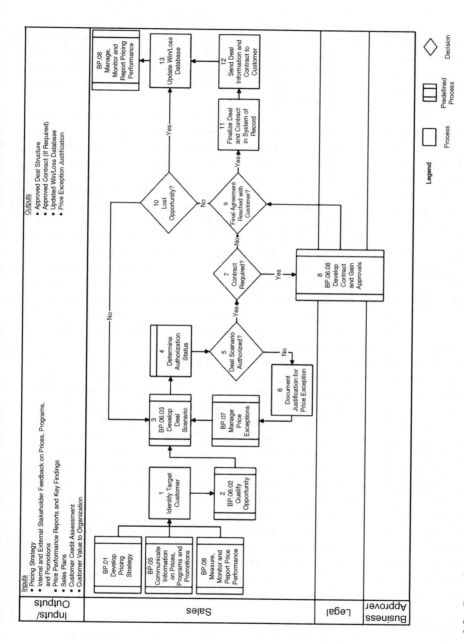

Figure 4.9 Development of Customer Deals and Contracts (Best Practice Framework, Level 1)

111

Developing the Deal.   Negotiations typically use contract or spot pricing. Contract pricing occurs more in business-to-business transactions where a buyer-supplier relationship is established and sales can be predicted, providing financial predictability for a company (i.e., a customer is anticipated to generate a certain amount of business in return for a price). This approach allows for accurate measurements of deal profitability. Conversely, spot pricing sets the price—which will often coincide with raw materials costs—at the time of the transaction.

A typical contract includes a price, customer terms (such as volume levels, payment terms, and exclusivity), policy agreements (such as customer service, support levels, and freight requirements), and an end date. Companies should explicitly incorporate buyer and vendor agreements into a contract to guard against customer negligence or product expectations that go beyond the scope of the deal and can result in additional costs to serve. While renegotiating contracts involves time, money, and risk, the effort generally proves worthwhile because it encourages periodic dialog with the customer and offers the opportunity to realign a deal as market conditions evolve. The enforcement of end dates and renegotiation of contracts provide two mechanisms for companies to maintain prices and customer value perceptions as well as their overall pricing strategies. In some industries, permanently extending contracts, or *evergreening*, is standard practice. Companies that operate in these sectors must be very aware of the trade-offs and ensure they find ways to capture the value expected from each client.

When dealing with a target customer, the sales representative that designs the deal should take into account the customer's needs, the value of the product (or service) to the customer, target pocket margin, value of the customer to the organization, credit risk, the product pricing strategy, any promotional programs currently being offered, and any other relevant market, competitor, or product information. The deal should then be evaluated to confirm it complies with established organizational parameters outlined in the company's operating procedure, such as the price ceiling and floor, payment terms, service level parameters, and volume discounts. This is the point at which overall deal (as opposed to product-by-product) profitability can be measured and controlled.

If the deal does not meet the established parameters, then the sales representative can continue to negotiate to bring it within the accepted range, or escalate the approval to try to justify an exception. If the deal is rejected, then it (along with reasons for the refusal) should be documented for future analysis.

Finalizing the Contract.   All finalized negotiations (regardless whether the deal is closed) should be logged into a tracking system. By following negotiations and their results, firms provide themselves with a mechanism to monitor sales team performance and improve standard contract agreements. Identifying commonalities between won and lost business can help firms improve their overall negotiation process and get a better understanding of their customers and target markets. Over time, the accumulated lessons should build on each other and sustain continuous improvement of the processes for negotiation, customer segmentation, and deal profitability.

Managing Price Exceptions

A *price exception* is a transaction that falls outside the business-defined threshold for deal profitability. This exception can be caused by the price itself (i.e., it is below the price floor or above the ceiling), or by the inclusion of other costs to serve that reduce the profitability of the entire deal. A price exception can also reflect a situation when an agreed-upon price has been altered, typically at the discretion of a customer service agent or other corporate representative.

The percentage of transactions resulting in exceptions can vary by industry, sales volume, or business model of the company. An excessive number of exceptions and an inefficient management process can contribute to unnecessary complexity, which inevitably increases costs. The impact and cost of price exceptions can be amplified in high-volume businesses. Consider this example. At a *Fortune* 50 consumer products company, target prices were created for each product, but the sales team ignored them. This practice resulted in 70 percent of new deals moving through a special pricing workflow. When exceptions were denied, salespeople made up the difference by using extra trade promotion dollars. This practice basically resulted in a 6 percent reduction in year-over-year, account net profit.

The process shown in Figure 4.10 should be used to document, track, and manage price exceptions to authorized base prices or acceptable price-band discounts. The following roles and responsibilities are defined for this process:

Role	Responsibilities
Price exception approver	Identifies price exception situation
	Knows price exception policy
	Understands approval hierarchy for price exceptions
	Verifies price exception documentation
	Notifies seller of price exception status
Price exception negotiator	Evaluates price exception documentation
	Recalculates price exception amount
	Submits price exception for approval
External price communicator	Notifies customer of price rejection
	Documents lost sale

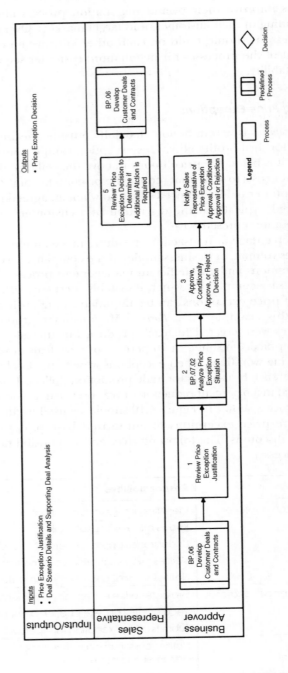

Figure 4.10 Management of Price Exceptions (Best Practice Framework, Level 1)

Once an exception has been identified, it should move swiftly through a predetermined escalation hierarchy. When possible, firms should use technology to help govern exception-granting authority and to capture the required contextual information. Using standardized request formats can help provide the decision maker with all of the necessary information to understand and evaluate the impact of a particular exception. This assessment must also take into account the strategic and tactical impact of the exception, which can not only impact the profitability of the deal, but also set a precedent in the market if the customer is large or particularly influential. The status conditions for a price exception are:

- *approval*, enabling the price to be used
- *conditional approval*, enabling the price to be used if certain conditions are met by the customer
- *rejection*, meaning the price cannot be offered to the customer.

The decision can be escalated through several levels before it is approved or rejected, depending on the hierarchical structure of the company's price exception process. Once a decision is reached, the customer must be notified either directly or through the sales representative and given a chance to respond.

Price exceptions should be monitored to understand when and how adjustments to the deal envelope are being made. Prices may need to be recalibrated if many substantial exceptions are requested for the same products. In addition, by tracking exception request rates by sales representative and sales manager, firms can determine whether anyone in the process is misusing his or her authority and so negatively affecting profitability.

Measuring, Monitoring, and Reporting Pricing Performance

In any organization, pricing policies and processes are more effective when measured. Organizations must use metrics to assess process efficiency, pricing strategy effectiveness, adherence to pricing policies, and alignment to corporate goals and objectives. Monitoring execution relentlessly can help reinforce management's high expectations and achieve the level of transparency needed to ensure that pricing improvements are sustainable.

Performance measurement is not a new concept. As the familiar business axiom reminds us, "If something is important, then it should be measured. If it is really important, then it should be measured twice and reported widely." However, applying this axiom to a discipline with as many potential inputs and that involves so many other functions as pricing can be as challenging as it is essential. At the end of the day (or quarter), nothing measures a company's ability to sell a product or service more than price. It represents the ultimate exchange and defines every interaction between supplier and customer.

To measure the effectiveness of a pricing strategy, a firm must identify what its goals were. Was it trying to grow market share or to incentivize customers to buy specific products? Was the objective to improve profitability through specific pricing or a reduced cost-to-serve? When it is designed, a pricing strategy should be tied to a tangible goal that can be measured and used as the benchmark for achieving the business objective. By identifying and communicating it up front, everyone can be aligned to that goal.

Performance monitoring should allow employees to see progress in the closing of gaps (between expected and actual performance) or prevention of margin leakage. Policy adherence measures should help strengthen, and bring greater discipline to, the pricing process. Similarly, by tracking process efficiency, firms can help continually improve critical activities, such as responding to customer quotes. The results of both policy adherence and process efficiency may serve as important indicators of changing market conditions or competitive positioning.

Because many areas of an organization impact pricing, each function must use the same underlying metrics to understand customers, products, and channels. For example, Finance may track and report on gross margin or operating margin, but Marketing and Sales may use a different metric that accounts for freight and delivery costs in an attempt to isolate true product and customer costs from supply chain costs. Once everyone shares the same metrics, organizations can achieve transparency more easily and bring the appropriate stakeholders forward for a discussion about pricing improvement.

A company needs contributions from multiple points within it to improve an underperforming product or service. Finance needs to determine the variable costs to serve; Purchasing should look to improve the cost of goods sold (COGS); Marketing should rethink the positioning of the product and the appropriate target market; and Sales should understand and communicate the value and ultimately make the sale. Converging these perspectives into a single version of the *truth* should help each person see where his or her actions can contribute to the bottom line.

Just as pricing strategies and related policies must be data driven, so too must any assessment of how firms are achieving goals and benchmarks. It may appear obvious that measuring requires data metrics, but which ones will identify root issues and allow a firm to adapt and adjust to changing market conditions? Often, picking the best measures can be the difference between success and failure as the firm presses forward with ongoing pricing improvements.

A medical device manufacturer decided to implement new pricing performance monitoring. At the beginning of the fiscal year the firm implemented a new quarterly measurement and incentive system aimed at growing total unit sales. The incentives measured quarterly volume, but—critically—made no adjustment for product mix or potential returns. As a result of these poorly designed performance metrics, the manufacturer found itself faced with surges of new orders right before the end of each quarter that it struggled to fulfill.

When monitoring pricing, three key performance indicators should be considered: process efficiency, process effectiveness and quality, and business unit alignment. They are interrelated, but each tracks a specific element of a business's performance. Examples of each measure are provided in Table 4.3.

Process Efficiency. Organizations with centrally controlled pricing often face complaints about slow responses to price requests, which jeopardize sales opportunities. By reducing the response time for quotes, sales representatives can more efficiently tend to customer needs. How critical an issue this is depends entirely on the market expectations, but it should never be a limiting factor in negotiations—forcing a customer to wait to hear a

Table 4.3   Pricing Performance Key Performance Indicators (KPIs)

Indicator	Examples
Process efficiency	Response time (when answering customer request for quote)
	Cycle time (when addressing competitor and market changes)
	Response time (for responding to competitor price changes)
	Response time (to approve pricing exceptions)
Process effectiveness and quality	Number of pricing overrides (by sales representative, region, channel, product)
	Number of pricing errors and corrections
	Quality of pricing data and information analysis
Business unit alignment	Product, service, and customer profitability
	Year-over-year profitability and growth targets
	Win/loss data
	Pricing alignment with corporate objectives

counter proposal should be a tactical decision and not a reflection of an inefficient pricing process.

In a decentralized organization in which pricing decisions are made by sales and business representatives close to the customer, response time is equally important. One of the most effective ways to speed up the response process is to share the key information affecting profitability decisions with those handling the negotiations. Tracking response time is critical because the findings can eliminate anecdotes that skew perceptions. Every organization can point to an instance where business may have been lost by a tardy response to a client; whether that was really the reason for the lost business can be determined by tracking and reporting the right metric.

When tracking process efficiency, one measurement is the cycle time required to react to market changes. For example, how quickly after a competitor announces a pricing adjustment (either up or down) can the business respond? If certain raw material indices affect pricing, how rapidly can the organization translate those movements into its end pricing in the market?

Process Effectiveness and Quality.   Metrics that measure process effectiveness can provide a *wellness check* of the company's overall price execution capability. They should indicate which processes are working as intended and which need to be refined. Too many pricing overrides, for example, can point to poor deal and contract management or an unintended loophole in the price exception process. Comparing and contrasting the number of pricing overrides between sales representatives, regions, or products can provide detailed insight into areas where processes are not followed or policies are not adhered to.

Similarly, a high number of pricing errors can reflect inadequate staff training or poor quality assurance processes. Further investigation should reveal whether additional training is required or if processes need to be added or modified to increase oversight of pricing data and a reduction in errors.

Business Unit Alignment.   Metrics used at the business unit level should indicate whether pricing policies and processes align properly with the overall goals of the firm. Measuring year-over-year profitability and the number of deals won and lost (including the reasons) enables firms to compare the results against overall targets and strategies and then to make the necessary adjustments.

Implementing the Tools of Performance Monitoring.   The process for regularly monitoring and reviewing pricing performance (see Figure 4.11) typically involves using both a standard dashboard and a systematic distribution method to identify opportunities for price improvement (e.g., through organizational and incentive alignment, or changes in marketing

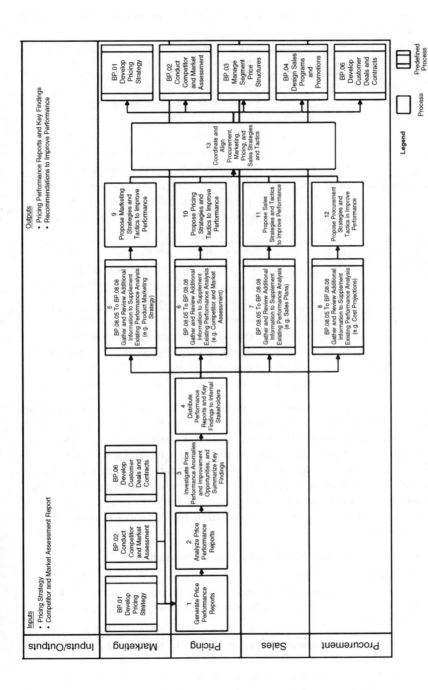

Figure 4.11 Measurement and Reporting of Pricing Performance (Best Practice Framework, Level 1)

119

and sales programs). The following roles and responsibilities are defined for this process:

Role	Responsibilities
Pricing strategy developer	Generates pricing dashboards
	Evaluates pricing dashboard metrics
	Generates pricing performance reports
	Analyzes pricing performance reports
	Prepares pricing and profit recommendations
	Develops pricing improvement plan
Sales strategy developer	Generates pricing performance reports
	Analyzes pricing performance reports
	Prepares pricing and profit recommendations
	Develops sales plan
Customer-facing strategy developer	Generates pricing performance reports
	Analyzes pricing performance reports
	Prepares pricing and profit recommendations
	Develops marketing plan
Supply-facing strategy developer	Generates pricing performance reports
	Analyzes pricing performance reports
	Prepares pricing and profit recommendations
	Develops sourcing plan

Continuous performance monitoring is critical to understanding where processes and pricing can improve, as well as the best ways to respond to changing market dynamics. Having a mechanism for periodically evaluating performance can improve price transparency and accountability throughout the pricing process. A monitoring system can also use repeatable pricing analytics that can be enhanced and automated through technology systems or pricing software. Because data must often be collected from multiple sources, a standardized format can improve comprehension by all stakeholders.

Generating dashboards and pricing reports for analysis

Monitoring pricing performance requires creating a dashboard, which can take many forms, and continually refreshing the data that feed it. The following performance indicators can be evaluated through dashboard analyses:

- Customer segmentation performance by revenue and margin trends
- Pricing performance targets by product and by contract (comparing current and historical pricing performance)

- profit performance targets by customer, salesperson, and region (comparing current and historical profit performance)
- price exception reports generated for a specified period of time
- core pricing analyses, including the pricing waterfall, SKU and customer velocity analyses, price-band analysis, and segmentation analysis.

Preparing pricing recommendations

Based on the performance captured through dashboards and reports, key stakeholders should prepare recommendations for pricing changes. These changes can vary widely across the spectrum of levers that impact performance, including sourcing (e.g., opportunities to make cost-savings and change suppliers, plant locations, or warehousing options); marketing (e.g., product or SKU rationalization, changes in customer segmentation, promotion strategy, and product formulation; brand image messaging and training); sales (e.g., changes in incentives and training, customer focus strategy, and regions); or pricing itself (e.g., increasing or decreasing base price and modifying allowances and deductions).

Through performance monitoring, a company can avoid losing margin by making course corrections; adjusting prices and campaigns as needed. All results and decisions should be fed back into the price-setting process to enhance and refine it further.

Maintaining Pricing Information and Support Systems

The process of administering and maintaining information systems (see Figure 4.12) includes making regular and accurate updates of pricing rules, storing customer-specific information, and verifying data accuracy. The following defines the responsibilities of the pricing system administrator in this process:

Role	Responsibilities
Pricing system administrator	Enters and maintains pricing rules
	Enters and maintains customer-specific information
	Verifies pricing data

Throughout the pricing lifecycle, pricing rules and data changes should be updated in real time. Examples include:

- Current and historical base prices per product or SKU
- Promotional information; namely, the percentage or dollar deductions and allowances for specific products or SKUs (including the start and end dates of the promotion)

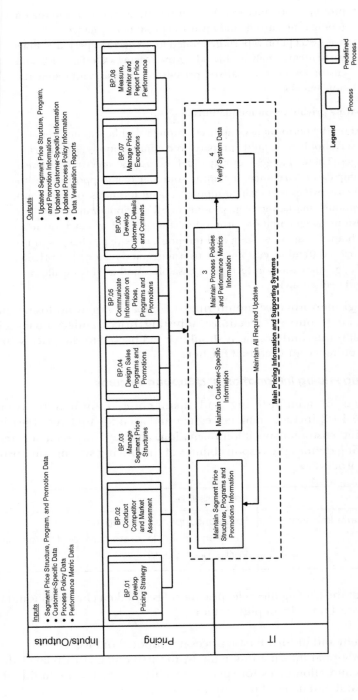

Inputs
• Segment Price Structure, Program, and Promotion Data
• Customer-Specific Data
• Process Policy Data
• Performance Metric Data

Outputs
• Updated Segment Price Structure, Program, and Promotion Information
• Updated Customer-Specific Information
• Updated Process Policy Information
• Data Verification Reports

Inputs/Outputs

Pricing

IT

BP.01 Develop Pricing Strategy

BP.02 Conduct Competitor and Market Assessment

BP.03 Manage Segment Price Structures

BP.04 Design Sales Programs and Promotions

BP.05 Communicate Information on Prices, Programs and Promotions

BP.06 Develop Customer Details and Contracts

BP.07 Manage Price Exceptions

BP.08 Measure, Monitor and Report Price Performance

1 Maintain Segment Price Structures, Programs and Promotions Information

2 Maintain Customer-Specific Information

3 Maintain Process Policies and Performance Metrics Information

4 Verify System Data

Maintain All Required Updates

Main Pricing Information and Supporting Systems

Legend

Process

Predefined Process

Figure 4.12 Maintenance of Pricing Information and Support Systems (Best Practice Framework, Level 1)

- Accrued rebate or chargeback information for specific products or SKUs
- Price approval authority (modifications to the workflow hierarchy for approving or rejecting base price, deductions, and allowance changes)
- Pricing and margin thresholds; that is, the fixed numbers below which net prices and margins cannot drop on an invoice without triggering an alert
- Percentage or dollar discount information for specific products or SKUs
- Pricing access and security rules that restrict access to certain data to certain personnel.

Examples of customer-specific changes include:

- Customer performance records; specifically, revenue and margin metrics and other account performance information
- Customer program information, including sales and marketing data and customer contact information
- Customer contracts or agreements and the data and information associated with them
- Customer segmentation models, covering attitudinal, behavioral, or geographical categories within buyer groups and their associated data and information.

Quality reports should be generated on a recurring basis to determine whether all changes have been correctly made to help avoid invoicing errors and unnecessary margin loss. In addition, standardized reports should be run to check *reasonability*. Examples of such reports include the following:

- *Pricing quality assurance reports:* Metrics and information used to check the data entered into information systems for accuracy
- *Pricing performance reports:* Metrics and information regarding the performance of current base pricing compared to financial targets
- *Promotions reports:* Data and information pertaining to the performance of deductions and allowances compared to marketing and financial targets
- *Contract and program reports:* Data and information regarding contract adherence and sales and marketing programs.

Setting Policies to Reinforce Pricing Processes

The Ten Commandments contain 297 words. The Bill of Rights is stated in 463 words. Lincoln's Gettysburg Address contains 266 words. A recent federal directive to regulate the price of cabbage contains 26,911 words.

The Atlanta Journal[4]

Pricing processes should be supplemented with complementary policies when a new pricing structure is implemented. These policies can help fine tune the execution of processes and drive closer organizational alignment with business objectives. In general, policies spell out leadership's expectations in support of a company's efforts to achieve its pricing objectives (e.g., increased revenue, market share, or profitability). Policies can be internally focused to govern the behavior of sales representatives, or externally focused to influence the purchasing practices of customers. Some examples of policies include setting rules for:

- minimum acceptable prices by volume range
- discounts for specific market and customer segments
- standard charges for freight and packaging
- surcharges for product or packaging customization
- service options and associated charges
- financing options and associated charges
- payment terms and conditions.

The framework in Figure 4.13 links the business and pricing strategies to help determine the dimensions for policy setting as well as the specific policies to define.

Pricing Policy Guidelines

The following guidelines can be used to devise pricing policies.

The Costs of Certain Customer Behaviors Should Be Determined and Recovered.   A pricing policy can help govern how sales representatives offer products or services that typically result in additional costs to serve for customers. It should help manage the profitability of a transaction, product, or buyer by specifying how much of, and in what manner, the costs to serve will be recovered (or, more accurately, how much will be given away in deal negotiations). The policy can also help encourage

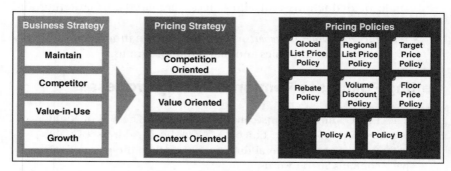

Figure 4.13   Framework for the Definition of Pricing Policy

desired customer behavior; for example, offering discounts for larger, less frequent orders to incentivize buyers to use a cheaper method of freight (i.e., full truckloads) to preserve margin on the deal.

External Pricing Policies Should Be Transparent to Customers. If the intent is to influence behavior, then the buyer must understand the policy and be able to choose among options that fall within defined parameters. In the example above of order size and frequency, the customer's purchasing patterns will be impacted only if the buyer is aware of the policy options.

Practicality Should Be the Goal in Implementation and Enforcement. Given the complexity of pricing analytics and the sheer volume of data available today, firms can get carried away with policy design as they attempt to capture every last bit of margin. However, the more convoluted the policy, the more difficult it is to implement and enforce. The number of pricing errors usually increases with complexity—as does the number of workarounds the sales team uses.

Policies Should Be Set Only When They Are Absolutely Necessary. An inordinate number of rules can confuse the sales team and customers, while becoming a burden to administer, monitor, and maintain. Too few policies can give excessive latitude to individual sales representatives and leave buyers with the impression that their own behavior doesn't matter.

Pricing policies are the guardrails that support the approved strategy throughout execution. Besides governing the types of concessions that can be granted, these policies should also cover areas of potential leakage that can subtly erode profits. Policies can be difficult to administer, particularly if they are customized from customer to customer, but they are critical to achieving the goals of an effective pricing strategy.

In setting policies, organizations struggle to find a balance between enforcing the tenets of a new strategy and tying the hands of salespeople. Many customers request or demand exceptions. The goal is not to disallow every request but rather to require consideration of the profitability, operations, and customer value implications of the exception to make an informed decision. The value of the exception should be quantified by using historical data and estimating the annual impact. The competitive environment should also be assessed: Are peer companies providing the same break? If so, are they achieving profits in some other way?

Compounding the problem is the fact that organizations often fail to craft policies that adequately consider sales incentives and the processes involved with price negotiations. For example, a sales team or partner channel might be compensated on volume and, perhaps, even on the product margin (i.e., selling price less any discounts). Initially, a salesperson may achieve margin targets when settling on a price with a customer. However, when he or she subsequently makes policy concessions (e.g., free overnight shipping or extended payment terms), the net profitability of the deal decreases and the strategy to achieve a certain price point is undermined. In some cases, the process may break down simply because existing policies were not considered when a deal's potential profitability was being evaluated during a customer negotiation.

While an organization should not grant exceptions frequently, there needs to be a mechanism for evaluating requests and determining when approval should be given to win a desirable piece of business. Pricing policies should be designed in the spirit of mass customization with a few structured options to offer some flexibility.

Of course, once policies are set, they must be communicated effectively. Team members may stray from prescribed guidelines because they are unclear on which ones are in force at any given time. For this reason, affected employees should be involved in establishing the price exception process, so that results are shared companywide. Key stakeholders should then participate in decisions to approve or deny customer requests to speed up response times. For example, if a client asks for free overnight shipping, then the decision should involve not only Sales, but also Logistics to determine the overall impact on the business. Finally, technology should be used to help enforce and implement the new policies. The more manual the administration, the more likely errors and deviations will occur. Automation can help eliminate these potential problems.

Pricing Policy Areas

To avoid new profit leaks occurring, similar policies need to be set across all major areas of customer interaction:

- price discounts
- order size and frequency
- freight and handling
- samples
- returns and warranties
- rebates
- payment terms.

The following section discusses each of these areas of concern, the key issues to consider, and examples of the types of policies that can be implemented.

Price Discounts.   Most organizations enact policies to determine the types of discounts that will be offered as well as how they should be implemented. A car manufacturer might introduce loyalty and competitor defection discounts for its products, varying the amount between the two depending on the business objective (retain the base or steal market share). These policies also specify the maximum size of the discount available and the differing levels of escalation needed to override preapproved limits. This section discusses five of the most popular discount policies: volume, promotional, off-quality, competitive, and portfolio. Organizations will often offer more than one type to customers; however, checks and balances should be in place to prevent the collective amount from exceeding a certain threshold and creating an exceptionally low-price scenario for a customer.

Volume discount policy

This policy stipulates that, in return for a customer's buying at certain volumes, the seller will discount the price, generally in tiers or steps that increase the price reductions. Volume discounts require the risk to be borne upfront by the seller. The customer, in essence, promises to purchase larger quantities in the future to secure the lower price.

When both parties uphold their agreements, volume discounts can be an effective way to align the incentives of the buyer and the seller. However, these policies typically run into problems when the buyer does not meet agreed-upon volumes. Because of this risk, some companies opt to use rebates instead, only paying the incentive to the customer if, during the period of performance, the volume commitment is met. Companies that use volume discounts need to develop tolerance levels for shortfalls and establish compliance policies. For example, a company might establish internally that an annual volume tolerance of 10 percent is allowable. In other words, a customer can miss its commitment, but if the shortfall is greater than the tolerance amount, then the customer must pay a penalty or have its contract reopened for negotiation. However, enforcement is more difficult with this approach because (unlike a rebate policy) a company cannot withhold delivery on incentives until after the customer has met its commitments.

Promotional discount policy

This policy outlines the conditions buyers must meet to qualify for a promotional price on a specific product or service. Promotional discounts should be aligned with the business needs and strategy, with the promotional conditions acting as the governing criteria. For example, if a promotion is available on a certain family of products (when purchased with other goods), then cross-referenced internal systems should be able to determine when individual transactions deserve a discount. These price reductions are typically reflected as a straightforward amount or percentage.

Policy designers should set clear start and end dates for the promotion, so that customers do not continue to request or receive the discount beyond the period for which it is intended to stimulate demand. In addition, companies should require coupons, codes, or other validation criteria for promotional discounts so that promotions are targeted, rather than serving as just another price cut by the sales team to close a deal regardless of whether the business benefits.

Off-quality discount policy

Organizations may establish prices and guidelines to help sell defective products to customers. When setting these policies, organizations should consider the value differential between the off-quality and the first-quality price and how it is perceived (or derived) by the buyer. When the value is almost the same, then customers may feel encouraged to purchase the disproportionately lower-priced, off-quality goods instead of the first-quality items. An additional challenge to discounting off-quality products is that the value of individual items within a batch may vary, making a single price hard to uphold. For these reasons, organizations should establish formulas to help price off-quality goods on an ad-hoc basis based on quality level and differences in customer valuation.

Competitive discount policy

Customers regularly request additional discounts from merchants and suppliers, citing competitor alternatives. Fearing a loss in sales, organizations often bend to the pressure and meet the price requested by the customer. A competitive discount policy should set limits on how much salespeople may yield, which rivals the company is willing to take on, and what information is needed from the customer before granting a request. Organizations should plan how they will react to each competitor: some challenges may be best addressed by a reduction that still maintains a premium price point, but certain regional or smaller rivals may warrant no price movement whatsoever.

In return for the discount, an organization should, at a minimum, obtain some intelligence on the competitor's price. A company can ask its salespeople to obtain the competing quote sheet or price list from the customer. Salespeople often resist making such a request, claiming it may introduce mistrust into their relationships with customers. However, sales and marketing executives should respond that without proof of competing offers, a customer can simply pit companies against one another in an effort to secure an even larger discount.

Portfolio discount policy

This approach offers the customer an additional discount for purchasing a prescribed mix of product. Portfolio discounts are useful when encouraging customers to expand the number of products they purchase or motivating them to buy higher-margin, complementary offerings along with their original selections. Many organizations establish policies offering a flat percentage discount depending on the number of different products purchased; however, that approach does not take volume into account—a customer may buy just a few products outside of its core set to fulfill the discount criteria. Portfolio discount policies should establish specific benchmarks, such as growth targets for products not currently being purchased by the customer, or a certain amount of spend in other business divisions.

Order Size and Frequency.   These policies should be designed to influence customer ordering behavior and to recover the costs incurred when fulfilling orders. Operations and Logistics can establish standardized processing times, production runs, and shipment methods to optimize productivity and to minimize costs. Without order size and frequency policies, some buyers may become costly to serve. For example, if a customer frequently places small orders with a company whose cost to process a single order is roughly fixed, the customer's behavior will erode profits. To address the issue, the company can implement a surcharge policy, assessing an additional fee when the order does not meet a minimum dollar amount. Some of the commonly used options for the order size and frequency policy approach follow.

Order quantity discount

A percentage discount when an order meets a certain threshold; for example, filling more than half a truckload to make shipping more economical.

Item quantity discount

A discount on a particular product or SKU when shipping an entire palette is easier for a company or helps it avoid breaking up production lots.

Minimum order surcharge

A surcharge that encourages customers to purchase large amounts to avoid the company incurring extra expenses on small orders.

Typically, order size and frequency policies are not profit generators, so they run the risk of discouraging customer orders altogether. They should be designed to provide the buyer with the option of conforming to more normal ordering patterns or paying a small fee to obtain services and support for nonstandard requests. The organization and its customers share the consequences that flow from irregular activity, and the right policies can incentivize both sides to devise ways to manage ordering behavior better.

Freight and Handling.   These policies represent agreements between the seller and the customer that establish how products will be routinely delivered and define what constitutes an additional service that will incur a surcharge. A basic freight and handling policy should outline the method of transportation, fulfillment service level, and rate determination criteria. All of these elements should be part of a standard contract. While these policies are generally adequate for routine business, companies sometimes fail to structure necessary supplemental policies to accommodate irregular or disruptive orders. For example, a customer who requests expedited shipping may be charged only the rush rate for freight, which may be insufficient.

Sellers must ask themselves: Will we recover our cost for interrupting fulfillment of other orders in the queue to rush this order for a single customer? Sellers should consider how expedited, drop ship, and various shipping restrictions affect freight costs. For example, if a customer can receive deliveries only during certain hours or requires a smaller-size truck due to its dock configuration, then the seller should consider passing along the added costs of delivery to the customer.

Freight and handling policies may include surcharges tied to volatility in fuel costs. Customers, however, are likely to resist these surcharges because they create unpredictability in the customers' costs. To mitigate objections to a surcharge, firms can tie their calculations of it to an industry statistic or government report—or any metric the customer can verify independently. This can help alleviate the perception that the firm is simply tacking on extra charges to increase profitability at the customer's expense. If freight exceptions are a critical negotiating point, firms can try modeling the variability in costs and only agree to a limited time frame so that the exception can be re-evaluated periodically.

Samples.   Organizations use samples to encourage customers to try a product or to use it in its point-of-sale display. When poorly managed, samples can become a source of excessive profit leakage for an organization. Policies should be devised that dictate how many samples customers can receive and at what cost. Pricing is often handled in one of two ways: partial charge and free of charge. An organization may opt to allow unlimited purchases of partial-charge samples because they cover the production costs, yet limit the free items to a prescribed threshold.

Equally important, organizations need to use adequate monitoring mechanisms in relation to samples. If a customer's spend and profitability increase over the course of the fiscal year, then the number of samples it is permitted should increase to support the greater volume of purchases. Sample policies should not be limited to customers. For organizations with a direct sales force, providing representatives with a fixed sample budget or allotment encourages their providing these products to only top prospects, rather than to weak ones (which can erode profits). Monitoring mechanisms should periodically evaluate salespeople and provide additional sample allowances only to those who are growing their business and meeting organizational goals.

Firms must also consider other charges. Samples usually require their own freight and handling policies independent of running line goods. Because they are usually a fraction of the size of their normal counterparts, customers might presume the shipping to be free or deeply discounted. While sample budgets may absorb these costs, customers should be educated to expect that the firm alone will determine how and when samples will be delivered. Firms often find profit leakage results from expediting samples at a customer's request. Sample offerings should also be standardized so that production lines are not subject to reconfiguration downtime and the costs associated with custom lots or quantities.

Returns and Warranties. Returns and warranties are designed to assure customers of product quality and to provide a mechanism for them to receive credit when items are defective or returned unused. Companies need to make clear, however, the difference between returns and warranties. Warranty policies are set for products that do not perform to expectations and tend to be more lenient than return policies, which cover products returned for reasons other than quality. Return policies should take into account the following considerations.

- Time frame within which returns are possible: Time frames are especially important for items that are perishable or diminish in value over time, likely resulting in the seller's needing to dispose of them at a significant discount.
- The policy should ensure the expense of accepting an item back from the customer is recovered adequately, thus reducing the risk of potential profit loss. If the item must be restocked and inventoried, then the policy should provide for a restocking fee.
- How value will be calculated when return is requested, particularly if the order has already been customized or a special production run has already been started.
- How the customer should make the request: If a customer service representative helps qualify a return, then he or she can instruct the customer on the required packaging and shipping.
- The manner in which refunds will be processed: Should customers be given credits toward future purchases or be issued checks (which adds processing and administrative costs)? Should a fee be charged if a customer requests a different form of payment than stipulated by the policy?
- How the return will be verified: Verifying returns is the process of inspecting the returned product to confirm the reason for the return stated by the customer and the amount of product returned.

Verification is a step that companies often ignore in the belief that customers will become annoyed when they have to wait for a refund and that the costs to verify will exceed any benefits. However, allowing this gap in a return policy can lead to its being exploited and result in profit leakage. At a minimum, companies should audit returned materials occasionally and inform customers of the results to discourage any potential "gaming" behavior.

While return policies are aimed at recovering costs and preventing profit loss when a customer returns a good-quality product, warranty policies should be designed to accommodate a customer after a poor-quality product experience. As with return policies, warranty policies should specify the terms a customer must follow to send an item back or to have it replaced. Warranty conditions need to be clearly defined. For example, should a minor scratch on the exterior box qualify an item as a return or as a warranty claim? The policy should also clearly describe the remedy, so the customer knows whether a replacement product or an account credit will be issued and how long the process will take.

Sellers should track their warranty and return items throughout the year to determine whether any customers seem to be returning abnormal amounts of product (by percent of sales or volume). These kinds of anomalies can indicate inventory management issues or that particular buyers are stocking extra product and then, when it doesn't sell, recouping the costs by returning it. If a seller finds potential abuse of its warranty policy, then it can take action to eliminate the behavior.

Rebates.   Rebates can help encourage customer growth and volume commitments, while incentivizing certain behavior. They often are more effective than upfront price concessions, because they reward customers after a period of demonstrated performance. Generally, where these policies fall apart and cause profit erosion is in the compliance phase. For example, a sales representative may negotiate a rebate agreement that discounts a product below its profitability target, or the representative may offer a rebate percentage based on an annual volume commitment, only to discover later that the buyer did not meet expectations. Problems can arise from the sheer number of programs a company administers. Typically, the more a company customizes rebate schemes for individual customers, the harder it will be for that company to monitor them properly.

Rebate policies should ideally be aligned with the firm's pricing strategy. If the firm pursues a skim strategy emphasizing a high price, then it should resist offering rebates at the outset. Conversely, when utilizing penetration pricing, it might consider rewarding customers and distributors for higher-volume purchases. When firms use many strategies, they should aim to set rebate policies at the product line or brand level: this allows for more customization than a one-size-fits-all approach, but it will not overwhelm the firm or the customer (who may also appreciate not having to deal with an array of policies, each covering different products).

When determining the appropriate rebate to offer, an organization should consider the profitability of the products in question, so that profit margins are not unintentionally lowered below specified thresholds. The organization should consider the product mix that the customer is likely to purchase and then how the offer may affect the customer's overall profitability. Custom rebate programs should be avoided if possible, especially those that don't drive substantial margin or volume with the business. Customers should be matched with standardized rebate programs by product line or brand. Organizations should carefully manage which programs are tied to which products or services. Organizations have a tendency to create double-dip scenarios inadvertently over time, enabling customers to receive two rebates for one purchase.

Tracking rebate compliance can be challenging; significant effort is needed to administer and monitor these policies, which can be quite complex, effectively. While companies do not like to impose penalties on customers who fail to meet agreed-upon goals, compliance tracking can highlight pricing issues that need attention and inform future negotiations with those and other customers. For instance, if a customer's volume rebate is based on forecasted purchases of $1 million or more, but the customer only purchases half that amount, then the company's tracking mechanism should identify this compliance issue. The sales representative or negotiating agent can then use that information to renegotiate prices or to discuss ways for the customer to reach volume goals.

Payment Terms. Although most companies don't acknowledge or factor the cost of payment terms into customer negotiations, they can greatly affect profitability. Many buyers request, and are granted, extended payment terms, allowing them to treat the supplier essentially as an interest-free lender. Aggressive customers sometimes negotiate early payment discounts that don't actually benefit the seller. Furthermore, when customers pay late and aren't subjected to late payment penalties, sellers condition these customers to continue this behavior or to take other payment liberties. Like rebates, payment terms have a habit of proliferating. Oddly, companies don't show the same fervor for addressing these issues as they do other problems. One reason may be that the costs associated with providing extended or more discounted payment terms do not immediately affect the income statement. However, disadvantageous payment terms do, at a minimum, deprive a company of cash flow and interest income, which means less money is available to make new investments.

As an example, here is a formula that one company uses to approximate the cost of payment terms associated with a sales transaction:

$$\text{Cost of terms} = \text{early payment discount} + \text{carrying cost of the invoice} - \text{late payment surcharges}$$

Based on the day the customer actually pays the invoice, an early payment discount may apply. Typically, this discount is a flat percentage of the overall invoice, so a supplier should consider offering one that benefits both it and the buyer. Does early payment enable the supplier to purchase raw materials sooner from a third party and thus to receive a discount in turn? Are there cash flow implications? If not, then the early payment discount becomes only another concession to the customer.

The carrying cost of the invoice should be determined next by combining the number of days to pay, the organization's daily cost-of-capital (weighted-average-cost-of-capital [WACC] divided by 365 days), and the invoice amount:

$$\text{Carrying cost of the invoice} = \text{days sales outstanding} \\ \times (\text{WACC}/365) \times \text{invoice amount}$$

This formula represents the financing cost incurred when providing terms to the customer (and the impact on profitability). The higher the *days sales outstanding*, the higher the overall carrying cost of the invoice. When key customers demand concessions, firms should determine which would have a larger impact on profitability: meeting the demand for an early payment discount or extending the number of days to pay. In addition, when firms establish promotional payment terms to stimulate the sales of certain products, they should assess how these terms will affect overall margin and whether they meet the profitability thresholds of the promotional campaign.

Finally, any interest or penalties recovered as a result of a customer's paying an invoice beyond the agreed upon due date (i.e., late payment surcharges) should be subtracted from the cost of terms. While a rare missed payment can be forgiven, frequent late-paying offenders should be subject to penalties.

When setting up payment term policies, companies should limit the number of available terms. Customized options can be provided for valuable customers, but most other customers should be placed into a few standard options. The policies should specify the methods of payment accepted and what surcharges will be assessed for processing more costly credit card and cash-on-delivery payments. Finally, technology should be used to monitor payment term compliance and behavior, and to report exceptions, so any problems can be quickly addressed.

Tips for Moving Forward

To make important process improvements, some redesign will likely be necessary. Typically, this begins with the documentation of existing processes so that gaps and inefficiencies can be identified objectively. Once these have been noted, firms can consider the Best Practice Framework (Level 1) processes discussed in this chapter as they begin their redesign.

Key Questions to Address Upfront

- What formal and informal pricing processes currently exist?
- What written procedures and guidelines are in place?
- What consequences will occur if guidelines are not followed?
- What are effective industry practices?
- How can existing processes be streamlined or improved?
- How much flexibility and enforcement should be built into the new process?
- How often should performance be measured?

Simple Process Options Achievable with a Redesign

- Redefine where and how an activity is performed
- Add or remove an activity, or move it to another process or subprocess
- Combine two or more activities into one
- Break an activity into two or more activities
- Change the sequence or timing of activities
- Make sequential activities simultaneous
- Automate an activity
- Employ a new tool
- Change responsibilities and roles
- Change an activity name or description
- Change linkages to other processes or subprocesses.

Principles to Keep in Mind

- *Focus on the customer.* Value can be created only by addressing the needs and goals of the customer. Pricing processes should be designed to reflect the customer's perspective and to optimize the entire value chain, regardless of organizational boundaries. One contact point should be established for each customer.
- *Improve coordination.* Companies should minimize the number of people involved in the execution of a process. This will not only reduce hand-offs, but also help break down barriers between team members because boundaries caused by current processes will likely be eliminated.
- *Aim for simplicity.* Non-value-added activities should be eliminated and new opportunities should be identified to perform remaining activities in parallel. Firms can also develop alternate routes for complex cases, rather than trying to create one path to handle all situations.
- *Fix processes first, then apply technology.* Existing tasks should only be automated after the company determines they have been adding value and have been handled efficiently. When processes are combined with technology, steps should be taken to ensure that data are

only entered once and are input by staff who understand them. This will eliminate many clerical errors.

- *Manage people effectively.* Work should be organized around outcomes, not tasks. People involved in a process should be given ownership for at least a meaningful component—if not all—of it.
- *Measure performance.* Firms should track those aspects of performance that reveal whether they are delivering superior results to the customer.
  - Challenge organizational assumptions
  - Who should perform the work (personnel mix)?
  - Where is work done (geographical limitations)?
  - When must work be done (time limitations)?
  - What resources does the work require (asset requirements)?
  - Under what conditions is work done (job requirements)?
  - Are there too many layers of governance controlling the work (non-value-added overheads)?
  - What does the customer really hope to achieve (process output)?
- *Question conventional thinking.* Firms should acknowledge and respect cross-business-unit considerations and nuances, but continually ask: What is the purpose of our performing activity X in this manner?
- *Focus on creating value.* When a requirement exists solely to maintain the status quo, it typically does not deliver value. The organization should be challenged to think in terms of economic costs, benefits, and customer value. Employees should ask: Are buyers paying us more to perform this activity in this manner? If the answer is no, then the task should be eliminated.

Endnotes

1. ManuCorp is a fictitious company created for illustrative purposes, but the situation described is a fairly common one.
2. AMR Research, "Research Alert 18038," February 23, 2005.
3. Steven Tom, "Transform Your Pricing Strategy into a Competitive Weapon," Journal of Professional Pricing, April 1, 2008.
4. Credited to The Atlanta Journal in a "Letter to the Editor" by Julian C. McCalla, *The Fayetteville Observer*, July 22, 2000.

CHAPTER

5

Advanced Analytics and Price Setting

Definition of a Statistician: A man who believes figures don't lie, but admits that under analysis some of them won't stand up either.

—Evan Esar

More than ever before, companies are gathering, storing, mining, and aggregating data to produce reports distributed throughout organizations in real time. Yet despite this massive information effort, companies still rely on reactive, speculative pricing strategies. Competitive pressures, shifting customer demands, and entrenched organizational cultures may collide, making people fearful of doing anything to disrupt the status quo. Consequently, companies generate few actionable insights from their data and are often reluctant to explore alternative approaches and methods to pricing.

Applied effectively, pricing analytics serve as a powerful tool to improve decision making and increase profitability. But to utilize these analytic methods, a unique, transaction-level view of a company's data is required. This perspective is very different—sharper—than the typical collection of sales information that business leaders find in management reports and financial statements. Unfortunately, the very act of aggregation produces misleading averages and *gross* metrics, which can mask critical truths about the business. The specific impact of hundreds of thousands of individual negotiations may become obscured in the cumulative totaling of a billion-dollar business. After reviewing several data sets, which produce highly counterintuitive results, an executive might remark, "I guess a lot of issues get buried in an average."

In conducting their pricing analyses, organizations often must integrate data spread across dozens of systems with different owners. It can be a laborious, time-consuming task just to identify and gather the right information, let alone determine what to do with it. However, organizations have been forced to address these issues as they increasingly understand the latent power of this data and how applying advanced analytics can help harness the data to achieve more profitable pricing. To help with this effort, organizations can use a simple framework to understand their sales environment at the most granular level. This framework comprises four distinct categories, each of which utilizes unique tools:

- the *costs* of doing business (transaction-level analytics)
- the *customer*—its various segments and segment attributes (cluster analysis)
- the *category/characteristics*—what the customer desires, and the product elements it may be willing to trade off (conjoint analysis)
- the *competition*—how it affects the customer experience (value equivalency analytics).

Ultimately, this focus on costs, customer, category, and competition allows an organization to understand the true dynamics of its market, and therefore to begin setting prices using optimization analytics. In this chapter we will explore various quantitative approaches organizations can use to get closer to their customers, and some critical ways pricing can be optimized to increase profitability and customer loyalty.

Building a Transaction-Level Data Set

The old adage "you can't manage what you don't measure" goes a long way to explaining why companies have struggled to improve their profitability. Companies often find themselves facing a glut of information with little or no underlying structure to make it useful. A wave of enterprise resource planning (ERP) implementations in recent decades has led companies to store massive amounts of data backed by armies of individuals who manage, manipulate, and monitor a variety of metrics, measures, aggregates, and outcomes. The challenge is not simply to measure activities appropriately, but to measure the right data at the right level of detail in the appropriate format.

Effective pricing and profitability management must begin with a solid foundational fact base. The lifecycle of each transaction must be traced in detail as well as the revenues and costs associated with it. This is where profitability-related efforts often go off course. The data in most systems are based on the financial reporting timeline; that is, the date when the transaction is recorded to the general ledger. Unfortunately, this practice biases the information toward the balance sheets because each notation reflects when the transaction was paid or received. For example, a product pallet purchased in January would appear in accounts receivable that same month, while the annual rebate earned on this same pallet will appear as a cost in accounts payable some 12 months later. This spreading about of critical data is further complicated by the sheer number of cost-to-serve elements associated with any transaction, whether they be costs for shipping, customer service and technical support, or sales and marketing expenses.

Because gathering, cleansing, interpreting, formatting, and packaging all this data presents such a complex challenge, a dedicated team must be assembled, which will follow a carefully designed plan of action. To manage profitability, data must be tracked in a holistic way at the transaction level. The sheer size of the task can seem overwhelming. For many firms a year's worth of business can produce millions (or tens of millions) of transactions, and electronic records of it can be dozens of gigabytes in size. In addition, this information will most likely need to be retrieved from numerous sources, including ERP, invoicing, order management, contract management, and shipping and distribution management as well as from various financial systems, including payments, accounts receivable, and credit. One must then determine how best to gather, decipher, and assign data so that profitability insights can be uncovered.

Data Management Strategies

Although the process of advanced analytics seems daunting, some tips and strategies for companies assembling the data and laying the groundwork follow.

Realize That Perfect Data Don't Exist.   Instead of trying to assemble the perfect data set, firms should go with what they've got. Though they may discover that they lack the data to test a particular hypothesis, simply going through the exercise of doing pricing analyses with imperfect data may generate important findings along the way (execution issues or operational inefficiencies or best practices, which can be leveraged across the organization) that can be acted on.

Know When to Say Stop.   There is a tendency to try to include every cost or customer element and every product or service demographic. This will result in an unwieldy data set and also will likely generate assumptions and calculations that fail to resonate with key stakeholders. The focus should be on the elements that contribute the most to revenue or cost and ignore (or make simple assumptions for) those that do not. Detail can always be added later.

Avoid the "It Can't Be" Trap.   Tribal knowledge is valuable to any organization. A healthy skepticism is always useful when considering a data set and the analytic outcomes it produces; it does not, however, trump the data, which may challenge accepted truths about the business.

Assign, Don't Allocate.   Cost elements that are not customer or product specific, such as business overheads, should be included. To incorporate these in the transaction-level data set, businesses often use arbitrary mechanisms or complex calculations to allocate them. In the end, these elements are spread throughout the business, resulting in profit reductions for all products and customers. If a business takes this approach, then it will have little or no ability to understand whether particular elements pose problems (or opportunities) that need to be managed. Businesses should strive, instead, to assign all costs to a customer, product, or transaction.

Find Natural Reference Points and Examples.   Large data sets are particularly hard to manage, and successful analytics are often built on millions upon millions of records. To make data sets more manageable, natural reference points can be selected that are easily verifiable from memory (e.g., monthly revenue totals). One way to make an internal team feel comfortable with the data is to select the company's highest-earning product and show numbers that everyone is familiar with. The total revenue for, say, a seafood company's tuna fish category may be the most recognizable figure, so using it as a benchmark can provide buy-in to the analytic exercise. Examples that support recommendations or hypotheses should be found. For instance, a large chemical company cited the price for a certain product as $3.00 per pound. However, overall profitability for the item was low because a single customer was purchasing a very large volume at less than half that figure. Although the price was reasonable considering the volume, subjecting a high-profile product to such a granular analysis produced a valuable insight that contradicted conventional wisdom in the company. In this case, one large customer's low profitability had obscured the high profitability of others.

Develop a System to Capture and Implement Data Improvements.   As people learn from the data, they should find ways to incorporate that knowledge into the data set itself; for example, a new allocation method to improve the distribution of costs or a completely new data collection process to improve outcomes. A system should be put in place to capture findings, assumptions, and *wish lists*. Where appropriate, all of these should be incorporated into the data set.

Conducting Transactional Profitability Assessments

All too many organizations have become comfortable managing at an aggregate level. In the past, this was necessary because the technology, know-how, and statistical tools to mine data efficiently at a detailed level simply did not exist. This, however, is no longer the case. Organizations can now take advantage of technological advances, beginning with a transactional profitability assessment (TPA, also known as "transactional analytics"). This basic analytic seeks to identify opportunities for an organization to improve performance through an enhanced understanding of transaction-level profitability. A unified data set brings exceptional—and invaluable— visibility to the core of an organization's business models. A TPA is designed to identify common pricing problems that can result from inefficiencies in sales, processes, policies, and cost to serve through close analysis of internal pricing practices and data.

Though businesses often factor supply, demand, and product positioning strategies into their decision making, many leave profit on the table at the transactional level, where product meets customer. Invoice price is generally used to measure revenue. Unfortunately, the difference between invoice price and actual price (after discounts, rebates, and other customer concessions are factored in) can result in significant reductions to the bottom-line profit. Businesses are not leaving this money on the table on purpose. The sheer volume and complexity of individual customer transactions make effective transactional pricing management nearly impossible to grasp fully on a customer-by-customer basis.

A TPA approach enables a company to recognize profit-leaking practices by identifying faulty price execution, such as in:

- sales—volume or bundled product discounts, inconsistent (or nonexistent) price list, and negotiated discounts based on customer relationships
- process—noncompliant contracts, inappropriate payment term discounts, and late payments without penalty
- policy—no-charge product customizations, free trials, and no-charge package or label customizations
- cost-to-serve—credits and returns, customer-driven testing or inspections, uncompensated field service, and express shipments.

Some of the typical areas of price execution that are explored and evaluated during a TPA are listed and described in the following.

- *Geographic pricing.* Are geographic price differentials justified? Are global customers buying from several regional price lists? Is a customer eroding prices by ordering products from lower-priced geographic areas and having them shipped to higher-priced ones? Is the customer negotiating globally to erode geographic price differentials?
- *Scale pricing.* Scale pricing should encourage customers to place fewer larger orders and cover any additional order (such as customer service representative and warehouse movements) or freight costs. Look at the number of orders per month versus the average

order size. High monthly orders for quantities representing less than full truckloads should be investigated. In addition, look at price versus freight differentials to see if scale prices are properly set.

- *Package differentials.* Package and shipment size can be highly correlated to cost and margin. Are there efficiencies in moving more customers to a larger package or bulk? Is pricing at the product or the material level? Do package price differentials cover COGS differentials?

- *Uncharged dilution costs.* A series of products may vary in concentration (e.g., the percentage of an active ingredient). When looking at a series, determine if its prices and margins are following the concentration elements in a logical way.

- *Noncompliance with lead times.* Lead times are necessary for the supply chain to operate efficiently. Noncompliance leads to higher inventory levels, higher freight, and so forth. Does the business allow lead time violations? How often? Is there a charge for expediting the order?

- *Rebate management.* Customer rebates commonly depend on sales targets. Are rebate conditions enforced? How are they monitored?

- *Standard freight charges.* Is the cost of freight a factor in setting prices? Does pricing reflect actual freight differentials? Look at pocket margin versus shipping zone for anomalies.

- *Free, expedited freight.* Are buyers charged for expedited freight when they request it?

- *Variable payment terms.* How many payment terms does the business use? How many are more than 30 days? What is the magnitude of discounts? Is there an allowable float? Are customers paying late without penalty or receiving discounts beyond the term conditions? What is the business goal for accounts receivable? Graph terms' cost divided by net revenue on one axis and annual net revenue on the other axis: assume the value is 0.01 for every 30 days of receivables the business wants to achieve (or their average). Identify customers who are significantly above target to see if pocket margins justify the extra receivables expense.

- *Service time productivity.* Service time includes costs for personnel such as customer service representatives (CSRs), sales, and field technicians. Are customer costs in this area justified based on percentage pocket margin? Are these services valued by the customer and reflected in the price?

- *Inventory carrying costs.* Graph inventory costs divided by cost of goods sold versus annual COGS by material. The business should have some historical average of the inventory days as well as a target number it wants to achieve. Assume the value is 0.01 for every 30 days of inventory. (If the business wants 45 days of inventory, then the number is 0.015.) Look for products above the target value, especially on

the right side of the graph. Causes for high values include safety stocks, improper channels, or customer-specific inventory.
- *Distributors*. Are distributors used? Are pocket margins comparable (by product) for distributor sales versus direct sales? Which channel is more profitable by customer size, and by how much?
- *Commissions*. Are commissions being paid for underperforming orders? Plot commissions versus percentage pocket margin by order. Investigate the cause of orders delivering a below-average percentage pocket margin for the business.

Opportunities for improvement are identified by both qualitative and quantitative means. The strength of the TPA approach lies in the combination of these two types of analyses: the former makes them real, indisputable, and quantifiable, while the latter ensures they are realistic, feasible, and implementable.

TPA: The Qualitative Approach

The TPA process must be hypothesis driven. Millions of lines of transactional data and innumerable graphs and charts will not reveal opportunities for improvement by themselves. Instead, firms must conduct specific analyses to prove or disprove hypotheses. For example, a manager may have a hunch that some of her sales representatives are giving away free freight too easily to win deals. To test that theory, she can design a data analysis plan that includes freight billed, the actual freight costs incurred by customer and sales representative, and the effects on pocket margin. She should look for buyers and products for which this practice has reduced pocket margins to an unacceptable level, or even a negative amount. In general, qualitative analyses can help managers refine initial hypotheses and then suggest where they might find improvement opportunities.

Interviews.   By questioning key contacts, firms can identify business processes deserving attention and leakage points in their price waterfalls. The information gathered produces a fairly accurate picture of the current sales situation; namely, the policies and processes governing pricing decisions. It may also generate useful hunches about the best (and worst) products and customers. The insights gained from the qualitative discussions will strengthen quantitative analyses, while any new hypotheses can be formulated and tested with the transactional data.

Listed in the following are examples of TPA opportunities that can be investigated through interviews and then quantified with the data.

- General
  - What is the current market dynamic the business is facing?
  - What tools (if any) does the business use to evaluate pricing data?

- Pricing
  - How have prices in this market been acting lately (e.g., moving, stabilizing)?
  - How transparent are prices in the marketplace?
  - Who is responsible for price setting in this business?
  - Are list prices used? If so, how often are they updated?
  - Which elements are negotiated at the point of transaction (e.g., terms, discounts)?
  - What pricing challenges (if any) is the firm facing?
- Sales management
  - How are sales representatives compensated (i.e., what are their performance drivers)?
  - What level of turnover exists in the sales force? What drives this turnover?
  - How is the sales force structured (e.g., territory, market, inside [primarily over the phone and small accounts] or outside [primarily a mobile sales force for larger accounts])?
- Marketing
  - Does the firm engage in cooperative advertising with customers?
  - Who is responsible for tracking promotional activity and discounting?
- Logistics
  - What are the common delivery terms of sale?
  - How many orders are typically placed each month per customer?
  - Where is material warehoused? Is consignment used?
- Financing
  - Are there standard payment terms in this business?
  - How important are prompt payment discounts to customers?
  - Is the customer being offered standard term lengths or a cash discount percentage?
  - Are unearned discounts being claimed by customers?
  - Are late payment fees charged?
- Freight
  - Is there a minimum order quantity for customers?
  - Are customers charged for expedited orders?
- Rebates and commissions
  - Are any outdated or unnecessary rebates being paid?
  - Can unprofitable, third-party commissions be eliminated?
- Returns
  - Are customers routinely sending back unwarranted returns?
- Technical Support
  - Are there charges for special services performed?
  - Should service to unprofitable accounts be reduced or eliminated?
- Contracts
  - Is the customer compliant with contract terms?

- Marketing
  - Are too many free samples or product trials being given out?
- Packaging
  - Is there a charge for special packaging or label customization?

Because the interviews will provide early and significant guidance to the transactional analysis (and the development of potential solutions), the selection of interviewees is an important step, but a potentially challenging one. Representatives from all business functions should be interviewed, including Marketing, Sales, Supply Chain, Customer Service, Finance and Accounting, Credit, and Shipping and Logistics, to get as broad a view as possible of the processes affecting pricing. In addition, personnel at multiple levels within the organization should participate so that all opinions and observations can be evaluated. Regional sales managers, for example, may have different ideas about how decisions are made than the sales representatives in the field.

Qualitative Analyses.   Interviews with key business stakeholders will suggest where to look first for opportunities in the transactional data. Qualitative analyses, which should be done concurrently with quantitative analyses, can identify the root causes of the problems identified through the quantitative analyses. Listed below are some typical qualitative assessments conducted by firms during a TPA and the key goals and activities associated with each.

- Pricing process mapping
  - Map existing processes.
  - Understand elements of pricing negotiated at points of transaction.
  - Identify improvement opportunities and elements critical to quality.
  - Assess process controls and measurements.
- Sales force compensation review
  - Analyze compensation structures that may encourage unintended behavior and drive poor pricing performance.
  - Identify loopholes in performance measurement frameworks that allow the sales force to work around the system.
- Sales force tools and support evaluation
  - Identify standard and nonstandard sales tools and capture best-in-class tools for standardization.
  - Evaluate margin leakage allowed or caused by tools currently in use.
  - Identify needs or gaps in sales force tools and support.
- Operations review
  - Develop a detailed understanding of operations and key cost drivers and how they affect cost-to-serve.

- Identify operational cost drivers that can be controlled or influenced at the time of the sale.
- Market and competitor review
  - Review currently available market and competitor data.
  - Understand the tools and methods of collecting market intelligence.
  - Identify gaps in market and competitor knowledge.
  - Assess quality and timeliness of information available to the sales force.

TPA: The Quantitative Approach

While qualitative analyses identify the conditions creating pricing opportunities and suggest how to benefit from them, quantitative analyses provide the proof that there is improvement opportunity. Transactional analytics, as the term itself suggests, offers a means to explore a data model at a transaction-by-transaction level. The actual TPAs are not themselves complex tools. They consist of Pareto charts, scatter plots, price bands, and other simple graphic mechanisms for analyzing data. The interpretation of these analyses, however, is more sophisticated than the average price versus quantity graph. During a TPA, data are manipulated through targeted segmenting and filtering techniques to make them meaningful, specific, and actionable, which ultimately enables better decision making (see Figure 5.1).

A set of basic transactional price analyses can offer insights at multiple levels. First, it can verify (or disprove) widely accepted facts about the business within an organization. These range from simple statements (e.g., "the average selling price for this product is $X") to complex assertions (e.g., "when we provide a rebate, we drive incremental, year-over-year volume"). Second, this analytic set can generate a common language to discuss pricing and profitability, encouraging organization-wide alignment around these concepts. When a team defines profit and profit drivers the same way, it also shares an understanding of what is important for profitable growth. Finally, and most critically, the analyses drive value for the organization by illuminating pricing improvement opportunities.

A typical transactional analytics initiative can shift 1–3 percent of revenue to the bottom line in the first 12 months *without adding new technology, making major adjustments in the operating model, or increasing costs.* This is possible because many firms have never before aligned their organizations around profitability. Once insights are drawn from the data set, action can be taken quickly, particularly to seize previously missed opportunities, such as enforcing unfulfilled customer contract obligations.

The goal of transactional analytics is twofold. First, it provides a means to understand the true cost of doing business, rather than taking the traditional approach of merely tabulating the COGS. This cost equation must include the realities of doing business at a detailed, programmatic

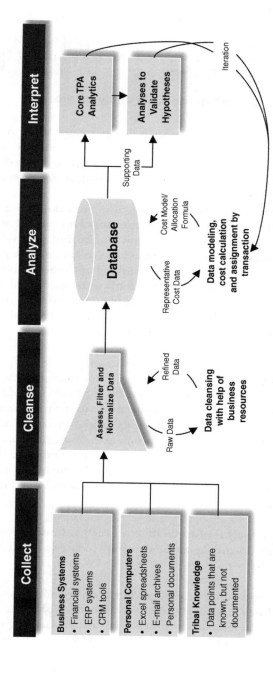

Figure 5.1 The Quantitative Approach to Transactional Profitability Assessment (TPA)

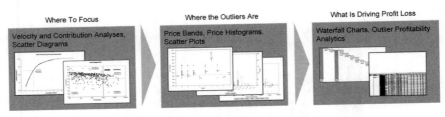

Figure 5.2   The Standard Transactional Analytics Process

level, including the costs-to-serve, such as customer service or shipping expenses. Second, transactional analytics creates an important opportunity to standardize operations and to identify key areas of profit leakage. This will lead, in turn, to tighter controls, more integrated operations, and better data.

Transactional analytics should not be considered as a once-off exercise producing transient results. Many of the opportunities identified will emerge again and again without review and monitoring. Firms should conduct transactional analytics on a regular basis to actually compound the benefits. The returns can be staggering, and the outcomes game changing.

This is not to say that applying the tools of transactional analytics is easy, as they have an infinite number of variations. Trying to use them all is both cost-prohibitive and of little incremental value. Firms should therefore follow these well-defined process steps when carrying out an initial set of analytics (see also Figure 5.2):

1. Use Pareto charts on products and customers to determine key focus areas, such as products that drive 80 percent of revenue or customers who contribute negative profit to the organization.
2. Use scatter graphs and price bands to identify areas of high variance across critical demographics, segments, and time periods. These graphic tools can indicate which elements are driving unexpected behavior and can generate insights that drive value.
3. Use specialized transactional analytics to model specific scenarios in the data.

Transactional analytics can include a nearly infinite amount of data and combinations, so they must be carefully focused. We discuss in the following how to do this.

Pareto Charts.   Pareto charts are a good data filter and can identify key areas to explore further. At its simplest, a Pareto chart plots the cumulative effect of individual elements in descending order (see Figure 5.3). In profit analytics, the most common Pareto charts focus on revenue and margin. By plotting the cumulative revenue (in dollars or percent) on the y-axis, how many (and which) elements drive the most significant business

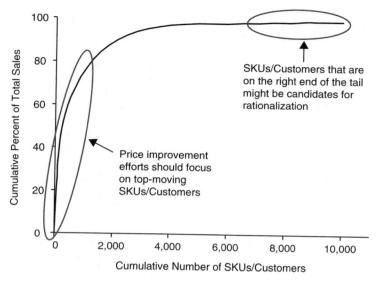

Figure 5.3   Velocity (Pareto) Chart

can easily be determined. Furthermore, the elements that contribute little or nothing to the company's overall objectives can be identified. Following the Pareto Principle,[1] or the 80/20 rule, the focus should generally be on the elements (customers or products or both) driving 80 percent of the revenue (highlighted in the first red oval in Figure 5.3) because that is where the biggest benefit will result from any improvement. Customers or products that are on the right end of the tail (the second red oval) might be candidates for rationalization.

Firms may start with a customer and product Pareto chart, but additional analyses can be conducted by region, division, channel, or product category. These can provide valuable insights into the ranking of products, customers, and channels. They can also point to areas where profitability management efforts would bear the most fruit.

Plotting some form of margin (e.g., gross margin or pocket margin) produces a similar chart, often with a large negative dip at the tail end causing the curve to resemble the outline of a whale (leading to the name *whale curve*). In these cases, it is best to invert thinking to focus on the elements that contribute to the decline in margin dollars.

In Figure 5.4, the first oval represents the products and customers that a firm should concentrate its pricing and selling efforts on because these will increase both profitability and volume. Products and customers in the second oval are potential candidates for repricing, SKU rationalization, product or service bundling, or customer attrition.

A large chemical company assembled a product Pareto chart. When each element on the graph was colored to indicate product classifications, management realized several of its core products had trickled into the tail of the curve, contributing little or no revenue to the bottom line. Conversely, several niche products had increased in revenue to such a degree as to mirror the revenue profile of core products. Most surprisingly, two discontinued products—no longer advertised and produced only upon request—had made it into the top 10. Each product's classification determined lead times, stock status, and a variety of other business drivers intimately related to cost. The result of the analytic: managers implemented a review of product classifications to drive a new portfolio strategy.

The intersection of the velocity chart and the whale curve can be revealing. If, for instance, a customer or product appears both in the first oval on the velocity chart (i.e., high-volume sales) and in the second oval of the whale curve (i.e., negative margin), then a firm will need to make changes immediately as it is losing money with each high-volume transaction.

Pareto charts have a versatility that should be leveraged. Within large waterfall buckets (described later in the section ''Profit Waterfalls''), for example, it is extremely valuable to run a cost Pareto chart. If the

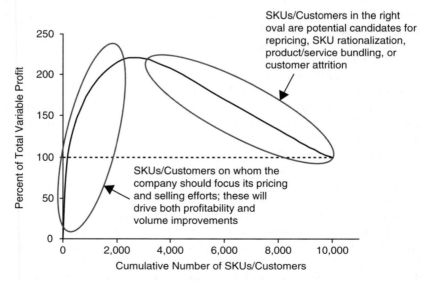

Figure 5.4   Whale Curve (Margin Pareto Chart)

hypothesis is that "X is driving freight costs," then a firm can identify the customers, products, states, transportation providers, warehouses, and so forth contributing to those costs. A firm should further analyze those categories where there is a steep incline to 80 percent.

Scatter plots.   Another relatively simple analytic—the scatter plot—can generate powerful insights by plotting one variable against another. These plots tend to highlight outliers meriting closer investigation. The scatter plot in Figure 5.5 uses data from the two common forms of Pareto chart—revenue and margin. A simple segmentation of the business can be created by plotting each customer, product, or category on a graph. By separating the graph into quadrants (generally using weighted average margin and the 80 percent line of revenue) the customers or products that serve as value generators for the business can easily be found.

Those points above the 80 percent line represent elements having the greatest cash impact on the organization, and small improvements in margin of those transactions represented by the dots above the 80 percent line of revenue can drive significant bottom-line results. Those that are above the weighted-average margin drive organizational profitability. The data points representing greatest revenue and the *magic quadrant* of high margin can be identified easily and learned from. Similarly, the key focus areas for the organization can be defined easily: large-revenue, low-margin customers who need aggressive management to prevent significant losses in organizational earnings. Small, high-margin customers should be

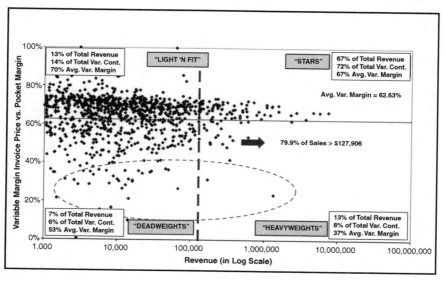

Figure 5.5   Margin and Revenue Scatter Plot

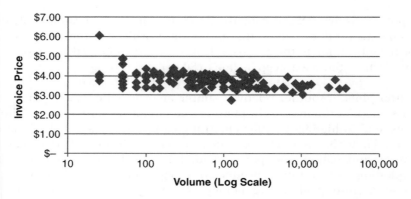

Figure 5.6   Scatter Plot Based on Volume and Price Per Unit

nurtured and grown. Modest, low-margin customers have little impact and may warrant limited sales focus (though some may serve as an attractive testing ground for new pricing strategies, which can later be rolled out to larger customers or higher-impact products).

Another common scatter plot analysis attempts to correlate volume to price per unit (see Figure 5.6). In these plots it is common to hypothesize that larger aggregate volumes drive lower prices per unit. Not surprisingly, the correlation seldom is as accurate as hoped for. This occurs for a variety of reasons, including cross-product, cross-business-unit, or channel spend as well as special discounts, promotions, and other price adjustments. Organizations often find a widely accepted paradigm within the organization is not reflected in the data. The elimination of these false assumptions has considerable value. Executives and senior leaders are freed to set out a new vision with clear benchmarks that can be tracked in the data.

Scatter plots are perhaps the most versatile of the common transactional analytics as they offer infinite opportunities for developing and testing hypotheses. A more precise version of this analytic compares the number of orders made by a customer in a year with the median size of those orders (see Figure 5.7). Upon examining the results of this analytic, several key insights can be drawn. First, if there is a demarcation at both 12 and 52 (number of orders made per year), customers ordering product more than once a month and, even more telling, more than once a week, can be identified. Some customers who order in great frequency purchase relatively modest quantities. It may become apparent that some of these customers are managing their inventories by warehousing product with the supplier, which will ultimately lower pocket margin because shipping costs will be high. The negotiating points are clear for the supplier's salespeople: balance discounts, price points, and terms based on order size and

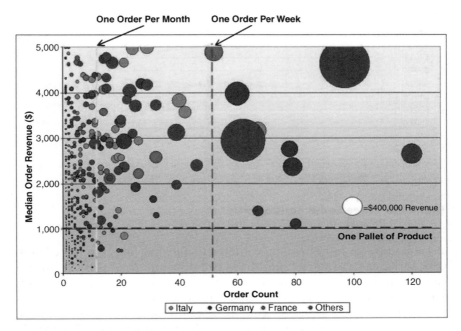

Figure 5.7 Scatter Plot with Number of Orders Per Year and Median Order Size

order frequency. A slight price decrease can be passed to the customer in exchange for larger order quantities and fewer orders per year. Paired with declines in shipping, warehousing, and customer service and order processing costs, *the decrease in price may still yield a higher profit.* This can be a win–win situation for the customer and the supplier.

When a scatter plot uses a time series on the *x*-axis, trends can be observed (see Figure 5.8). This is useful, for instance, when looking at changes in raw material costs and the relative impact they have on price over time. These fluctuations may not be able to be captured in real time, and it is common to see leakage when price increases are pushed in the marketplace. Time series plots alone cannot identify correlative effects, but they can raise the questions that help drive valuable change. For example, these plots can indicate when:

- an organization needs to better control the cost of terms (e.g., if days sales outstanding (DSO) increase over time);
- rebates need to be rethought (e.g., if small customer rebates become more frequent than large customer rebates); or
- shipping needs to be more tightly controlled (e.g., when the frequency of air freight over time increases considerably).

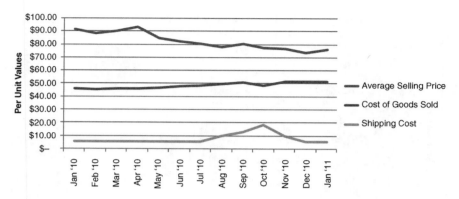

Figure 5.8   Time Series Scatter Plot

Price Bands.   Another common transactional analytic is the price band. This variant of the scatter plot shows the distribution of prices among a number of categories, segments, or attributes. For instance, a consumer packaged goods company may choose to plot the spread of prices for a food product by package size. The price per unit would be expected to be lower for the 32-ounce can than for the 15.5- or 6-ounce cans. This hypothesis can be tested by comparing the sales prices for each package size. The results may be surprising. In the price band shown in Figure 5.9, oval A represents *fix-or-flush* customers—those who should either have their prices increased or be eliminated altogether. Oval B represents *grow-and-own* customers. These customers and their transactions can be targeted for increased selling efforts. As always with transactional analytics, improvement efforts should be focused on best and worst performers.

The options for price-band analysis are quite extensive. The three major variants include the segment choice, the measure to use on the *y*-axis (price per unit, revenue, volume, margin, and so on) and the aggregation method. Each dot represents a transaction, a customer average, a customer month, a region, and so forth. Additional variations make these graphs even more useful (e.g., coloring or changing the shape of the data points to add another dimension). Weighted averages, targets, or price guidelines can be plotted to indicate when a sale was made outside of defined norms (see Figure 5.10). Bubbles can be used in place of data points to make volume or margin easily apparent. These variations are just some of the ways these graphs can be modified to identify key outliers. The data generated can help rule out general operating practices as the reason for a variance and make it easier to identify a specific transaction or set of transactions as outliers.

Segment Performance Analysis.   Segment performance analysis allows a company to evaluate the performance of its current segmentation

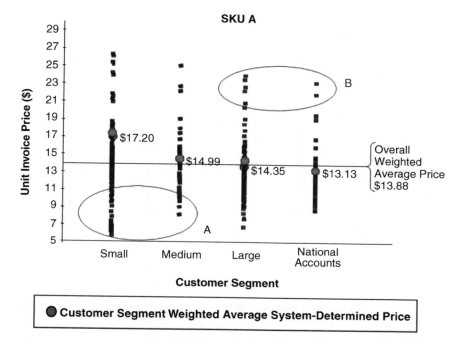

Figure 5.9   Price-Band Analysis

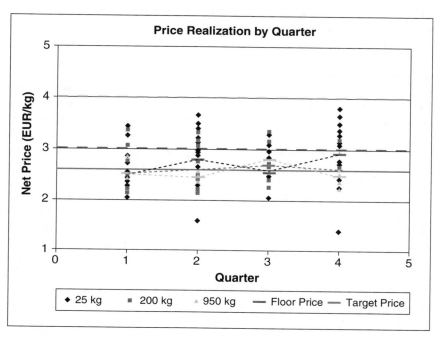

Figure 5.10   Price-Band Variation

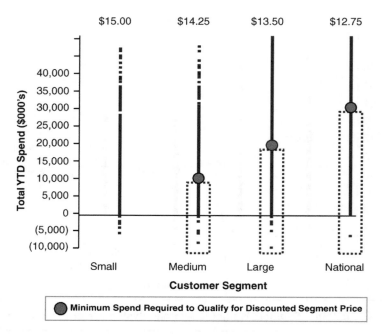

Figure 5.11   Segment Performance Analysis

schemes. It is similar to a price-band analysis, but instead of variance analysis, this method highlights unjustified prices based on current segmentation models.

For example, the graph in Figure 5.11 shows small, medium, large, and national accounts. This is a size-based scheme, which is widely used as a framework for differentiating pricing. In essence, it is merely an easy tool for classifying customers based on revenue data. Many organizations use these groupings as default segments in the absence of a proper segmentation scheme. To be effective, however, rules must be enforced. In Figure 5.11, $50 million in sales were made at prices unwarranted by customer volumes on a revenue base of $500 million. As a result, the company lost more than $2.5 million in operating profit.

Other relatively simple analyses become even more valuable when applied to a well-structured transactional database. Histograms, for instance, show the frequency distribution of data and are particularly useful in looking at prices because bi-, tri-, or other multi-modal outcomes become readily visible (see Figure 5.12). Histograms like Figure 5.12, which reveal multiple price points with significant volumes passing through, dispel the often mistaken belief that the average, or weighted average, price is a meaningful reference point in the marketplace. Clearly, if the average happens to occur at a price point at which little or no throughput occurs, then

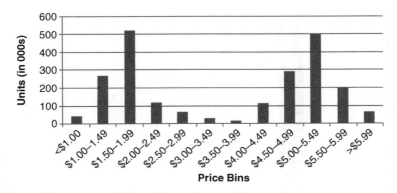

Figure 5.12   Histogram with Multi-Nodal Outcome

it is not as meaningful for analysis. More important, multiple high-frequency outputs can reveal key segments in the data set. These segments could be tied to the purchasing patterns of customers (why certain customers settle for one price over another) or variations in product or service characteristics that are valued in the marketplace.

Profit Waterfalls.   Since being described in 1992 in the *Harvard Business Review*,[2] the profit waterfall has become the definitive transactional analysis and an icon of pricing and profitability management. The profit waterfall consists of value *pillars*, including both common and uncommon metrics for measuring business performance across product categories, channels, or customers. The common metrics include the list price or market-based reference price, the invoice price, the net price, and the pocket price (see Figure 5.13). Pocket price represents the amount of money left over after all of the discounts, rebates, promotions, and other concessions have been subtracted from the list price. Many organizations have extended their use of waterfalls to pocket margin, which is a measure of the margin retained by the organization after all sales, discounts, promotions, payment adjustments, and other directly attributable costs are removed. This can be an extremely useful metric for managing a business if an organization is aligned around this concept.

Between value pillars are cost buckets and adjustments. These elements add to or subtract from the values set in the market or placed on an invoice. These buckets are designed to help aggregate and organize important, manageable elements of the business process to improve analysis and decision making.

Every organization has a distinct set of pillars and buckets, which produce a unique profit waterfall. This creates both challenges and complexity for an organization's waterfall design. Thus, when structuring a waterfall, it must be made flexible enough to accommodate the business

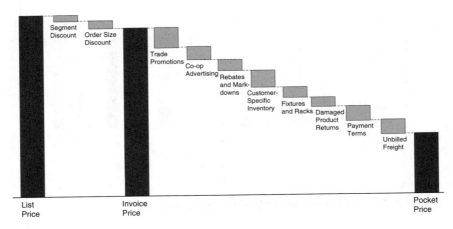

Figure 5.13   Profit Waterfall

models across the entire organization, and common terminology and definitions should be developed that apply to, and can be understood by, every segment of the organization. It is rare, though, for an organization to share the same waterfall buckets across the enterprise. One business unit may need additional disaggregation of elements; for example, freight (inter- and intracompany shipments), promotions (flyers, coupons, and special discounts), or terms (offered payment terms and actual days sales outstanding). As individual units often differ fundamentally in how they approach the market, managers must ensure the underlying data set is aligned with the business model.

The profit waterfall's distinctive view of profitability makes it an important tool, though businesses often struggle when they try to reconcile its elements to financial statements. The fact is not every pillar or bucket will fit because the waterfall is an economic, not a financial, model. It includes cost-of-capital calculations that are generally viewed as opportunity costs. For example the *cost of terms* is a calculation assessing the financial consequence of giving a customer extra days to pay. This does not appear in financial statements, despite being an inevitable liability in the natural course of business. These types of cost should be incorporated into the waterfall because they will suggest opportunities for process, behavior, or price improvement. However, once this occurs, the numbers in the waterfall will no longer directly correlate to financial statements.

Complexity can be added through the demographic variables associated with each transaction. Customers and product demographics form the baseline for this activity. The former often exist in a hierarchy; that is, a parent customer, business unit, division, or specific location. For example, a particular transaction may reflect a sale made to both a supermarket

—Canned Meats
   ᴸTuna
      ᴸSolid
         ᴸPacked in Oil
            ᴸ3 oz. (85 g)
            ᴸ5 oz. (142 g)
            ᴸ9 oz. (255 g)
            ᴸ12oz. (340 g)
         ᴸPacked in Water
      ᴸChunk
         +Packed in Oil
         +Packed in Water
    +Salmon
    +Chicken
+Canned Vegetables

Figure 5.14   Product Hierarchy

chain (the parent) and a grocer in Lakeville, Massachusetts, that belongs to the chain. The data, to be fully functional, must capture all of these variations. Product hierarchies (see Figure 5.14) should be similarly layered so the company can look at, for example, the profitability of tuna as an entire category or merely at 1.5-ounce cans packed in water. With a well-structured, demographic data set, specific questions can be asked, such as: Do customers in the Midwest buy tuna in larger or smaller quantities during the summer than at other times of year?

In essence, once the cost drivers have been identified and allocated at the transaction level, the visual representation becomes self-evident. Pillars are graphed with buckets between them. The profit increases and decreases reaffirm an important maxim: profit is made (or lost) one transaction at a time.

Profit waterfalls are powerful analytical tools. They can be used by salespeople during negotiations to evaluate the attractiveness of a particular deal. Pricing analysts can use them retrospectively to measure and compare product or customer profitability. Waterfalls may also offer executives a snapshot of their entire business operation using aggregate metrics that do not unintentionally mask true profitability.

As we've demonstrated throughout this section, a TPA can create opportunities to improve profitability at the transaction level. Many of these are actionable immediately or in the short-term and can produce benefits so significant that they can offset the costs of an even larger profitability transformation project. That being said, when an analysis produces results, more work will likely be necessary to understand fully the customer, product, and competitive situation—the necessary prelude to setting truly optimal prices.

Opportunity Quantification, Validation, and Prioritization

The process of capitalizing on opportunities uncovered through the TPA is a mix of science and art. It generally follows three steps—(1) quantification, (2) validation, and (3) prioritization—and it can draw on innumerable techniques and tools along the way. We won't try to capture all of the approaches here (each opportunity is unique and will require a customized method to assign a dollar value to the improvement), but we will offer simple examples showing how the process might play out.

Quantification.   Customers or products in the *tail* of a contribution analysis (whale curve) are potential candidates for repricing, SKU rationalization, product or service bundling, or customer attrition. To evaluate below-average margin customers, a table can be created that shows those clients who fall below the average, or target, pocket margin for the business. The quantified opportunity to fix these below-average accounts depends on how aggressive the business chooses to be in its approach.

Generally, few good or strategic reasons exist for supporting a negative-margin customer. In Table 5.1, we show how a firm can calculate the benefit of bringing all of its low-performing accounts to at least a break-even point.

Calculating a reasonable benefit for below-average-margin customers can be somewhat complex because an average, by definition, has data points falling beneath it. Ideally, organizations will have a target margin that can be used. If one does not already exist, then it can be set—for the purpose of analysis—in consultation with organizational leadership.

Table 5.1   Bringing Accounts to the Break-Even Point

Customer	Product	Country	Market	Pocket Margin ($k)	Pocket Margin/ kg	Added PM at 0% Floor ($k)
Cust01	Prod001	Mexico	Pipe	$392	$0.47	$392
Cust01	SKU02	Guatemala	Pipe	$113	$0.84	$113
Cust02	Prod007	Guatemala	Pipe	$63	$0.48	$63
Cust03	Prod007	Mexico	Tubes	$41	$0.29	$41
Cust02	Prod001	Guatemala	Pipe	$38	$0.19	$38
Cust03	Prod001	U.S.	Pipe	$37	$0.20	$37
Cust05	Prod001	U.S.	Tubes	$29	$0.23	$29
Total				$713	—	$713

To accommodate uncertainties in implementation, the size of each opportunity should be calculated as a range based on several outcomes such as the following:

- All below-average customers being raised to average or target price or margin
- All below-average customers being raised halfway to average or target price or margin
- Fifty percent of customers being raised halfway to average or target price or margin.

The largest value serves as the maximum potential benefit for this opportunity. The second and third, smaller estimates may be used if businesses find themselves in a competitive marketplace where such increases are not practical. The more *sold out* an enterprise is, the more aggressive it will likely be in pursuing such an opportunity.

For more complex scenarios, the 10/20/30 rule may be helpful to estimate the size of the improvement, depending on the degree of the problem. For example, a minor issue involving $10 million in freight would be estimated as a $1 million opportunity, a significant concern should produce $2 million, and a severe problem would likely create a $3 million opportunity. Another example: a severe problem involving freight returns of $100,000 could still generate a $30,000 opportunity for a business.

Validation.   Unfortunately, not every opportunity can be taken for a variety of business reasons (e.g., competitive situation, or contract or business structure). Validation can generally be pursued in one of two ways. Typical process or policy opportunities tend to impact a number of customers and should be confirmed by the company resource responsible for that aspect of the business. For example, to validate opportunities involving payment terms, team members in Accounts Receivable and Finance should be consulted, while those tied to freight would require consultation with personnel in Distribution Logistics. More tactical opportunities, such as raising prices for negative- or below-target-margin customers, are account-specific and need to be validated by individual sales representatives or their managers.

Prioritization.   Once quantification and validation are complete, opportunities should be prioritized based on potential value and ease of implementation. They can initially be classed as high, medium, or low priority. Further quantification and evaluation will occur iteratively as the analyses are refined. The list should be organized in decreasing order according to "potential value" or "ease of implementation." Because some cases may be classified as "high potential value" or "difficult to implement" or "medium value" or "easy to implement" and therefore involve tougher decisions, the ranking should be arrived at by consensus within the business.

The objective of the TPA is not to analyze every scenario, but to identify the most important one. Here are two general guidelines to help manage the scope:

- Significant opportunities should be completed in less than four weeks.
- The process should end when the last opportunity is greater than 1 percent of the largest one (e.g., if the greatest opportunity is estimated at $10 million, then a firm should not investigate any one that is less than $100,000).

Of course, the actual guidelines will vary with each TPA, but they should be established before beginning prioritization.

Critical Success Factors.   Gathering and cleansing all of the necessary data for a TPA arguably present the most difficult challenge. Several other factors are also critical (see Table 5.2). Most of these relate to organizational challenges encountered in the face of change.

Table 5.2   Critical Success Factors of a TPA

Success Factor	Description
Ability to Challenge Long-Standing Assumptions	To succeed in shaping a pricing strategy, the organization must be able to challenge openly, long-standing assumptions about price, markets, customers and products and services.
Visible Executive Commitment	Proposed changes in the pricing function must have visible executive commitment including the endorsement of a C-level executive.
Clean, Accurate Data	The availability of clean and accurate data, as well as organizational cooperation in obtaining the information, is crucial to performing elasticity modeling and TPAs.
Significant, but Manageable, Scope	The project's scope must be large enough to produce meaningful benefits, but small enough to be manageable.
Access to Key Personnel	Success is dependent on daily access to the required personnel in Operations, Finance, Marketing, Sales, and Pricing.
Ability to Make Change Sustainable	A message must be sent to the organization that any pricing improvements made are not temporary fixes. The supporting processes, technologies, and organizational structures must be changed accordingly to make the changes sustainable.

Prioritized Improvements	Initial improvement efforts should focus on the process areas that favor quick wins and offer the largest payoffs for expended effort. Participants want to demonstrate quickly to the organization that the effort is worthwhile.
Ability to Standardize and Deviate	The design objective for the pricing process should be to eliminate as many potential variations in outcome as possible. Standardization should be the general rule, with some differentiation and deviation allowed when necessary.

Integrating Cluster Analyses to Segment Customers, Products, and Services

As discussed in Chapter 3, "Developing an Effective Pricing Strategy," advanced analytics support key elements of customer needs analysis and attribute clustering, helping to pair the right products with the right customers. These analytic techniques provide a thorough, reliable mechanism to analyze key customer attributes that should not be left to intuition or chance. Cluster analysis combines buyers, products, or services into relevant categories with the goal of differentiating how a company serves them. Organizations seeking to improve profits can often do so by:

- shifting customers from a lower-margin product to a higher-margin one within the same cluster
- targeting similarly clustered customers for high-profit offerings
- pairing higher- and lower-profit services in the same cluster.

Assessing the Competition: Value Equivalency Analytics

While understanding customer segments and their needs is important, so, too, is grasping competitive positioning. Unfortunately, most organizations rely on secondhand information and market studies that provide limited comparative analytics.

Competitive positioning requires understanding the consumer's perception of value. There are two distinct *value equivalency* analytics, both rooted in the same conceptual framework. The first attempts to compare how consumers perceive differences in value and price between one company's products and those of its competitors (both in-kind and not-in-kind substitutions). Through this comparison, the landscape of price perceptions can be understood; that is, how well a company's value proposition has been delivered to consumers. The second value equivalency breaks down the specific attributes that make up a product category and compares how rival offerings match up with each other.

Consider Kmart, which lost its dominant position as a discount retailer by failing to react to the competitive threats of Target and Wal-Mart. According to a 2003 Forbes Magazine article, the company's leaders "believed that they had invented discount retailing, and they knew best what the marketplace wanted."[3]

Had Kmart been better able to predict the changes in the market, how would it have responded to the forecasts? What analytics could the company have done to determine how best to compete? Clearly, it is possible for firms to win against the lowest-cost provider. Rivals beat back Kmart, and retailers such as Kohl's and Target continue to challenge Wal-Mart, the most recent winner in the budget category. Kmart simply did not understand the complex dynamic of value and price as well as it thought it did.

Both of these methods require incorporating primary research, which carries the risk of bias, in both survey design and respondent answers. However, because these approaches focus primarily on *consumer perception* of competing products and their attributes, this bias is often described as *real.* Surveys (generally run by third-party organizations to protect a company's identity) collect absolute and relative rankings of products versus price and attribute performance. The data are consolidated and indexed to create a value equivalency matrix.

An example of a value equivalency matrix is shown in Figure 5.15. Note the various competitors for this key product. Several of them are *low-cost providers*, as indicated by the relatively modest perceived price (PP) index. Their products are considered as being of relatively lesser value than the more expensive products. The red pure value equivalency line (VEL) reflects the market relationship between PP and perceived value (PV) and is calculated by producing a linear regression on the individual data points. This line represents the trade-off in the market between price and value, and indicates when a product is marked too high for what it delivers, or, conversely, when price may be increased to match consumer perception of value.

The yellow line is the mean value line and is always set at 1.0 in the price index. It represents the PV of the product set. By comparing it to the *theoretical* PV equivalency (always set at a 45 percent angle where value and price are directly correlated), the price sensitivity of the market can be determined, as well as which competitors are best positioned for success. In our example, ACME has the highest PV, but remains below the VEL. This means that the company can afford to raise its price further to reflect the value consumers place on its product. Competitor 4 appears to be extracting significant price value for this product far in excess of the VEL. This is a company ACME could aggressively compete with for market share.

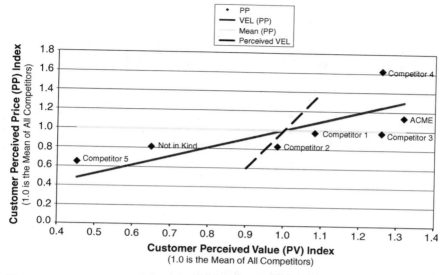

**Figure 5.15   Value Equivalency Matrix Showing the Value
Equivalency Line (VEL)**

Companies need to determine what product (and customer service) attributes determine the consumer's perception of value. This analysis will help answer two critical questions: What drives the customer's purchase decision and what advantage (or disadvantage) does each company have vis-à-vis its competition? Is the product or service attribute a *must have,* a *like to have,* or *irrelevant to the decision to buy?* Obviously, the must-have attributes are most important to the consumer; these may turn out not to be tied to the product itself, but to be features such as on-time delivery or service response time.

Analysis of the value equivalency matrix provides valuable insight into what is or is not working to an organization's competitive advantage. In the example shown in Figure 5.16, the attributes that are considered pluses appear above the 50/50 line: these are areas where a significant value proposition has been successfully communicated. Note the various attributes that are not well positioned (though several represent critical factors in the purchasing decision). The attributes falling within a tight range (standard deviation is a commonly used method to measure this) indicate areas of the greatest vulnerability, or, conversely, areas offering organizations the best opportunities to make a strategic shift to their advantage. In these cases, neither the organization nor its competitor has created sufficient product differentiation to produce the kind of notable *perception gap* that drives purchasing behavior.

This analysis can help create a road map for a firm to improve its competitive positioning and to optimize its pricing. It provides a macro-level

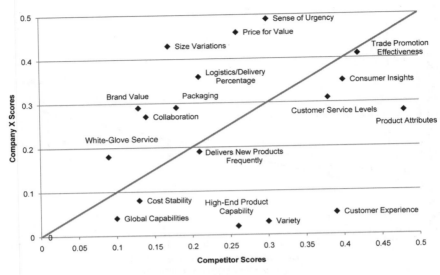

Figure 5.16   Value Equivalency Attribute Analysis

view of not only price and value (indicating relative price position and flexibility), but also those attributes that can be managed to produce higher PV (or to take some value from the competition). Combining this analytic with conjoint analysis often produces critical insights that contribute to improved financial performance and market position.

CASE STUDY: Challenging organizational assumptions

A large chemical company created a product that proved to have many potential applications. The company's engineers were forced into extra duty as salespeople to pitch the new offering. Historically, the company prided itself on the strength of its science and high standards, which were reflected in its first-class technical capabilities, quality testing, and superior product literature. The product's premium price was based on these attributes, as well as on the cost of having highly educated and talented support staff accompany the prized offering through the manufacturing process of nearly every industry it was used in.

Despite these apparent strengths, however, the company was losing market share. New competitors were identifying not-in-kind solutions that were more cost effective and served as reasonable substitutes for the product. As a result, two key questions emerged for the chemical company: How could it segment its customers to differentiate prices based on what they valued? How could it identify opportunities to adjust pricing to compensate for losses in various market segments? The company decided to commission a formal market review, including a conjoint study and a value equivalency assessment (see Figure 5.17).

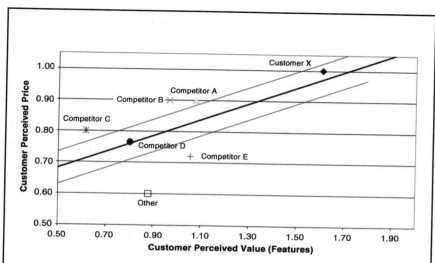

Figure 5.17   Value Equivalency Assessment

The value equivalency assessment produced some good news. The company's product clearly had greater value than the in-kind offerings of its competitors and was extracting an appropriate price advantage for this value. But the overall study produced a major surprise. A significant segment of the market expressed indifference to receiving additional support and even preferred not to have it on site in some cases. Similarly, clients did not value their access to advanced technical resources—they cared primarily about price. The market study forced the chemical company to conclude that its operating model was generating significant costs, while providing little or no additional value.

Although the company found it shocking at first to consider overturning a decade-long paradigm in the business, management understood the considerable cost savings (and therefore profit advantage) that could be realized by decreasing the level of technical service and product literature provided to a significant segment of the market. The team also took the added step of scrutinizing the company's discounting policy to eliminate unnecessary price reductions to the customer. The tradeoff produced millions in additional income and helped remind the company that its brand was built on what the customer perceived rather than on what the company was pushing in terms of brand identity.

Demand-Based Optimization Modeling to Improve Price Setting

The list of products that have failed due to a mismatch between price and customer perception is incredibly long. For example, IBM's PCjr, which entered the early computer market and was priced far higher than the roughly equivalent Atari and Commodore models. The consequence? PCjr faded away.[4-6] Unfortunately, IBM's woes did not stop there. The company also made the mistake of underpricing the IBM 7030 (Stretch) to such a point that it lost money on every sale until it ceased production in 1964.[7,8] The Apple Newton is another example.[9] Arriving ahead of its time in the early 1990s, this $700 handheld was priced too high to break into the market. When personal digital assistants (PDAs) became more popular in the late 1990s, Apple had already dropped the brand for being unprofitable.[10-12]

Even McDonald's has fallen into the pricing trap. The company created the Arch Deluxe hamburger and marketed it to the fast food consumer market as a more sophisticated offering for an adult palate. It was expensive. To launch the new burger, McDonald's distributed coupons allowing it to be purchased, initially, for only $1.00. But the Arch Deluxe failed to catch on and became a costly mistake.[13-16] Ultimately, the market always has the final say on whether new products and pricing decisions were well conceived.

To a company with multiple entries in a complex market, setting the prices of all the products in its portfolio can be an imposing task, particularly if some compete with each other. Moreover, any price adjustments will undoubtedly trigger responses from competitors. It is not surprising then that, facing these myriad issues, companies choose to use ad hoc methods and to make each product decision separately.

However, certain analytic tools and methods can help firms deal far more effectively with these challenging decisions. To use them, firms need to understand how sales will be affected by pricing. Specifying this demand function, particularly as it involves the interactions between many products, is often the most difficult element of an analysis to carry out when devising an optimal pricing policy.

It Starts with Really Understanding Demand

To grasp the true demand for its products or services, a company needs to find a way to quantify the relationships among price, promotions, seasonality, and other sales drivers. Several methods can be used to estimate price elasticity, such as correlation, regression, and discriminant analysis. Statistical methods are generally used because companies find it nearly impossible to carry out experiments that rely on testing a single variable against a control group to determine causality. This is almost impossible to do in a complex market. There are some exceptions; for instance, structured market tests[17] and controlled market simulations.

Another approach, historical analysis, presents many challenges such as multicollinearity, omitted-variable bias, and a host of other problems that must be addressed through a proper model validation process (both technically and from a business perspective). Hence, most demand calculations that draw on historical data make a rigorous effort to screen out the many *noise* elements that these data often contain.

The initial step in any statistical analysis is to obtain, cleanse, transform, format, and (occasionally) normalize the data. Depending on the goal of the modeling effort, different data sets will be used. To look at demand-based price optimization, raw sales transaction data must generally be obtained along with cost, promotional, and product information, which can then be manipulated into multiple forms such as time-series data (generally used when seasonality and promotions play an important role in driving customer purchases). Ultimately, data manipulation and preparation are the most time-consuming element of any price optimization project.

The price elasticity of demand (PED) can be determined by measuring the ratio of how demand reacts to changes in price. PED is mathematically represented as follows (where Q is quantity and P is price):

$$E_d = \frac{percent\ change\ in\ quantity}{percent\ change\ in\ price} = \frac{\Delta Q}{\Delta P} = \frac{\partial Q}{\partial P} \cdot \frac{P}{Q}$$

For example, let's say that the price of a good increases by 2 percent, leading to a 1 percent reduction in quantity sold. The result: -1 percent$/$ 2 percent $= -0.5$. For the most part, elasticities tend to be negative, so they will often be reported as an absolute value. When PED is greater than 1, it means the relative shift in quantity is greater than the relative shift in price. This is referred to as being *price elastic*. Usually, luxury goods and discretionary items (e.g., premium brands of clothing, food, and automobiles as well as cruises) are highly elastic. When PED is less than 1, it means that the relative change in demand for a good or service is smaller than the change in price. This is referred to as being *price inelastic*. Commoditized, essential products with limited competition or supply are often inelastic (e.g., specialized medical devices and fuel).

Elasticity measurement—the sensitivity of demand to price change— encompasses many of the ideas within this chapter. Elasticity provides a clear measurement of a company's relative strength when considering demand (the products and features that consumers desire) and the competitive environment (what influences those consumers' purchasing decisions or leads them to change to in-kind and not-in-kind competitors). Shifting the demand curve is nearly impossible, but understanding it and manipulating the underlying structures (in terms of cost, consumer perception, category demographics, product and service rationalization, and so on) can help a company find the right price for the right product for the right consumer at the right time.

The quantitative analysis of demand, therefore, helps to answer some key questions:

- How will the sales volume of a product or service change as the price is adjusted? This may be the hardest question to answer because so many considerations, externalities, and other caveats affect the outcome.

- How, and to what extent, do cannibalization and affinity impact demand? Frequently, to measure price elasticity, companies must understand how price changes within a set of products can affect the demand of other items in the set (positively or negatively).
- When a product (e.g., a car) is made up of other intermediate goods or inputs (e.g., steel and engines), how will the price of the overall product be affected by price changes to the inputs? In some cases the impact on demand may depend upon how important the particular input is to the total cost of the product.
- How are different customers affected by price changes? By developing an effective way to segment customers according to how they react to these changes, firms can develop a granular and coherent understanding of how price adjustments affect demand—and, in turn, positively impact the bottom line.

Building a Model

Models are mathematical representations of reality. Generally speaking, they can be built deterministically or stochastically. In the case of demand models, the goal is to create a series of calculations that will estimate demand in the form of sales volume or customers' propensity to buy a service or product when given inputs such as prices, competition, customer profiles, and so forth.

To build a statistical model representing demand, one generally begins by understanding what drives sales and customer choice. Although statistical models can be constructed in several ways, the most effective ways appear to be those that draw upon business insight and experience rather than simply letting the data drive the building process.

Today, software tools allow for a multitude of choices when developing demand models, from complex neural networks to simple ordinary least squares algorithms. Making the right choice will be a function of the data, the model objectives, and the modeler's expertise, the latter of which is particularly important when building a robust model.

Modeling involves many steps and interactions between business people and analysts. Many individuals with basic statistical knowledge tend to fall in the R^2 *trap*[18]—the belief that R^2 is the most important measure of a statistical model's effectiveness in predicting variations in a real-world data set. Unfortunately, a high R^2 (i.e., greater than 80 percent), does not necessarily reflect a good model; skilled statisticians can actually increase the percentage without really improving model's accuracy.

To overcome this problem, companies sometimes use the *adjusted R^2* measurement. This formula allows R^2 to increase only if variables added to the model strengthen its predictive ability more than would be anticipated by chance. A high R^2 is usually associated with another phenomenon called *overfitting*, which occurs when a model tries to incorporate every small fluctuation in the data, resulting in a poor predictive performance.

The example in Figure 5.18, derived from real data, exemplifies both a high R^2 and the overfitting traps. In this case, a company has decided it wants to quantify the relationship between the number of hours in a project and the number of full-time-equivalent (FTE) resources that will be needed to complete the work. Common sense dictates a positive correlation between project hours and resources (as one number grows, so does the other). Indeed, that is what happened in reality. Yet the two models (represented by the black and red lines on the chart) interpreted the results differently. The red line shows an overfit model, with multiple variables and degrees of freedom and, as expected, a higher R^2. But clearly, the predictions for projects with greater than 17,000 hours are unintuitive. In fact, for projects with more than 30,000 hours, the model shows that less than zero FTEs would be needed! In contrast, the black line (using just one variable) has produced a much more logical prediction.

The most time-consuming tasks when building a model can be choosing the variables correctly and validating the results thoroughly. The goal is for the design to combine simplicity and robustness—this requires creativity, experience, and skill. Fortunately, the validation stage is more technical and straightforward. Once it is completed, the model can be used in an optimization process to help the company find the right price (or prices) to help maximize profits.

Ten Steps for Robust Demand Modeling

1. **Base the Model on Business Experience**
   Always begin by hypothesizing relationships between the key predictors and a dependent variable. For example, when trying to estimate the price elasticity of beer, the dependent variable would be beer sales in units, and the predictive variables could be price, month, channel, or promotional indicators. Think about the impact the beginning of summer might have on beer sales as captured by the month variable.

2. **Look Critically at Cause and Effect**
   Causality is the relationship between two events, where the second (the *effect*, represented by the dependent variable) is a direct consequence of the first (the *cause*, represented by the predictive variables). Remember the often-repeated expression: "correlation does not imply causation," (i.e., the correlation between two variables does not automatically imply that one causes the other). A famous example of causality versus correlation is the ice cream and drowning relationship that is often used in statistics classes. Ice cream sales correlate highly to the rate of drowning in the U.S., though it can hardly be seen as a cause. Ice cream is consumed more during

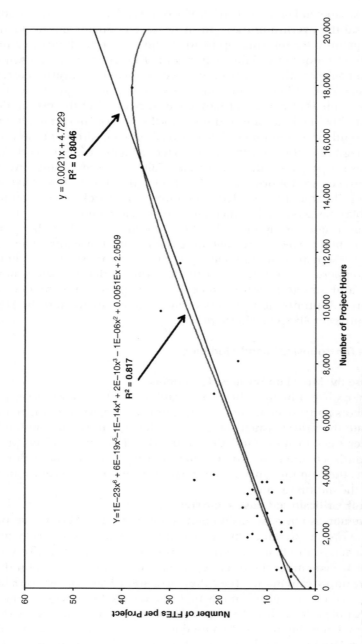

Figure 5.18   Example of a Model that Overfits Data

summer, which is when more people swim, and it is *that* activity that causes more drowning. Remember causality because the vast majority of statistical models are based on correlation.

3. **Obtain, Format, Normalize, and Cleanse the Data**
   Regression techniques work hard to fit the outliers. They try to minimize the squared residuals, and outliers, particularly, can have really large ones. It follows that one bad data point can really mess up an analysis.

4. **Match the Data and the Model Assumptions to the Business**
   Data can be classified as either primary or secondary depending on how they affect the dependent variable. Again, think about causality. For example, R&D spend is probably a good proxy for know-how when trying to measure how these investments affect the success of a new product. In other words, R&D can easily be measured and correlated with know-how. A good proxy variable is easy to measure and captures the essential truth of the underlying theoretical variable of interest.

5. **Aim for Simplicity to Start**
   The analysis should begin with a simple model that includes the most important predictor variables and *excludes* unnecessary or synthetic ones (as well as any interactions that have been created). The model can evolve from there.

6. **Before Choosing an Empirical Methodology, Examine the Relationships among the Variables**
   Starting the modeling process with a univariate analysis can be helpful as it separately explores each variable in a data set. This approach allows the user to look at the range and trend of the values by describing how the independent variable relates to the target variable being measured or forecast. Despite the attention it receives in introductory statistics classes, multicollinearity (a statistical phenomenon in which two or more predictor variables in a multiple regression model are highly correlated) is rarely considered a problem in real-world empirical research.

7. **Choose a Fitting Model**
   For instance, are any of the independent variables categorical? If so, then basic regression models may work, but *dummy* variables may need to be created. A determination should also be made as to whether *interaction terms* are needed and whether a log (an n degree-polynomial) could be used instead. For example, look at the three models in Figure 5.19. The first is a straight-line regression and the second is a second-degree polynomial—neither of these fits the data well. The third is a third-degree polynomial and clearly offers the best fit for the data.

8. **After Implementation, Test the Model's Effectiveness**
   A model is robust when small changes in its structure do not affect its predictive power and accuracy. If a single dropped variable

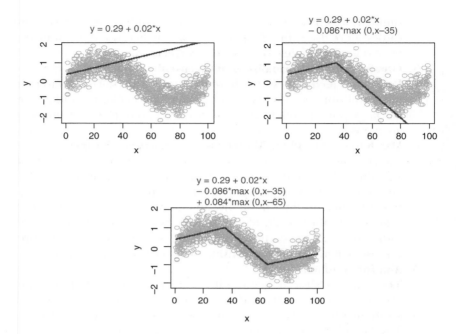

Figure 5.19   Fitting Models

causes significant deviations from the expected results, then the model may need to be reviewed.

9. **Assess the Error Structure**

   Investigation of the error structure is key to identifying and quantifying bias (e.g., whether the model consistently underpredicts or overpredicts the dependent variable). If the error structure presents itself in a nonrandom way, then the model and its predictors may need to be re-evaluated.

10. **Interpret the Results**

    If numbers are tortured long enough, then they will tell you anything. After all the mathematical and statistical analyses are over, check the results for reasonability and coherence. Domain expertise (or tribal knowledge of the business), although often overly relied on, can be useful when making a commonsense interpretation of statistical results.

From Demand to Optimization

Optimization models are generally decision support systems or tools built on mathematical functions. The primary objective of these models is to establish the optimal set of prices for an organization subject to organizational, regulatory, operational, and strategic constraints. A wide variety of algorithms and approaches can be used but each attempts to solve the same problem: given the demand model and the strategy, what is the *optimal balance* between price and volume needed to maximize the company's profit? Often these models, rather than producing a single output value or price, provide a range that meets the overall objective being considered.

At its most basic level, an optimizing engine will use the demand functions described in the previous section to test a large number of potential scenarios. Initial values are generated and passed through the demand model to estimate broader market impact and cannibalization on both the product itself and related offerings (often grouped using clustering algorithms as described in Chapter 3, "Developing an Effective Pricing Strategy"). This process iterates many times to identify the set or range of prices that achieve the strategic objective.

Price optimization models are also used throughout the product lifecycle. For instance, they can be designed to determine the initial or base price of a product. This is their primary use in industries with long lifecycles and infrequent price changes. Promotional and discount prices can also be calculated with an optimization model. In general, these are used in markets with short product lifecycles subject to regular price fluctuations, such as service industries (e.g., hotels and airlines) and retail organizations (e.g., groceries and clothing stores).

A distinction should be made as to what type of price is being optimized because the demand curves, constraints, and objectives may differ depending on the anticipated outcome. For example, the base price may be designed to optimize long-term profit while a promotional price may try to increase volume in a short period.

Optimization algorithms may be highly variable, but the overall approach remains consistent, as follows.

1. *Collect historical data,* for example, raw transactional sales information, promotional calendars, competitors' prices, macro-economic conditions, and cost details.
2. *Understand the business objectives and constraints.* This step both defines what objective needs are being addressed (e.g., how the firm can increase market share, improve its profit per transaction, or push more volume through the channel) and what constraints must be placed on the algorithm. Constraints can be at the macro level (e.g., if a firm's potential customer base is only 1 million people, then the market size should be a factor to ensure the model is scaled appropriately) or micro level (e.g., the model may be limited to testing price increases of no more than 10 percent if the company knows that this is the most its customers will accept). Whatever the desired limits are, they can be incorporated as constraints into the algorithm. This will help ensure the results are realistic from a business perspective.
3. *Choose the right optimization approach.* Generally, the complexity of the demand models will impact the decision on which algorithm to

use. Because there are so many mathematical methods to choose from, companies should make their decision based on the time they have and the level of precision they need. In some cases, speed to market is more important than accuracy. That is, a simple algorithm that successfully points a company in the right direction may prove more useful than more complex options. In tightly controlled and regulated markets where prices are set less often, a more accurate and sophisticated method may be chosen.

4. *Load, run, reassess, and update the model.* Optimization models are evolving tools that can be continually improved and updated to incorporate new data elements. Once the initial model is in place and has been tested, it can be adjusted over time with new constraints included to test additional what-if scenarios. For example, initially the impact of a 5 percent price increase on demand might be tested. Later, that constraint might be adjusted to an 8 percent increase. In other words, the model can be changed continually to meet the needs of the business.

5. *Obtain buy-in and make sure optimization results are easily understood by all stakeholders.* No model will be successful unless it is incorporated into business processes and broadly understood. To that end, stakeholders should be kept apprised of outcomes. A model may well suggest a price increase on a product or service that many in the organization believe is unwarranted, so, like any other development in business intelligence expectations, the impact of the possible changes needs to be managed accordingly.

6. *Monitor results and upgrade data input to improve the model at regular intervals.* Periodically, the organization may need to change constraints, improve the root data source, or incorporate new products. The models (and algorithms) should be rerun regularly because markets shift and organizational dynamics change. At some point, they may need to be completely replaced as they outlive their capacity to predict future outcomes accurately.

Optimization models provide a detailed roadmap for pricing actions and can help assess the impact of these actions on financial and operational metrics, such as average selling price, net profit, or inventory. Until recently, many of these decisions were made on instinct—in terms of both setting a price to meet an objective and predicting the outcomes of these actions. However, optimization models now merge critical business intelligence tools (valuable, accurate data sources), increased computing power (vehicles that can analyze the data quickly), and improved economic theory (robust methods to analyze the data) to allow organizations to understand more precisely their unique market and competitive situations. The result has been an increase in profits for many organizations.

CASE STUDY: Price optimization

XYZ Mortgage, a hypothetical direct and indirect mortgage lender, primarily serves prime and Alt-A customers and has operations in 40 states. The firm's management believed that a significant opportunity existed to improve profits, but it was unsure how to take advantage of it. The key questions XYZ wanted to answer were:

- If our rates increase or decrease by 10 basis points, what will happen to the origination volume?
- How should we respond to a promotion offered by two of our top five competitors, but not offered by the other three?
- What strategy should we adopt in order to launch operations in a new state?
- Our sales managers made price exceptions in 20 percent of all loans funded. How much value, if any, did those rate exceptions represent?

XYZ Mortgage decided to look into pricing more quantitatively through an optimization program. The firm had experimented in the past with promotional rates, but had difficulty tying price reductions to the volume increases because other factors (occurring simultaneously) may have helped drive demand. The price-setting process at XYZ was mainly determined by its secondary market operations and the cost to produce a loan.

As a first step, the lender quantified price elasticities at a granular level (i.e., on every cell of the rate sheet). This required sophisticated tools and mathematical and statistical analysis beyond the skills of XYZ's analytical team. The firm hired a consultancy to help, but the ensuing task of quantifying price elasticities still proved challenging as each calculation came with an expiration date.

Because a single loan can have multiple features, mortgage or home equity pricing can be a complex undertaking. In the case of XYZ Mortgage, 40 rate sheets—each with six FICO bands, five loan-to-value (LTV) bands, two lien positions, five property types, five bands for loan amounts, and two bands for occupancy status—produced an astonishing 120,000 different product combinations, each of which potentially had a different elasticity. To further complicate the process, not only would these 120,000 rates require biweekly update, but also the rates were given to a sales force with authority to override every single one, within certain parameters.

Despite these challenges, XYZ Mortgage was able to get the right technical support and complete the elasticity study in three months. The results demonstrated to management that mortgage elasticities could differ in excess of 100 percent depending on product characteristics such as FICO, LTV, or even lock-rate length. Across different channels, they varied by more than 400 percent. XYZ also realized that elasticity estimates would require constant updating as market and consumer behavior changed. Thus, having a self-adjusting demand model with a feedback loop was essential.

(*continued*)

(*Continued*)

The lender next worked to optimize profits by devising a new price-setting strategy. In general, optimization would require lowering rates to generate more volume on selected rate-sheet cells, while *increasing* other rates to improve margins *without* losing volume—a delicate balance. However, the firm determined that the overall approach would generate an additional $1.5 million in potential profit for every $1 billion in business, assuming that XYZ's overall risk profile and total origination volume remained constant. This represented an almost 20 percent lift in profitability for the firm with a very small investment in underlying infrastructure.

Price elasticity analysis also identified which competitors mattered most in each market XYZ operated in. After the optimization program was completed, the firm was able to react more intelligently to competitors' promotions. It quantified proposed reactions to the moves of competitors and responded only when it could be shown that the reactions would not negatively affect profitability. The model also acted as a filter for competitive price movements. Competitors that were responding directly to XYZ's promotions were separated from those that were changing prices based on other factors beyond the firm's control.

What about management's third question, regarding how to define an optimal pricing strategy in a new state? How could XYZ calculate optimal rate sheets if no historical information was available for that geographic region? The answer was to use competitive environment, market, and demographic data to identify similar patterns between the new state and the 40 others in which the firm was currently operating. After a statistically suitable market had been found, the self-adjusting nature of the demand model took care of the rest, constantly updating itself and thus routinely positioning XYZ's rates at, or near, its optimal point in the new market.

As the pricing program was being implemented, a few members of the management team were skeptical that optimized rates would reach the borrower intact, especially in the wholesale channel. The firm had allowed a 20 percent exception rate on its prices. But strict compliance to rate-sheet pricing is not necessary for a successful optimization program. The most robust models take into consideration discounting behavior. As long as exception rate patterns do not change dramatically overnight, the optimization engine will incorporate such behavior when setting prices. Furthermore, by utilizing a what-if functionality embedded in the software, XYZ was able to quantify whether rate exceptions were generating additional volume and increased profits. This feature turned out to be a preferred component of the program for the mortgage company.

Tips for Moving Forward

Advanced analytics and optimization techniques can provide companies with a substantial competitive advantage. As customer behavior becomes harder to predict, rival firms become more aggressive (and sophisticated) and channels begin to blur. Faced with these challenges, a company can lose its ability to leverage data into a more effective strategy and an improved capability. The latter problem has been mitigated in large part by better technology and data availability, more advanced techniques in statistics and econometrics, and new developments in management science. What has not been easy is melding these tools into a successful strategy to improve profitability. The specific tools outlined in this chapter are by no means a comprehensive list, but they do provide organizations with a sense of how analytics can effectively be used to drive the benefits they seek. Following are some key points managers should keep in mind—technically and organizationally—when using advanced analytics to improve price setting.

Structuring and Implementing an Analytics Initiative

- *Develop a quantitative and qualitative fact base* to drive improvement. By drawing on a solid foundation of information, suggested improvement opportunities will seem more credible to the organization and more likely to be implemented successfully.
- *Create a transaction-level data set* based on a sales or transaction-centric timeline.
- *Analyze transactions in detail* to uncover immediate savings. Understand the cost structure and determine whether the business model being used matches the strategy as defined.
- *Create customer segments that allow individual subgroups to be analyzed* based on their key attributes. This allows for basic price differentiation.
- *Develop an understanding of the needs, profiles, and elasticities* of key segments.
- *Determine how competition affects the organization's segments* and how to win in the marketplace. Value equivalency analytics is one method that enables organizations to separate specific attributes within a product category, so that rival offerings can be compared with each other.
- *Use econometrics and statistics to determine the demand curve and elasticity.* Use these figures to optimize the value the organization captures in the market.
- *Prioritize initial improvement efforts* on the process areas that favor quick wins and the largest payoff for expended effort. Quickly demonstrate to the organization that:
  - The solutions work and will generate significant benefits.
  - Management is serious about implementing the identified improvement opportunities.
  - The organization will be held accountable for realizing the results—progress should be measured against quantified expectations.

Ensuring the Organizational Culture and Goals Support the Initiative

- Align performance measurement systems and compensation with the overall corporate objectives for achieving revenue and profitability goals. This will ensure that benefits will be sustainable and repeatable.
- Ensure project scope and objectives follow a clearly articulated vision and detailed business case.
- Involve business users and all other stakeholders from the start; communicate the benefits of the changes starting from day one, and repeat core messages frequently.
- Develop a customer communication strategy that complements existing ones.
- Focus on getting the sales organization to adopt the changes mandated by the pricing improvement initiative. This will require employees to develop the necessary skills and competencies to ensure effective implementation of the improved pricing capabilities.
- Because ultimate success requires the involvement and support of the entire organization, management should make certain all stakeholders have the necessary skills and capabilities required for success.

Endnotes

1. Vilfredo Pareto and Alfred N. Page, trans., *Manual of Political Economy* (New York: A. M. Kelley, 1971).
2. Michael V. Marn and Robert L. Rosellio, "Managing Price, Gaining Profit," *Harvard Business Review,* September/October, 1992, 83–93.
3. Kern Lewis, "Kmart's Ten Deadly Sins," review of *Kmart's Ten Deadly Sins: How Incompetence Tainted an American Icon,* by Marcia Layton Turner. *Forbes Magazine,* October 10, 2003, http://www.forbes.com/2003/10/10/1010kmartreview.html.
4. Michael B. Brutman, "PCjr History," October 2000, http://www.brutman.com/PCjr/pcjr_history.html.
5. Charles Eicher, "Christmas 1984: The Great Apple© vs. PCjr Battle," *Disinfotainment,* December 23, 2002, http://weblog.ceicher.com/archives/2002/12/christmas_1984_the_great_apple.html.
6. David Haskin, "The 10 Biggest Technology Flops of the Past 40 Years," *Computer World,* July 9, 2007, http://www.computerworld.com/s/article/295810/The_10_Biggest_Technology_Flops_of_the_Past_40_Years.
7. Jake Widman, "IT's Biggest Project Failures—and What We Can Learn from Them," *Computer World,* October 9, 2008, http://www.computerworld.com/s/article/9116470/IT_s_biggest_project_failures_and_what_we_can_learn_from_them.
8. Ionut Arghire, "IBM's Inventors Celebrate Fifty Years Since Stretch Appeared," *Softpedia,* October 15, 2008, http://news.softpedia.com/news/IBM-039-s-Inventors-Celebrate-Fifty-Years-Since-Stretch-Appeared-93509.shtml.

9. Roman Pixell, "Why Apple's Newton Failed in the Market Place, a Retrospective" (paper presented at the Worldwide Newton Conference, Paris, September 4–5, 2004), http://wwnc.newtontalk.net/2004/program/romanpixell/.
10. Tim Berry, "Product and Brand Failures: A Marketing Perspective," *Mplans*, http://articles.mplans.com/product-and-brand-failures-a-marketing-perspective/.
11. "The First PDA: Case Apple Newton," *Failures—Exposed, Reflected Upon, Considered*, September 17, 2008, http://fail92fail.wordpress.com/2008/09/17/the-first-pda-case-apple-newton/.
12. Richard A. Shaffer, "Don't Give Up on the Newton," *Forbes*, November 8, 1993.
13. Jane McGrath, "5 Failed McDonald's Menu Items," *HowStuffWorks*, October 20, 2008, http://money.howstuffworks.com/5-failed-mcdonalds-menu-items3.htm.
14. "Products Hurt by Too Much Hype," *MSN Money*, November 25, 2009, http://money.ca.msn.com/investing/gallery/gallery.aspx?cp-documentid=22 705354&page=6.
15. "Top 25 Biggest Product Flops of All Time," *Wallet Pop*, http://www.walletpop.com/specials/top-25-biggest-product-flops-of-all-time.
16. Shannon Stevens, "$150M Later, McD Axing the Arch," *Brandweek*, January 19, 1998.
17. Deloitte Touche Tohmatsu (Risk and Performance Management), "Structured Testing: A Comprehensive Testing Framework for Financial Products" (white paper, March 2009), http://www.deloitte.com/assets/Dcom-Switzerland/Local%20Assets/Documents/ch_en_Structured_Testing.pdf.
18. In statistics, R^2 is the coefficient of determination and measures how much variability in the data is accounted for by the model. In essence, it indicates how well the model will predict the future.

C H A P T E R 6

Achieving Effective Organizational Alignment and Governance

You're messing with a company's DNA when you change how you do prices.

—Richard Braun, VP of Corporate Strategic Pricing, Parker Hannifin Corporation[1]

A global medical device manufacturer was taking two-to-three times as long as its competitors to get proposals out the door. Every time a new request for proposal (RFP) came in, the firm had to scramble to get input from Sales, Finance, Marketing, and Legal—each with its own agenda—to develop its pitch. At the strategic level, the device that was intended to be the firm's single most profitable product had target margins of 80 percent. But because the pricing process involved so many people and was so dysfunctional, sales representatives were cutting corners to close deals. The result? Massive revenue and margin leakage on virtually every transaction. Because contracts ranged from one-off sales to independent physicians (averaging $14,000) to huge deals with large medical groups (worth hundreds of thousands of dollars), this organizational disarray resulted in significant losses.

Unfortunately, this scenario is not uncommon. Most companies have their pricing stakeholders scattered throughout a variety of functions. But without establishing a companywide understanding of, and commitment to, their pricing strategies, businesses will suffer. Inevitably, they risk losing market share, foregoing opportunities for higher margins, or otherwise failing to respond adeptly to market pressures. Yet despite its importance, a surprising number of companies fail to take this fundamental—and critical—step. As a result, they find it virtually impossible to sustain the pricing model they have chosen to help maximize long-term profitability.

Weak governance is a separate, though related, issue. Even when a management team believes it has achieved high-end agreement on a strategy, it must still put in place the necessary tactical processes and procedures for that strategy to be effectively implemented. Organizational alignment defines *what* will be accomplished, while governance covers *how* it will get done through the assignment of specific roles, responsibilities, and decision-making rights to various individuals.

Five Key Components for Aligning a Pricing Organization

Various factors can prevent an organization from operating effectively, but the most serious problems arise when the following factors are involved.

- *Roles have not been adequately defined.* A surprising number of businesses fail to determine which departments and individuals contribute to setting, executing, and monitoring prices, undermining a potential reorganization from the start.
- *Pricing lacks clout.* The value of functional areas such as Finance, Marketing, and Sales is widely recognized, but Pricing still struggles to get internal recognition and the authority that comes with it.
- *Communication between stakeholders is poor.* Individuals and departments that belong to the pricing organization may not be kept abreast of corporate objectives or important shifts in strategy.
- *Decision making is fragmented.* Coordination is critical between the often disparate members of the pricing organization. Unless the right mechanisms are put in place, execution may be inconsistent across product lines and distribution channels.
- *Agreement cannot be reached on profitability metrics.* Without consensus on how to calculate profitability, an organization likely won't be able to determine whether it is actually making money on specific customers, which threatens the very viability of its business model.
- *No clear lines of authority have been established.* Decentralized organizations—particularly those such as pricing, with cross-functional boundaries—suffer because no one takes ownership of the process. And when different stakeholders have different priorities, the pricing function can become chaotic and ineffective.

For most companies, transforming their current organizations into cohesive, well-managed units can seem an overwhelming task. The challenge

Figure 6.1   Five Key Components of Organizational Alignment and Governance

appears even greater when the company is simultaneously implementing a larger, more integrated approach to pricing. The process can be successfully navigated by recognizing five key components that must be addressed to help align the pricing organization and develop a supportive governance model for it. The five components are described below and are reiterated in Figure 6.1.

1. *Aligning Sales to support pricing and profitability goals,* which includes addressing incentives, tools, territories, accounts, and performance management
2. *Identifying and empowering pricing leaders* so that they can play a decisive role in the management of systemwide changes
3. *Designing robust organizational and governance structures* to reinforce new attitudes and behaviors to support overall pricing strategies
4. *Implementing change management and adoption processes* to facilitate transformation by identifying issues that must be communicated to stakeholders
5. *Evaluating and managing talent* to ensure the organization has the right skill sets to execute the pricing strategy.

In the following sections of this chapter, we discuss how best to put these five components in place to ensure the proper execution of a new pricing strategy.

Aligning Sales to Support Pricing and Profitability Goals

Of all the departments and functional areas in an organization, Sales has the most influence over pricing (and pricing the most influence over Sales) because everything depends on that moment when a customer agrees to buy a product under certain terms.

To achieve profitability goals, organizations must reward the right behavior and decision making among their sales teams. This means managing every element of the Sales function, as follows.

Incentives

Nothing can undermine a pricing strategy faster than a sales team whose incentives are not perfectly aligned with it. For example, a company might use *value pricing*, which means the same product (with the same cost to produce and ship) is priced differently according to the perceived value in different markets. For example, the company might sell a tank of oxygen for $10 to an automotive repair shop and for $40 to a hospital that uses it for life support. Obviously, the company would want to encourage its salespeople to sell more products into health care facilities. Yet if the salespeople are compensated based on the total volume of products they sell, then they may focus more on the automotive repair shops even though they are less profitable for the company.

Tools

For salespeople to implement a pricing strategy, they must have the right tools. For instance, they can use a profit waterfall (see Chapter 5, "Advanced Analytics and Price Setting") when calculating the potential profitability of a particular deal. Numerous software applications exist to collect and crunch numbers and to help determine whether salespeople are adhering to target margins.

Accounts

Not all accounts are created equal. A client that buys at the highest volume may not be the most profitable. In fact, a firm may actually make more money on a client that is ranked only tenth or even one-hundredth by total sales. But to make the correct determinations—and decisions—a firm must allocate resources in a manner that supports its company-wide pricing strategy.

Territories

Because certain customers share a zip code does not mean they have equal value. The sales team must focus its attention and resources only on those accounts that will contribute to the organization's profitability or strategic goals.

Performance Management

To align compensation to a pricing strategy, firms must devise sales incentives that take into consideration different facets of their cost model. In terms of the profit waterfall, salespeople typically have discretion over three major variables that impact the total cost to serve of customers: (1) volume or loyalty discounts, (2) rebates, and (3) trade or marketing dollars. Some compensation systems reward salespeople by total sales regardless of how much profit they give away through each of these mechanisms. Yet if salespeople resort to excessive discounting to close deals, then this will directly impact profitability—perhaps resulting in a net loss on the affected sales. These types of activities must therefore be factored into compensation schemes.

Defining and Gathering Sales Effectiveness Data

Sales organizations routinely collect massive amounts of information on:

- amount sold, at what price, by whom, and to whom
- sales by product and service line, by territory, and by account
- sales patterns that may have changed during promotions, or through loyalty programs or volume purchase incentives
- incentive compensation plans, training manuals, sales tools, and other internal qualitative and quantitative resources.

In addition, extraordinarily valuable data can be uncovered in interviews with stakeholders (inside and outside the company), who can share insights—sometimes radically different—into the role that Sales needs to play to ensure effective price setting. Field representatives, internal salespeople, and service and operations professionals should all be interviewed along with sales leaders and customers (who may make the most useful contributions to the discussion).

Some areas firms should probe these populations about are:

- How much leeway do field representatives currently have when negotiating with potential customers? How much leeway *should* they have?
- Does this discretion vary by product? Should it be based on margin potential?

All the necessary data that will help identify the costs to serve customers, including after-sales service, shipping expenses, and marketing and related activities should be collected. Neglecting to calculate all costs can obscure customer profitability and lead to suboptimal pricing decisions.

Conducting a Sales Effectiveness Assessment

Armed with the data that have been collected, companies can conduct sales assessments by first comparing their existing practices to effective ones used by market competitors (or even other industries, if relevant). The current sales environment can then be compared against a future state in which the company meets its pricing and profitability goals.

A large, global business-to-business manufacturer experienced this problem firsthand. The company had customers who crossed business units, but the individual units remained narrowly focused on selling their own solutions. Because no one collected or shared metrics internally, some customers were getting product-level rebates from some business units *and* large, customer-level volume discounts from others. Not surprisingly, these were unprofitable customers, though it took some time for the manufacturer to realize this.

A *Fortune* 100 firm conducted a profitability analysis and wanted to institute an across-the-board price increase. Because it understood, however, that the market would only accept a hike of 2 or perhaps 3 percent, the firm decided to look at its total cost to serve. Management realized it could make up the extra profitability by charging for add-ons that were formerly given away (e.g., extended warranties and a liberal return policy). Whereas it would have been a mistake to raise prices, the company successfully improved its profitability in these other ways.

These assessments should almost certainly include a compensation evaluation. Incentive plans that are not well structured frequently cause unintended—and unwanted—behavior that affects pricing.

When analyzing compensation plans, firms should track the performance of sales professionals over a three-year period. They should exclude both new hires and people who have left the firm to produce accurate numbers over several years on a consistent sales force population.

An evaluation of compensation should not only provide a better understanding of an organization's current incentive structure, but also offer insights into the behavior of individual salespeople.

One assessment tool—an account management evaluation—can yield valuable additional pricing information by demonstrating how a sales organization handles accounts, and how this impacts customers. Some questions firms might ask during this assessment are:

- Do clients receive visits from multiple sales representatives from different divisions? If so, then the company is probably not optimizing its entire product or service portfolio for profitability.
- Is excessive discounting occurring? Profitability can be eroded in many different ways. Only by looking at all them—including marketing dollars and discounts for volume and for fast payment—can management drill down to the barriers to greater profits.
- Are savvy procurement officers looking for the lowest total price by asking sales teams from different territories to bid? Transparency

A global manufacturer paid commissions based on the volume of products sold—a losing strategy. Though the firm loudly proclaimed that it wanted to emphasize profitability, it was not successful until it changed the sales force's compensation structure to reward profitability over volume.

Another company paid a 3 percent commission rate on all deals and customers. Each sale was treated equally. Consequently, the bottom line suffered because the company didn't discriminate between those accounts that had a high strategic value or were most profitable and those that did not have or weren't. As a result, even though the company's sales volume increased, its margins actually slipped.

Profitability may not be the only measure of a good deal. For example, one service organization interviewed its sales team, whose members admitted to not selling some basic products because they were relatively low margin. Instead, because representatives were compensated on contribution margin, they preferred to sell the organization's higher-margin specialized products. Management realized that if the organization did not continue to sell both basic and specialized products, then customers would migrate to competitors who did. To overcome the problem, the organization established a *strategic products* designation to motivate its sales team to continue offering the lower-margin, basic items at competitive prices. With proper incentives in place, the organization was able to keep its sales team happy, while ensuring its strategic growth and profitability.

and communication between sales teams can block this practice effectively.

- Does compensation cost of sales (CCOS)—the percentage of a sale that gets paid to the representative—vary significantly from person to person? If so, then sales incentives could be misaligned.

The account management evaluation should also analyze how different customer touch points impact the cost of serving customers. For example, how does margin vary on sales made through a company's call center, its direct sales force, or its distributor channel? The answers may prove surprising.

Regardless of their size, companies that exercise stringent account management can avoid these kinds of costly deals—and hurting their bottom lines.

Once an organization completes its internal review, it should compare its practices to the most effective ones used by its competitors. The

> A global consulting firm's single biggest customer was a *Fortune* 500 office equipment manufacturer, which racked up $30 million in sales annually. But a detailed analysis revealed that the firm was not making any money from this relationship because of the high costs associated with it; for example, the dedication of expensive management resources to service the client and the high level of investment needed to secure new contracts.

organization can assess such things as the level of trade and marketing spending as a percentage of sales; the proportion of deals that have to go to the pricing exception committee; and the compensation structure. This comparison can help identify, evaluate, and prioritize areas for improvement, such as the following.

Sales Processes.   Sales processes include each step in a transaction, from pursuing the initial lead to the closing of a deal and post-sale activities. Many organizations make it a priority to reduce the number of steps—and therefore the amount of time—needed to get a particular contract approved. Others assess how to respond more swiftly to the market dynamics that affect pricing.

Sales Tools.   Companies frequently experience margin leakage due to deficient tools, so must identify more effective ones—both standard and non-standard—to prevent unwanted erosion. The profit waterfall is one of the best vehicles for understanding the cost of serving clients at a granular level, whether by SKU, customer, or sales territory.

Sales Reports.   Firms need to determine which data are being tracked and how frequently, while assessing whether they are being used in a way that is meaningful to the firm. Sales reports need to present metrics that reflect both the value and the profitability of each deal, product, or market.

Sales Pipeline Metrics.   How many deals are in the pipeline? How many are expected to close in the next 60 days? In the next 90 days? By collecting data and analyzing the potential size of individual deals, the investments needed to land various accounts, and the probability of the deals closing, companies can better determine what business to go after and in what order.

(Re)Designing Sales Incentive Plans

Depending on where a firm is in its lifecycle, it may take different approaches to sales incentives. A growth company may develop revenue-based incentives to spur market penetration and increase scale, while a manufacturer with a more mature product line may focus on rewarding salespeople who optimize a combination of margin and revenue. An organization that struggles with profitability may reward high-margin sales, while one facing cash flow problems may consider offering incentives for deals that generate the most immediate revenue.

The incentive plan used must directly reinforce a company's pricing and profitability goals. If not, then the company will likely end up with unhappy salespeople, high turnover, and even larger business challenges because it failed to meet its basic financial objectives. Following three basic steps can help a company implement a sales incentive plan that supports institutional objectives:

1. Determine the most—and least—profitable customers. Everything follows from this analysis.
2. Align selling resources to accounts strategically. For example, the most profitable accounts may be assigned to the best sales representatives, the less valuable accounts to entry-level sales representatives, and the least valuable accounts to inside sales or call center personnel.
3. Allocate a significant portion of compensation to the profitability (and other goals) of the account.

When firms modify one part of their incentive plans, they will likely need to update others, as none of the individual components functions properly in isolation. For example, a change in how sales territories are created and assigned will probably require account management methods to be adjusted, too. Similarly, a pricing increase may cause sales representatives to issue larger discounts unless they are evaluated on margin-based metrics.

> The management of a major appliance manufacturer wanted to increase pricing by 3–5 percent across all product lines. To help ensure that salespeople did not dilute the results by giving away extended warranties, floor samples, or other forms of free product, incentives were changed to reward sales only to clients that achieved the overall profitability goals—including all costs-to-serve.

Senior management needs to support changes to sales incentives to ensure adoption. But sponsorship alone will not guarantee success; champions will also be needed at lower organizational levels. For example, an incentive plan will likely not succeed if the CEO orders it to be implemented—untested—without the sales leadership first having had a chance to preview it and weigh in on it. Frequent and transparent communication from the top of the organization to all relevant stakeholders is critical to success.

Establishing Performance Metrics and Evaluating Results

To analyze the effectiveness of these internal actions (defining and gathering sales effectiveness data, conducting a sales effectiveness assessment, and redesigning sales incentives plans), companies must use predetermined indicators to assess them on a regular basis. These metrics must be tied to the pricing and profitability strategy. For example, pocket margin provides a snapshot of the actual costs to serve for every deal, including such things as providing free technical support, offering rebates, taking returned goods, or generally giving better terms and conditions to customers. By making the pocket margin explicit, companies can educate salespeople on the true costs of a transaction—something that can be an eye opener for salespeople who have only thought about profitability in its most basic form. Once one knows all the costs—both direct and indirect—that go into pocket margin, profitability can be calculated across a number of dimensions, including account, product, territory, market, or salesperson.

A *feedback loop* can facilitate continuous improvement. It can take the form of periodic surveys or focus groups that include sales managers as well as field representatives. Feedback loops may spark helpful changes in employee behavior. For example, tighter controls on pricing may inspire salespeople to talk to customers more about the value of the company's products and services rather than price alone. Generally, wholesale changes take time to achieve, but companies should see signs of success as sales managers and other employees begin to understand how the changes will benefit them.

Identifying and Empowering Pricing Leaders

Pricing organizations tend to be spread across many functions and departments, so effective management can be challenging. Yet companies must overcome this fragmented structure to pull together a cohesive organization. To accomplish this, companies should firms should:

- *Identify pricing leaders.* These managers will make the key decisions and set policies. They can be selected (1) from those people already in positions of authority (even if not in a dedicated pricing department) or (2) from early adopters of new processes and technologies who demonstrate a willingness to take risks or to accept challenges.

- *Align the leaders.* Senior pricing professionals in the organization may well disagree on key issues initially. Organizations must find ways to get them to agree on a vision and direction. For example, the leaders may need to focus on pocket margin as the basis for measuring profitability or plan a transition from cost-plus to value-based pricing. Without buy-in from the designated leaders, organizations will have trouble getting the other pricing professionals to go along with the changes.
- *Ensure the leaders provide tangible support.* To create a united pricing organization, leaders must dedicate the time, equipment, and technology resources necessary to effect massive changes—both financial and cultural. For example, if the pricing organization has an IT leader—and it should—then he or she should make the implementation of new pricing software a top priority. Similarly, the human resource leader for pricing should ensure employee incentives are aligned with profitability.

Selecting the Pricing Leaders

Leaders need not come from the pricing department, and they should not necessarily have offices in the C-suite. Instead, they should represent a broad group of stakeholders, both inside and outside the formal pricing function, and they should be capable of driving the pricing strategy. The organization must know who will have the power to set, execute, and monitor pricing if employee buy-in is to be achieved. Potential pricing team members could include functional leaders from Marketing, Sales, and Finance, or leaders with positional or political power who routinely become early adopters. Corporate initiatives often succeed simply because employees recognize the quality and shared philosophy of the group behind them. Organizations should particularly look for leaders who are recognized as capable risk-takers or assemble an informal group who employees associate with action and progress.

One of the challenges of bringing together executives from different functional areas is that their goals—and underlying motivations—frequently conflict. The chief financial officer (CFO) will almost certainly press for cost reductions and margin improvements, while the chief marketing officer (CMO) may focus on overall market share, and the sales manager may emphasize revenue and sales volume. All these differences have to be reconciled. To reduce potential tensions, many businesses establish multidisciplinary pricing councils. These councils provide a mechanism for individuals from different functions and locations to offer ideas about pricing and governing policies.

Because market forces can create dynamic pricing environments, many businesses using these councils have developed processes to fast-track the handling of time-sensitive issues. In such cases, the council typically reviews expedited decisions before final sign off to ensure they align with corporate objectives. These councils can also help move an organization toward a more centralized pricing strategy.

> A global medical device manufacturer's pricing function was initially embedded in the finance department. Because this department had no enforcement authority, it could not ensure adherence to its policies. Real pricing responsibility lay with regional sales representatives. A first step toward bringing some discipline to the pricing process was to establish a council that evaluated decisions being made in the field and set guidelines to help achieve some consistency and common metrics. Although the council's role initially was limited to advice and consent, eventually it became responsible for issuing rigorous pricing rules that applied to all functional departments. Though each business unit was still able to operate autonomously, the council provided a forum for best practice, ideas, competencies, and lessons learned to be shared (among other benefits), while ensuring that pricing issues were correctly elevated to the leadership level.

Whether a council becomes an interim institution to help put a new strategy in place or whether it becomes a permanent part of the organization depends on the needs and culture of each organization. In every case the pricing strategy (and the organizational changes that go with it) must be fit to the corporate culture and not the reverse.

Engaging the Leadership Team

Once the pricing leaders have been identified, their views should be solicited on current pricing strategies and organizational issues. This information will help senior management to gauge the extent of internal support and the conflicts that might arise among the pricing leaders. Using the intelligence garnered from interviews, the firm can perform a leadership alignment analysis (see Figure 6.2). This analysis should determine the degree to which pricing leaders support current policies and decision-making guidelines and are committed to making any necessary changes.

The results of the alignment analysis can be used to create a leadership engagement plan (see Figure 6.3). This plan should foster candid discussions about the changes required by the new pricing strategy, the business issues likely to arise, and the risks involved. It can also outline ways to close the gaps between leaders and to transform them into a harmonious team that works together to achieve pricing goals. The plan need not be complicated—it can consist merely of three or four actions that the team commits to executing over the next few months. For example, the team could assign

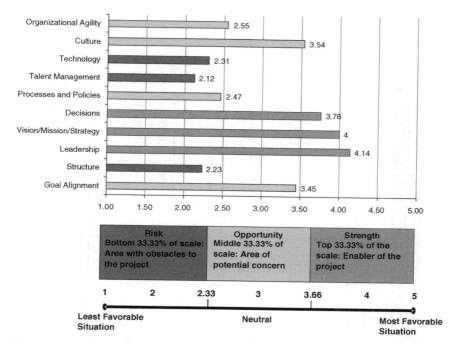

Figure 6.2   Leadership Alignment Analysis

a specific pricing-related research task to each individual and agree to re-convene in six weeks to report on results. Or each team member could submit his or her desired metrics for measuring a successful pricing initiative with the goal of coming up with a shared yardstick that could be used across the enterprise.

Developing the Leadership Action Plan

After selecting and engaging the pricing leadership team, the organization needs to create an action plan whose purpose is to specify the activities that the leaders will engage in to drive support for all agreed-upon changes across the pricing organization. This plan should have four major objectives.

1. *Set strategic pricing policy guidelines.* These directives govern pricing procedures, alternative strategies, and standards for strategic decision making.
2. *Identify and prioritize high-impact pricing issues.* For example, a major contract may be up for renewal, and pricing it correctly could be of considerable strategic importance to the firm. Or, a business might decide it needs to transition swiftly to a value-based pricing model and quickly put the right tools and scripts into the hands of the

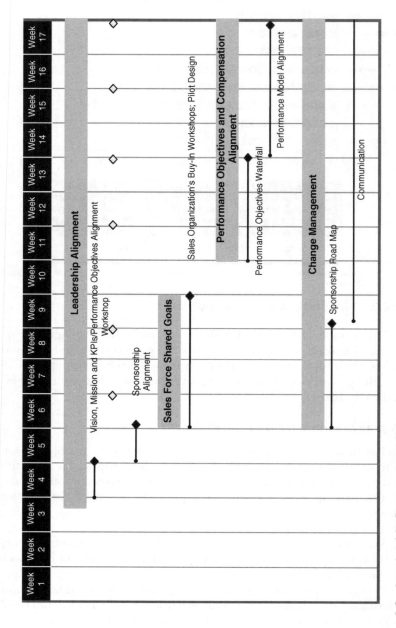

Figure 6.3 Leadership Engagement Plan

sales team to use with customers. The action plan will prioritize these issues.

3. *Ensure leaders drive behavioral changes within the organization.* Simply announcing a transformational strategy is not enough. Leaders have to enforce the new policies and procedures—and do so in a very public manner. For example, the company might decide that the price of a software product should no longer include custom on-site installation—yet sales engineers may still be hopping on planes to go to customer facilities to do exactly that. Pricing leaders need to stop behaviors that conflict with their strategic decisions.

4. *Establish key performance indicators (KPIs).* Leaders and other pricing employees need to have their performance measured. Deciding on KPIs—both general standards that all pricing leaders will be held to and ones that are specific to each role within the pricing organization—is a critical first step.

Designing Robust Organizational and Governance Structures

The challenge with any corporate restructuring is to redesign the organization so that it reflects the company's culture and serves its objectives without becoming co-opted by political considerations. In essence, the structure is a framework of rules and policies through which an organization defines roles, including their assigned rights and duties. The structure also determines the flow of information through formal—and informal—communication channels. The term *governance* refers to the rules that define and regulate an organization's decision-making authority and reporting relationships, as well as the ways stakeholders from multiple functions and lines of business interrelate. It also defines to what extent power and responsibilities are centralized.

Companies with effective organizational alignment and governance capabilities:

- align incentives and performance metrics with pricing strategy
- engage leadership to drive pricing excellence and cultural change
- clearly define areas of responsibility and accountability for all aspects of pricing
- focus on processes for continued improvement
- offer career paths for people involved in pricing processes so a firm can retain high-performing talent
- focus on creating buy-in and ownership for change, which will accelerate full optimization of the pricing strategy
- align the vision of the pricing organization with the company's culture.

As difficult as people find it to change, organizations can prove even more resistant—particularly when a transformative approach to pricing is being implemented. The challenge is twofold. First, management needs to determine which structure most effectively supports its pricing plan, as it must be tailored to the organization's unique strategy, corporate culture, and the willingness of people at all levels to work within it. Second, change must be consistently reinforced. Assigning pricing analysts with dotted-line responsibilities to both Finance and Marketing will not work if the analysts choose to communicate with only one division's managers.

Senior management must be realistic when communicating the challenges posed by the organizational changes. These are frequently underestimated. All stakeholders must be told that progress may be slow and setbacks likely will arise, particularly in the early stages of the restructuring initiative. But, most important, the objectives, which are as follows, should be communicated.

- *Design efficient pricing processes.* As outlined in Chapter 4, "Price Execution," nine critical areas must be considered when creating an appropriate structure.
- *Assign pricing roles, responsibilities, reporting relationships, and decision-making authority.* A ground-up approach, which starts with basic tactical actions, moves up through the required competencies, and ends with reporting structures, usually proves the most efficient.
- *Specify metrics to track successful completion of processes..* In addition to setting yardsticks to measure progress, management should also ensure employee incentives are tied to those metrics.
- *Reinforce behavior that supports the firm's pricing processes.* Once the right metrics are in place, they should be used and referred to continually in department meetings and performance evaluations to help ensure they have the desired effect.

Assessing the Effectiveness of the Current Organization

An organizational restructuring inevitably affects existing work processes, so management needs first to analyze the ways that the current pricing structure fits the firm's needs as well as the ways it does not. The leadership team must start by determining how people are using their time. Are they performing analytical or administrative activities? Do they add value to the pricing function or detract from it? Do they work directly with customers or labor in the back office?

The organization must document, as precisely as possible, what activities are being performed, by whom, and how they contribute to the profitable pricing of products and services. Pricing-related activities may be

> The benefits of restructuring can be tangible and encourage employee buy-in. A medical device manufacturer experienced this first hand. The company had been using an average selling price to determine the proper pricing window for a particular product. Over a six-month period, 1,000 units of the product had sold, on average, for $10,000. To help ensure new contracts reflected this market-tested price, the company decreed that any sale that dropped below $9,500 or exceeded $10,500 would have to be approved by both the VP of Sales and the CFO. Generally, some 20 out of 50 deals fell outside the official pricing parameters. Because of the exceptions, the company was taking 14–21 days to respond to RFPs, and was losing business to competitors who gave approvals in less than a week. The company realized it needed to re-evaluate its governance model to allow the field representatives greater latitude to give approvals (according to revised guidelines). This change dramatically reduced the number of exceptions requiring sign off by senior executives, benefitting both the sales team and the company as a whole.

difficult to identify if they are wrapped up in complex processes. For example, in a business where bundles of products or services are aggregated from various suppliers and sold to customers as a single unit, the activities of procurement professionals—and the prices they negotiate with vendors on the supply side of the business—can directly affect pricing on the sell side.

Other activities in this process range from the mundane (e.g., checking prices in an order entry system for accuracy) to the complex (e.g., figuring out the cost of providing after-sales support to customers worldwide when determining the price of the base product). Even customer service representatives can have an impact on pricing, as they may be authorized to accept returns of products, give coupons, or offer discounts on future purchases to appease disgruntled customers. In short, every process must be broken down into its most basic elements to identify each employee action that affects pricing.

Once a firm determines what its employees are doing, it must also examine how much time is being spent on these activities. This information can be gathered in different ways. Employees can be asked to participate in a survey. Online tools exist that can help firms carry out surveys quickly and inexpensively. Another option is to sponsor a focus group or live forum drawing on individuals with pricing responsibilities from throughout the firm. A leadership council meeting can be convened, and each stakeholder can be asked to offer a rough assessment on how his or her reports (direct and indirect) spend their time.

Regardless of how the information is assembled, the results can lead to important business improvements.

> One large and otherwise successful manufacturer learned that its highly trained pricing professionals were spending more than 50 percent of their time performing administrative tasks. This not only was a massive—and unproductive—diversion of valuable resources from pressing responsibilities, but also resulted in capable individuals frequently resigning to pursue career opportunities elsewhere. Once senior management realized this problem, it was able to rectify it by freeing up its pricing experts from administrative chores to focus on their primary mission.

The responsibilities of pricing organizations are to:

- set pricing policy or make policy recommendations
- monitor policy adherence
- establish profitability thresholds for deals
- approve pricing exceptions
- set and adjust base prices
- determine deal envelopes (price floors and ceilings)
- conduct pricing analytics
- report on pricing performance
- make pricing strategy recommendations
- monitor pricing of competitors
- communicate price changes
- monitor effectiveness of promotions
- maintain pricing data.

Identifying Key Decision Makers

After completing the documentation stage, management should next determine where the pricing leaders fit within the organization. Are decisions being made in the field? At the district level? At headquarters? Responsibility for different pricing decisions may in fact be (correctly) distributed through different functions and organizational levels. There will be many considerations that are unique to each organization: the overarching corporate strategy, the circumstances of the competitive environment, the skills of individual employees who will be making decisions, and the pricing-related risks and opportunities of each decision. All of these considerations will need to be revisited later when allocating decision-making authority to specific roles.

Examining Non-Sales Incentive Compensation

A key determinant of organizational effectiveness is the incentive compensation of *non-sales* personnel. (Firms should already have evaluated and redesigned the sales team's compensation as discussed in the "Aligning Sales to Support Pricing and Profitability Goals" section of this chapter.) Customer service performance is frequently measured by surveying buyers. Yet service representatives may be giving away excessive discounts on next purchases, or promising free maintenance or parts replacement to keep customer satisfaction levels up. Thus, these employees may receive high performance ratings, but their actions actually damage profitability because of the increased cost-to-serve.

Similarly, product marketing departments, which are rewarded for driving demand, frequently use promotions and rebates to increase sales. Such actions—particularly the dumping of excessive promotion dollars into the market—can kill margins and harm the business. This tends to happen particularly at the end of quarters to stimulate sales artificially. At the top of the organization, some executives are compensated based on the gross margins achieved rather than on performance metrics that would help ensure that products and services are being optimally priced to benefit the business better. Because so many employees in different functions can affect the pricing strategy, organizations need to identify them all carefully and examine how they are incentivized as well as the metrics being used to evaluate them.

Mapping Existing Processes

Another essential component of an *as-is* assessment is the mapping of current pricing processes, which can be a complex undertaking. Firms should first consider how information flows through the pricing organization. Where are the decisions made, and by whom? What tasks are performed, by whom, and what is the output? If such graphic documentation already exists, then management should have it independently validated. Unauthorized workarounds to processes, which have never been recorded, frequently emerge. Some of these may have created pricing efficiencies, while others may have had a detrimental impact. Once this information is gathered—usually through a combination of employee interviews and a review of existing documentation—the as-is pricing process can be captured in a new, or updated, graphic representation showing the organization's workflow. The firm can then begin an analysis to determine what is working, and what needs to be improved. In general, any decisions on a new structure—who will do the work—should be driven by the pricing processes—what tasks must be accomplished and how. (See Chapter 4, "Price Execution," for a discussion of the design of pricing processes.)

Determining an Effective Structure

Because pricing involves so many internal stakeholders and functions, it requires commitment from all levels of the organization. Consequently, management will generally have to change decision frameworks, processes, approval workflows, span of control, execution, and compensation metrics, or the implementation of advanced pricing tools will likely not result in the hoped-for margin improvements.

Adjustments will probably also need to be made in other areas, such as how segments and channel prices are determined, and in the messages the sales force communicates to customers to ensure new prices are adopted. Fresh approaches to improving how functions work together should be considered and pursued. Pricing will need to open its processes so that management may participate more actively; Sales will have to share control of negotiations through the approval workflow; and Procurement will need to take guidance from Pricing. IT, too, will play an important role as it must maintain the data needed for pricing analyses and applications—if the company selects and implements any. The company's systems may also need to be upgraded to support new functionality.

Future success requires an organization to embrace a disciplined, systematic approach to price setting, while adhering to a well-established and mature methodology. Figure 6.4 shows an overview of the new organizational design process.

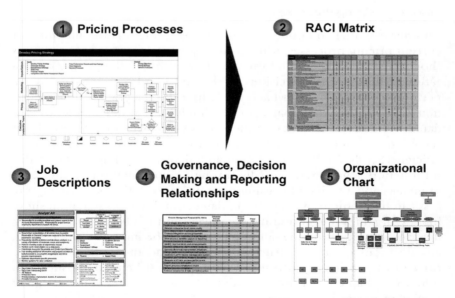

Figure 6.4   Gathering Requirements for New Organizational Design

The requirements for a pricing organization flow first from the roles that are defined in the pricing processes. An effective way to determine these is by creating a responsible, accountable, consulted, and informed (RACI) matrix (an example can be seen in Figure 6.4). A RACI matrix lists the participation and ownership of every role in completing an activity. The activities and their tasks are listed on the vertical axis (i.e., leftmost column) and the organizational roles (extracted from the process maps) are listed on the horizontal axis (i.e., top row). The responsibilities are indicated at the intersection of task and role by the assignment of an R, A, C, or I:

- *Responsible:* Employees who execute a task or activity. More than one person can be assigned to the responsible role, although it is advisable to keep the number to a minimum.
- *Accountable:* Responsible employees report to those in accountable roles, who provide guidance and remove obstacles, but may not actually oversee execution. Accountable personnel are ultimately responsible to the organization for the completion of the activity.
- *Consulted:* Employees who participate in discussions and offer opinions, particularly regarding issues and decisions that impact their areas, but who do not have approval authority or make final decisions.
- *Informed:* Employees who are notified of decisions and activities that may affect them. Communication is one way; their input is not sought for completion of the activity.

From the RACI matrix, the organizational structure can be (re)defined by:

- *Mapping grouped roles.* Almost certainly, firms will discover that some roles overlap, even if they are scattered through various functional areas or involve employees reporting to different pricing leaders. For example, the sales and product marketing departments may both have analysts—the first focusing on customer profitability and the second on product profitability—so management needs to map out how they fall within the organization.
- *Formally defining jobs.* A precise job description should be created to detail the responsibilities of the person filling each role.
- *Identifying the ideal reporting relationships.* All pricing positions must be examined to determine how they relate to one another and to the pricing leadership. To whom should a sales profitability analyst report? A marketing pricing analyst? How can duties best be aggregated? What is the decision-making model?
- *Creating an organizational chart.* This chart should represent the structure graphically so that it can be easily communicated and broadly shared.

Implementing and Sustaining the New Pricing Organization

Maintaining a reorganized pricing function can be a challenge over the long term. Companies can do this by:

- *Redefining governance structures.* By formalizing rules, decision-making authority, and policies, firms can strengthen overall process management. They can develop a manual or manuals to document reporting and divisional structures, future-state process maps, information flows, procedures, and general policies as further reinforcement.
- *Identifying new pay-for-performance metrics for the sales team.* These metrics should reinforce the desired behavior of salespeople based on corporate objectives.
- *Updating non-sales incentive plans to align with the new organizational structure.* It is important to remember that non-sales departments and individuals also need incentives that motivate them to take pricing actions in support of corporate profitability strategies.
- *Establishing baseline metrics for comparison purposes.* To help ensure performance goals are realistic, management should agree upon initial metrics and then test them in short-term pilot programs.

Careful redesign and implementation of organizational and governing structures can strongly benefit a company.

A large truck manufacturer had a highly decentralized pricing function with a strategy in disarray and activities scattered throughout the company. Predictably, the firm was leaking profits across most of its product lines. Determined to staunch the flow, the firm documented its as-is organizational structure. This exercise revealed that 54 professionals were spending 25 percent or more of their time on pricing. Of these, 18 were contractors with a very high turnover. After interviewing all employees in depth about their pricing responsibilities, the firm undertook a restructuring that consolidated all pricing activities under 30 full-time employees and included additional steps to improve the caliber and capability of the pricing workforce. The result? Profit leakage was substantially reduced, increasing profits across all affected product lines.

Implementing Change Management and Adoption Processes

Many business leaders report that managing the change associated with improvement initiatives and technology implementations presents them with their biggest challenges. When the change relates to pricing, the obstacles can be even greater as the effort can be emotionally charged. Practices that are deeply rooted in a company's history may be challenged, and individual compensation may be affected. All of these factors can inspire organizational resistance. Some of the obstacles that must be overcome follow.

- *Convincing stakeholders about the value of pricing and its validity as a discipline.* As a relatively new corporate function, pricing's importance tends to be undervalued by established business disciplines such as finance, marketing, and research and development (R&D), which discourages cooperation at many levels.
- *Implementing data-driven pricing techniques in the field.* Calculating profitability and other metrics in real time often requires changes to unify technology, business processes, and culture. Yet sales professionals are notoriously reluctant to change how they are compensated, adopt new tools, and accept additional oversight and guidance.
- *Fostering cross-functional collaboration.* Pricing activities are typically scattered throughout an organization, and most businesses struggle to find a way to get loosely connected employees with pricing responsibilities to realize their shared mission and work together to realize corporate profitability goals.
- *Persuading stakeholders that change is necessary.* Most organizations erroneously believe they are doing a good job on pricing. Unless they are provided with compelling evidence to the contrary, they will continue to resist efforts to adjust current practices.

Effective change management and adoption requires execution of four key steps, described in Table 6.1.

Effective communication with stakeholders is critical to winning their whole-hearted support. Unlike the implementation of new quality assurance (QA) or customer relationship management (CRM) systems—technologies with well-established track records—pricing initiatives usually require management to develop a powerful business case for change. This should include a careful delineation of both financial and non-financial benefits to overcome internal objections.

The primary reason employees resist change is because they do not understand how it will impact them personally. Most businesses have active rumor mills, which contribute to fears that a sweeping reorganization will affect job security, compensation levels, and daily work habits. Clear, frequent communications are essential. Management must explain to employees how they will be affected; how they will benefit from the changes.

In essence, change management efforts seek to move stakeholders—individuals and groups—up the commitment curve (see Figure 6.5), from *contact* to *internalization*, as they increasingly accept the initiative.

Communications must go through both top-down and bottom-up channels. Firms that choose just one channel risk having their message distorted, misheard, or ignored. For example, if executives simply issue memos to senior pricing leaders and expect them to pass the messages

Table 6.1 Change Management and Adoption Activities

Activity	Deliverables and Outcomes	Description	Goals
Analyze Stakeholder Groups	• Detailed stakeholder and audience needs analysis	Analysis of individual users who are accountable for the success or failure of the project, or who can affect the outcome of the project	Determine the current and targeted level of support and interaction of these individuals, including business signoff and issue resolution.
Develop Stakeholder Engagement Strategy	• Stakeholder engagement strategy – Stakeholder role descriptions – Specific adoption, change management and challenges list – Engagement tools and approach	A comprehensive strategy that identifies all the major components of a successful engagement effort, including audiences, tools, description of stakeholder roles and a list of specific adoption challenges	Provide a consistent resource for stakeholder activity planning and build the business case for engagement.
Develop and Refine Stakeholder Engagement Plan	• Stakeholder engagement plan – Stakeholder engagement calendar – Stakeholder action-and-decision inventory	A detailed matrix listing relevant audience groups, adoption events and messages to be delivered to these audiences	Provide a comprehensive, tactical, one-stop guide to activities that changes as new planning occurs.
Measure Stakeholder Engagement Progress	• Stakeholder engagement metrics • Adoption metrics by business unit • Leadership progress report – Periodic discussion document – Stakeholder engagement dashboard/ scorecard	Set of metrics used to measure success in engaging stakeholders and promoting adoption, and reporting tools used to support periodic discussions with leadership on progress	Provide real-time status updates to leadership and solicit its assistance in mitigating risks identified.

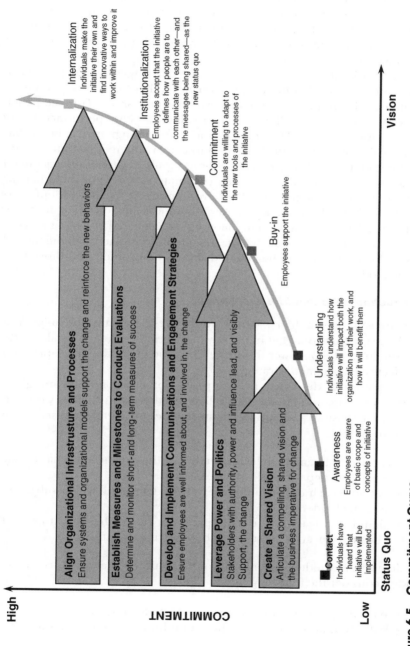

Figure 6.5 Commitment Curve

207

down through the ranks, then this could make people on the front lines of the pricing changes feel slighted and disenfranchised. On the other hand, if pricing managers thoroughly brief lower-level pricing employees without first separately briefing corporate leadership, then they risk losing the executive buy-in and sponsorship that is absolutely necessary for any transformative change to be successful.

The corporate culture can also present challenges to change management. For example, if individual performance rather than group success has traditionally been rewarded, then change may be resisted. Top salespeople may expect to do very well even if their colleagues have performed poorly over a quarter or a year. This could be such a deeply ingrained cultural characteristic that attempting to change it during a pricing reorganization would be a futile endeavor. As a general rule, firms should map their pricing organizations and strategies to the existing corporate culture, not the other way around. All stakeholders should receive training to facilitate adoption of changes; training, for example, on new software, selling on *value*, instituting decision-making procedures, and following reengineered pricing processes.

To execute a successful change and adoption initiative, all the individuals and groups who will be affected should be profiled and thoroughly understood.

Conducting a Stakeholder Assessment

Who are your stakeholders? Where do they reside organizationally? What are the issues that could get in the way of successful change? A stakeholder assessment can help answer these questions and guide the development of an effective engagement strategy.

As previously discussed, pricing professionals are found throughout Sales, Marketing, and Finance, as well as in other areas such as Customer Service, Purchasing, and Supply Chain. To identify all affected stakeholders, firms should:

- confirm that any high-level overview of the organization has considered every department
- examine each department carefully to determine which subgroups are stakeholders
- identify key leaders in each department (and subgroup, if needed) who are critical to the success of the pricing initiative.

To determine whether an entire group should be identified as a stakeholder, consider the following:

- Will changes in the pricing organization affect it in any way?
- Will the individuals within the group find their day-to-day activities affected?
- Does the firm need support from this group to achieve success?

Table 6.2   Stakeholder Analysis Criteria

Criteria	Definitions and Ratings
Current State of Awareness	Assigns H (high), M (medium), L (low) ratings, reflecting each stakeholder's current knowledge of the project or impending change
"To Be" Awareness	Assigns H (high), M (medium), L (low) ratings, reflecting desired level of knowledge regarding the project or impending change that each stakeholder should acquire in order for the project or impending change to be successful
Importance to Success	Assigns H (high), M (medium), L (low) ratings, reflecting each stakeholder's ability to impact the success of the project or impending change
Expected Behavioral Change	Assigns H (high), M (medium), L (low) ratings, reflecting the amount of expected behavioral change that each stakeholder will experience (i.e., impact on day-to-day activities)
Perception	Assigns P (Positive), T (Neutral), N (Negative) ratings, reflecting the stakeholder's attitude toward the initiative
Information Needs	The type of information required by the stakeholders to help them understand the effort and to engage them in the change
Individuals and Groups They Influence	The relationships between stakeholders that may positively or negatively influence the success of the project

Once the stakeholder groups have been identified, each should be evaluated against key criteria (e.g., size, specific role in the pricing organization, resource requirements, and the impact the change will have on its members) to consider its needs and—more important—to assess its potential to disrupt or impede the desired changes (see Table 6.2).

The results of the stakeholder analysis can be prioritized and summarized in a stakeholder map and an engagement strategy: these visually depict all stakeholders and how they should be engaged to ensure success. In the example stakeholder map shown in Figure 6.6, three different types of stakeholders are shown. They are categorized according to their required level of awareness and the degree to which their approval is necessary for the pricing changes to succeed. Figure 6.7 illustrates the engagement strategy that should be pursued with each group.

The stakeholder analysis can bring to light interdependencies between groups and help assess the risks associated with the implementation of planned changes. Firms should also assess the *change readiness* of the

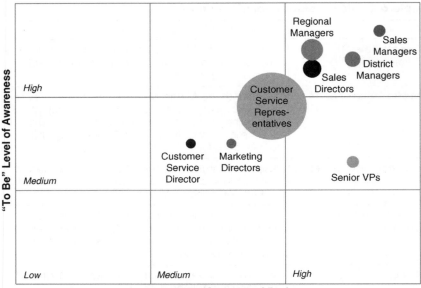

Figure 6.6   Stakeholder Map (Size of Bubbles Represents Stakeholder Group Size)

stakeholders and determine the most effective communication option to reach them. For example, one global manufacturing firm had recently lost almost 50 percent of its customer service division due to turnover and because the manufacturer was cutting costs, and the remaining personnel had literally no time to devote to implementing a new pricing structure.

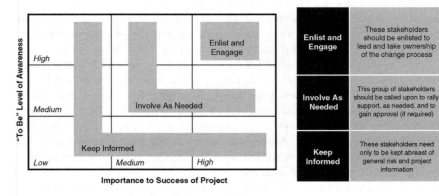

Figure 6.7   Stakeholder Map and the Engagement Strategy for Each Group

However, by engaging pricing specialists from other functional areas to step in and assist the customer service representatives, the firm was able to carry out the restructuring successfully without overburdening the customer service division.

Developing a Stakeholder Engagement Plan

The stakeholder analysis will define the outcomes expected for each group and make the case for change (see Table 6.3).

To minimize confusion during the restructuring and to help maximize effectiveness later on, a stakeholder engagement plan should be developed

Table 6.3   Stakeholder Groups and Expected Outcomes

Group	Expected Outcomes
Business Unit Leadership Group	• Demonstrate visible project support to all employees • Facilitate and cascade communications to all employees • Collect feedback from all employees • Model new behaviors and promote buy-in among all employees
Pricing Leadership Groups (Leaders of All Affected Areas: Sales, Marketing and Others)	• Demonstrate visible project support to managers, power users and end users • Facilitate and cascade communications to managers, power users, and end users • Collect feedback from managers, power users, and end users • Model new behavior and promote buy-in among managers, power users, and end users • Designate participants and ensure appropriate resourcing for Pricing activities (e.g., transition projects and testing) • Assist in execution of change activities and resolution of related challenges • Ensure employee enrollment in, and completion of, training
Pricing Manager Groups (Managers of All Affected Areas: Sales, Marketing and Others)	• Demonstrate project support to power users and end users • Facilitate and cascade communications to power users and end users • Collect feedback from power users and end users • Model new behavior and promote buy-in among power users and end users • Participate in Pricing activities (e.g., transition projects and testing) • Assist in execution of change activities and resolution of related challenges • Validate enrollment in, and completion of, training

(continued)

Table 6.3   (Continued)

Group	Expected Outcomes
Power Users	• Demonstrate project support among end users • Provide peers and end users with regular, informal Pricing updates • Gather informal feedback from power users and end users • Model use of new procedures and technology among end users • Participate in Pricing activities (e.g., transition projects and testing) • Assist in execution of change activities and resolution of related challenges • Work with training team to develop practice exercises and business scenarios • Receive training and then train end users in turn

(see Table 6.4). This plan should detail the overall strategy for involving key groups and for achieving expected outcomes. Key themes and messages should be refined for each stakeholder to address the "What is in it for me?" questions tied to implementation (the benefits). Firms should also determine what activities should be used to reinforce them. This frequently involves training. If employees will be expected to use a new tool or template, then conducting a workshop—whether online, via teleconference, or in an onsite meeting—can be helpful.

Implementing a Well-Designed Communications Plan

A strong communications plan helps engage stakeholders (see Figure 6.8 for an illustration of the communications process). The plan should keep all affected employees up to date on every element of the restructuring by:

- *Identifying the key messages needed to execute the pricing program.* This includes the message date, delivery mechanism (e.g., email, memo, telephone call, or webinar), message owner, and audience.
- *Proactively communicating key project messages, milestones, and upcoming events.* Repetition is key. Firms should begin issuing memos months in advance of planned changes and reiterate the timeline, the extent of the changes, and the expectations for each stakeholder. Employees should be given sufficient time to adjust to the changes and to ask any questions they may have. Communications should include high-level messaging about strategic direction as well as tactical instructions on how changes will play out on a very practical level.
- *Publicizing the training schedule.* As part of the communications plan, firms should notify stakeholders about training classes, workshops, documentation, and other resources that will enable them to transition to the new ways of doing things.

Table 6.4 Stakeholder Engagement Plan

Activity Event	Target Audience (Stakeholder Group)	Media Vehicle	Objective	Content/ Message	Feedback Mechanism	Delivery/ Distribution Timing	Signoff Date	Developer	Approver	Status

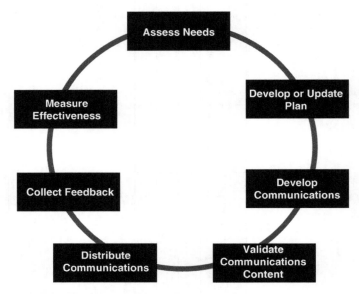

Figure 6.8   Effective Communication Process

Table 6.5 identifies the type of information that should be captured in a communications plan, and what vehicles should be used to reach each audience. Table 6.6 shows an example communications plan.

The objectives of a communications plan are as follows.

- Build understanding and support for the pricing improvement effort by establishing forums for discussion.
- Strengthen the communications capabilities of managers and leaders by providing resources and tools (including frameworks, guidelines, and key talking points) to facilitate a consistent dialogue with stakeholders.
- Support employees and managers as they adjust their activities and work processes to meet reconfigured (and clearly defined) expectations and benefits.
- Build commitment, ownership, and trust.
- Monitor and measure feedback.
- Use lessons learned to plan other communications efforts.
- Accelerate adoption, engagement, and commitment to use the new tools to achieve pricing benefits.

Reinforcing the Pricing Changes

Too often, a company will do almost everything right when planning for and implementing a major pricing transformation, but because the

Table 6.5   Communication Plan Elements

Element	Description
Stakeholder Group	Who is the target audience for the communication activity or event?
Objective	What is the purpose of the communication activity or event?
Key Message	What are the content and sources of information?
Vehicle	What is the appropriate method for distributing content to particular stakeholder groups?
Frequency	How many times (or on what date) will the communication activity or event occur?
Feedback Mechanism	How is feedback being gathered on the communication activity or event?
Developer	Who is creating the communication material?
Reviewer and Signoff	Who reviews and signs off on the communication material?
Status	What is the status of the communication activity?
Release Date	When will this communication be delivered to the identified stakeholder group?
Signoff Date	When does the leadership team need to sign off on this communication material?

company fails to put mechanisms in place to ensure that messages and training stick, employees forget what they have learned, stop using the new processes and tools, and return to their old habits.

Continual reinforcement must be an essential part of any change management plan; it is a crucial weapon in the battle against organizational regression. Firms can reinforce through a variety of methods, including refresher lunch and learn sessions, monthly feedback forums, and focused training on advanced topics. Firms must also anticipate how to deal with stubborn resistance among some employee groups. If this happens, stakeholders should be reminded that their job performance, and perhaps even their compensation, will be impacted if they do not adopt the changes.

Evaluating and Managing Pricing Talent

No pricing strategy can be successfully executed without the help of the right talent in key positions. As recently as 10 years ago, prices were primarily set by salespeople, marketers, or product managers.

Table 6.6 Pricing Communications Plan

Date	Communication	Audience	Message and Purpose	Medium
Roughly one month prior to training	Training enrollment announcement	All trainers	• Describe training enrollment process, timeline, curriculum and criteria (tool kit).	• Email • Intranet
Roughly one month before approver training	Approver training enrollment announcement	All approvers	• Describe training enrollment process, timeline, curriculum and criteria (tool kit).	• Email • Intranet
08/02/12	Bi-weekly update	District managers, VPs	Delivered by project leaders: • Bi-weekly call with key stakeholders to field questions, communicate status, and provide new information and an update on changes	• Conference call • Q&A session • Virtual meeting
08/16/12	Bi-weekly update	End users	Delivered by district managers to their respective stores and sales representatives: • Bi-weekly call with key stakeholders to field questions, communicate status and provide new information and an update on changes	• Conference call • Q&A session
08/30/12	Bi-weekly update	District managers, VPs	Delivered by project leaders: • Bi-weekly call with key stakeholders to field questions communicate status and provide new information and an update on changes	• Conference call • Q&A session • Virtual meeting
09/02/12	Monthly e-newsletter	End users, approvers, trainers	• Describe what to expect regarding training. • Offer prerequisite training information. • Provide users with an understanding of where the project stands as it approaches go-live date.	• E-newsletter • Intranet
09/13/12	Bi-weekly update	End users	Delivered by district managers to their respective stores and sales representatives: • Bi-weekly call with key stakeholders to field questions communicate status and provide new information and an update on changes	• Conference call • Q&A session

A global specialty materials company spent many millions of dollars formulating a new pricing strategy and putting supporting processes in place. Despite investing such a significant sum of money, the firm neglected to establish mechanisms to ensure that employees were actually adopting the new tools and processes. As a result, the firm realized less than 20 percent of the return on investment (ROI) it had expected for its pricing transformation.

Today, more and more companies recognize that pricing activities require unique skills, ranging from the ability to perform complex analytics using the latest technological tools to assessing price elasticity in a volatile marketplace.

Organizations have also increasingly grasped that pricing professionals need to straddle different functions. Thus, individuals with experience across Sales, Marketing, and Finance can prove invaluable. Because mature pricing professionals are still a relatively scarce resource, many businesses recruit them from other companies. But some companies are putting programs in place to nurture their talent. The most successful of these companies make their pricing specialists highly visible and reward them for what is increasingly viewed as a strategic position.

An effective talent management program enables a company to:

- ensure the company has the right expertise to execute its pricing strategy
- equip candidates for pricing positions with the appropriate training so they are capable of implementing the improved practices
- create viable career paths
- identify promising candidates to develop
- retain high-performing talent.

Whether it is within the Sales function or in other functions, Pricing should be established as a distinct discipline within the organization by:

- developing methods for attracting and recruiting new talent
- deploying pricing talent within the organization in roles that enable professionals to reach their full potential
- involving pricing managers in decision making and design activities to increase their sense of ownership
- providing pricing resources to employees along with professional development opportunities to keep them up to date on market trends.

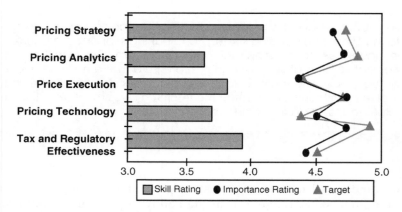

Figure 6.9   Current Employee Skill Set Gap Analysis

Evaluating Current Talent

When assessing an organization's talent needs, management must first assess what pricing skills it currently has in-house in the five core competencies:

- price execution
- pricing strategy
- pricing analytics
- pricing technology
- tax and regulatory effectiveness.

A gap analysis should be performed to determine which of these core competencies might be missing within the current resource pool (see Figure 6.9). Management should then create a plan to fill those gaps as illustrated in the talent management roadmap in Figure 6.10.

Developing a Talent Management Strategy

As with other employees, pricing professionals want to understand what career paths are open to them, and which skills are needed to advance. A firm's talent strategy should achieve the following.

- *Define a pricing career path.* The career development framework (see Figure 6.11) provides the steps employees can take to build their pricing experience and skill sets to advance within a pricing organization. The framework specifies rewards as well as opportunities for promotion.
- *Create customized training and leadership development programs.* Pricing curricula should be tailored to the specific needs of an organization and include a recommended timeline for completing courses in sequential order as well as benchmarks to track the progress

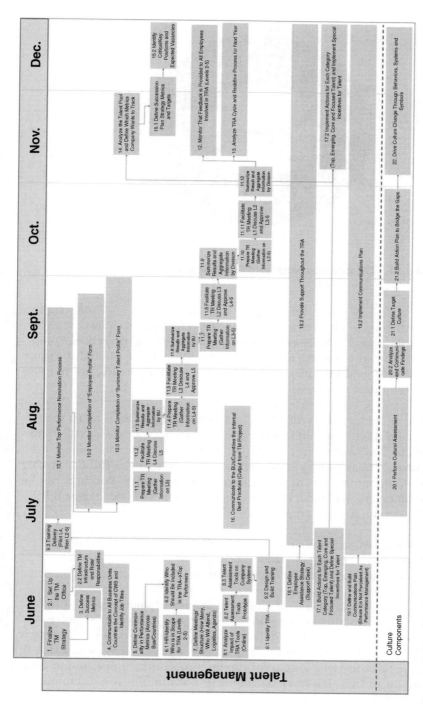

Figure 6.10 Talent Management Road Map

BU, Business Unit; CWS, Critical Workforce Segments; HR, Human Resources; TM, Talent Management; TR, Training; TRA, Training Requirements and Audience.

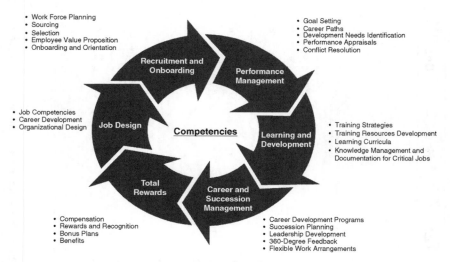

- Work Force Planning
- Sourcing
- Selection
- Employee Value Proposition
- Onboarding and Orientation

- Goal Setting
- Career Paths
- Development Needs Identification
- Performance Appraisals
- Conflict Resolution

- Job Competencies
- Career Development
- Organizational Design

- Training Strategies
- Training Resources Development
- Learning Curricula
- Knowledge Management and Documentation for Critical Jobs

- Compensation
- Rewards and Recognition
- Bonus Plans
- Benefits

- Career Development Programs
- Succession Planning
- Leadership Development
- 360-Degree Feedback
- Flexible Work Arrangements

Figure 6.11   Career Development Framework

employees make in developing their skill sets. In addition, employees must be offered access to formal leadership programs.

- *Offer professionals attractive compensation, awards, and recognition.* Companies need to ensure that pricing professionals are offered the same rewards and incentives for performance as their colleagues in more established functions.

The talent management plan should establish pricing as a lucrative career path if it is to succeed in attracting and retaining the most skilled professionals. The plan should signal the importance of the discipline to the organization by requiring all high-potential employees to fulfill a pricing role during their tenure, as a developmental experience. Positions can be found for entry-level, mid-level, and executive employees (see Figure 6.12).

Pricing can provide employees with:

- Rotational assignments that facilitate cross-functional learning
- An understanding of business economics
- More developed and refined analytical skills.

In a 2009 study of 317 pricing professionals,[2] many reported having moderate to substantial organizational status and influence: 81 percent of study participants were in middle management or above, and 42 percent were VPs, directors, or C-level executives. These results suggest pricing will continue to evolve as a long-term career choice with compensation commensurate to the high-level skills and responsibilities the discipline requires (see Figure 6.13).

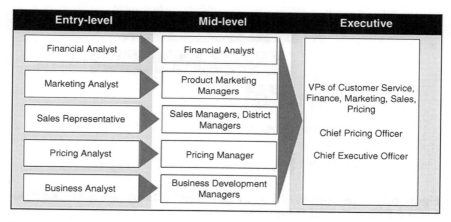

Figure 6.12   Pricing as a Career

In that same survey, 85 percent of the respondents "agreed" or "strongly agreed" that their current pricing role was a "very strong" career enhancer (see Figure 6.14). This finding indicates that business professionals find this growing discipline attractive and suggests that, in coming years, companies should be able to find, develop, and retain the talent they need to execute and manage their pricing transformations successfully.

Managing Cross-Country Pricing Cultures

Although pricing is and should be treated as a core competency throughout any business, multinational organizations face particular challenges. Even those that have implemented consistent pricing strategies within a given country or region may find it difficult to do so across borders. In

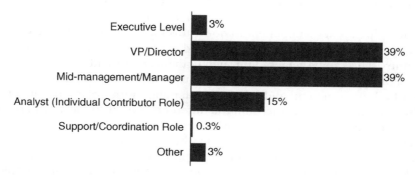

Figure 6.13   Distribution of Pricing Roles

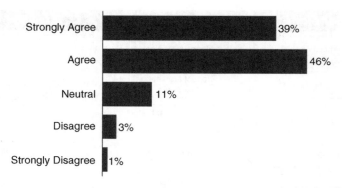

Figure 6.14   Responses to Survey Question "I Consider My Pricing Role to be a Strong Career Enhancer"

fact, a one-size-fits-all approach rarely works in international markets that operate under very different conditions and dynamics. Even a question as seemingly basic as when to apply end-of-life pricing to a mature product can vary significantly from country to country. For example, a major durable goods manufacturer wanted to retire a particular technology across the U.S. and Europe, but got pushed back from its leaders in two countries where the product was still viable and carried a high price premium. If the company had attempted to force uniform pricing across all countries, then it would have missed out on significant revenue.

In some countries, local cultural practices simply will not change in response to a directive from a U.S.-based headquarters. In the U.S., receivables are typically paid within 60 days. But in other countries, average receivables age can exceed 700 days. To a U.S. pricing manager that represents millions of dollars in additional cash flow. However, a local pricing professional would state—correctly—that to attempt to change the business culture to one in which bills are paid more promptly would be a futile endeavor, and the attempted change could cause significant harm to a company's reputation and its ability to conduct business.

Where possible, effective pricing practices should be shared across geographies. A key component to doing this successfully is to acknowledge that these practices need to be customized to fit the specific culture of each country. This can be achieved through both incentives and pricing roles.

For example, a pricing initiative that includes revising incentive pay (for both management and sales) to better align with pricing profitability objectives must take into account the different cultural and legal and regulatory requirements that exist within each country. How incentives are aligned in Japan, where the culture may be to use more team rewards and smaller amounts, may differ from the approach in the U.S., where individuals are often motivated by large, personal rewards. In China, for example, the local practice may be to allow companies to use more variable-based compensation schemes instead of salaries, whereas in Germany and France, firms would consult with national work councils to design and implement compensation structures.

Similarly, a multinational company undertaking an initiative to improve pricing may consider changes to the global organization. At the country level this might mean looking at job titles and job structures. In Europe, one might find an organization that is led by managing directors in key countries. In emerging markets (e.g., Eastern Europe, Africa, and South America) firms might set up pricing organizations that are much more autonomous and entrepreneurial in structure to support the opportunistic nature of these regions and to seize their evolving market opportunities.

Making the Organizational Commitment to Change

Convincing an entire organization to modify long-established practices can be a wrenching experience for everyone involved. But properly managed it can lead to changes that will benefit virtually every member of the organization.

A consumer products manufacturer realized it needed to overhaul its organization to strengthen its pricing and profitability management after years of rewarding sales on volume alone. Unfortunately, the company had very few pricing capabilities, lacked a strategy to develop internal talent, and the leadership itself had minimal understanding of effective pricing management. The CEO realized that to transform the organization, strong leadership would be required. He designed an approach that focused less on building consensus than on a command and control style in which he was the involved and visible leader. He also appointed the CMO as the owner of the initiative; not because of his knowledge and experience, but because he was diplomatic and had a track record of building bridges across the different functions in the organization. Both the CEO and the CMO knew these qualities would be critical in building a pricing organization that needed to be effective across the existing functional silos (a silo being an organizational function that works largely on its own).

Together, the two executives designed a pricing organization that reported to the CMO. Where possible, they integrated the existing organizational structure and aligned the pricing activities to it. However, they weren't afraid to create new teams when necessary. The skills and capabilities required to execute the pricing-related activities were defined and matched against the current structure. After assessing internal capabilities, they realized they would need to hire

(continued)

(Continued)
outside talent for about half of the positions. Finally, the executives examined existing metrics—reporting and feedback loops that had been constructed entirely around the volume goals that had prevailed over the past 50 years. The CMO decided to leverage the reporting mechanisms and relationships that were already in place and simply changed the messages that were communicated through these channels. Rather than rewarding volume sales, a new incentive and compensation system was created for employees that aligned with the company's new profitability goals. As a result, the sales organization made a relatively smooth transition.

The entire transformational process would take three years. But the results were substantial. The company increased its pocket margin by approximately 2 percent of its total revenue. Critically, the vast majority of improvements proved sustainable over the long term. The manufacturer is now recognized as having leading-edge price-setting capabilities, which can incorporate competitive and point-of-sale data from end customers in demand models. The company's pricing process has become a critical vehicle for maintaining optimal performance and for understanding when to make strategic tradeoffs to benefit the company.

Realigning an organization to improve its pricing function can be challenging. But, as the example above shows, a committed leadership team can achieve a successful transformation by systematically planning each step of the process; by accommodating the internal culture, structures, and processes where possible; and by communicating continually with employees at every stage.

Endnotes

1. Timothy Aeppel, "Seeking Perfect Prices, CEO Tears Up the Rules," *The Wall Street Journal*, March 27, 2007, Section A1.
2. Larry Montan and Mike Simonetto, "Is There a Career in Pricing? An Insider's View of the Pricing Profession" (white paper, Deloitte Development LLC, May 14, 2009).

CHAPTER 7

Pricing Technology and
Data Management

*Not all problems have a technological answer; but when they do, that is the
more lasting solution.*

—Andrew Grove, Senior Advisor, former Chairman and CEO,
Intel Corporation

A large manufacturer and distributor of consumer products had invested considerable resources to create and maintain its pricing spreadsheets over the years. Various complex processes supported the flow of data into and out of the tables. But the firm had encountered two big problems with its existing tools. First, management didn't know whether optimal prices were being set. Each time it moved to adjust prices, the process took months to complete and was performed mostly through intuition and guess work. No one was sure if the firm was leaving money on the table or driving customers to competitors.

Second, the leadership team had a limited understanding of how the sales team was negotiating with customers. Once price lists were distributed, management had to wait for invoices from the billing system to find out what had actually been agreed to. Moreover, without clear and enforced guidelines, the sales team took it upon itself to set its own prices, which only compounded the firm's problems. Realizing that it needed to impose more discipline on the process, the leadership team identified and implemented a pricing software solution, which brought about several transformational changes:

(continued)

(Continued)

- A new revenue and cost framework was adopted, which established a common organizational language based on a profit waterfall and transaction analysis tools.
- Rich visual representations showed clearly which products, customers, and sales representatives were contributing to—or eroding—margin. Management now had the information it needed to collaborate actively with the key internal stakeholders in setting pricing strategy.
- Policies governing the pricing of specific offerings, individual or bundles, as well as the use of various commercial terms, were established and enforced.
- A specially designed workflow enabled management to approve prices that fell below established thresholds. The time required to set new prices dropped from three months to three weeks. This allowed management to not only react more quickly to changes in the market, but also implement more effective promotions and product launches.

The net impact? Annual bottom-line earnings increased by $50 million, more than five times the total amount spent on the project to implement the software and its accompanying process and policy changes. This example shows the significant case that can be made for firms to consider the replacement of spreadsheets with modern pricing technology.

What Is Pricing Software?

Pricing software is basically any commercially available application containing tools to automate pricing analytics, optimization, and execution to help organizations in their efforts to make efficient, effective pricing decisions. Organizations are increasingly looking for ways to integrate these applications into their existing technology infrastructure to help ensure that the improvements implemented by management are sustainable over the long term.

Standard Functionality

Pricing software solutions address four distinct areas of functionality. The first one focuses on analysis and the three others are process oriented:

1. *Pricing Analytics* allow finance, marketing, sales, and pricing professionals to perform real-time assessments of customer, product,

marketing, and pricing data to inform decision makers of trends and opportunities. Key areas of functionality are:
- waterfalls and scatter plots to provide a view of price and margin performance
- profit potential and business risk assessments across segments
- segmentation analysis to support differentiated pricing
- dashboards and alerts to monitor pricing activity
- simulation programs to define and run pricing scenarios.

2. *Pricing Optimization* implements mathematical and statistical methods to help calculate recommended prices for a product or service. Key areas of functionality are:
- managing inputs from multiple internal and external economic sources
- analyzing defined microsegments within a given market
- forecasting product demand and costs
- determining price elasticity
- recommending optimized prices.

3. *Price Management* allows organizational specialists to set conditions and rules that can populate an order entry or enterprise resource planning (ERP) solution to provide guidance across the organization. Key areas of functionality are:
- managing price lists by market, customer, and product structures
- defining and implementing pricing rules and policies
- performing mass price updates
- checking consistency, compliance with, and appropriateness of pricing policies
- drawing master data from, and sending price updates to, ERP solutions.

4. *Deal Management* pulls together pricing data to enable sales professionals to negotiate more profitable quotes and contracts. Key areas of functionality are:
- providing scenario modeling for quotes and contracts to negotiate the most advantageous prices and terms
- helping to enforce compliance with corporate pricing and profit policies
- creating a platform to capture win/loss and competitive pricing data
- capturing price approvals and workflow for contract evaluation and signoff
- loading customer-specific prices and terms into an order entry or ERP solution.

Software with Limited Pricing Applications

In the market today, only those applications dedicated to customized pricing solutions provide all of the necessary analytics, deal management,

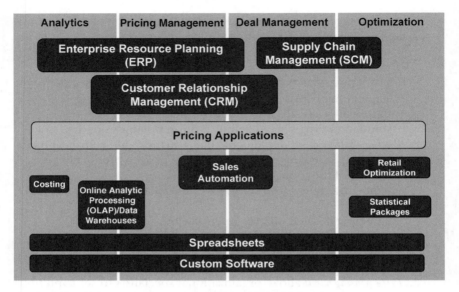

Figure 7.1   Pricing Software Functionality and Software Solution Categories

pricing management, and price optimization tools. However, other software may have related or overlapping functionality, or may interface with core pricing applications. For example, while the ability to measure sales activity and review order entry information are key advantages of pricing analytics, the actual data and transactions for these activities occur within their respective systems. The following software categories are not considered *pricing software*, but they can have related capabilities (see Figure 7.1):

- Enterprise resource planning (ERP), which provides end-to-end business process support for order-to-cash transactions, procurement, inventory management, accounting, and other activities
- Supply chain management (SCM), which helps optimize production planning, scheduling, procurement, and resource management
- Customer relationship management (CRM), which supports the sales function, including contact management, account planning, and sales pipeline and promotion management
- Business integration (BI), which often uses tools such as online analytic processing (OLAP), data mining, benchmarking, and predictive analytics to improve an organization's understanding of its historical and future operations as well as its overall decision making
- Statistical analysis packages, which can be used to model customer and market behavior in an effort to help optimize pricing

- Spreadsheets, which serve as general purpose financial modeling tools
- Custom software, which provides programming environments that allow the development of unique systems.

While some organizations have made strides by deploying and leveraging enterprise solutions, the most widely used pricing tool today by far is still spreadsheet software. Many factors have contributed to its common adoption. For sales representatives maintaining a price list, the spreadsheet software's ease of use makes it very appealing. In addition, the dearth of more advanced solutions in the market (until relatively recently) has meant that these applications have had little competition. Because of pricing's cross-functional nature and historically decentralized management, spreadsheet software has been just robust enough to manage each individual's contribution while being sufficiently accessible, easy to use, and low in cost.

However, as we describe in this book, the requirements of pricing management have progressed in recent years beyond the functionality of spreadsheet software. More advanced analytics and optimization tools can handle large volumes of transactional data, which easily surpass the limits of desktop applications; for example, a retailer that has tens of millions of transactions in a year could exceed the capacity of a spreadsheet application after just a month or two. In addition, to distribute pricing factors (e.g., price floors, segment-specific base prices, and pocket margin targets) and up-to-date product, customer, and cost data, companies require centralized repositories and systematic business processes. Many companies also need to establish a workflow for price approvals and an audit trail for regulatory compliance. Desktop spreadsheet packages are simply not robust enough, and they were not designed to be the kind of comprehensive, truly effective pricing management solution discussed in this chapter.

Pricing Software Architecture and Component Technology

The design of pricing software has evolved rapidly over the past decade. While customization for particular industries and clients has become increasingly common, the pricing solutions nonetheless tend to share key elements.

Interfaces. Pricing applications are typically implemented with automated interfaces (as well as manual feeds) to allow margin forecasting and historical profitability reporting (see Figure 7.2). Here are three common types of information that travel through robust interfaces between pricing applications and both ERP and CRM software solutions:

1. Customer-specific pricing data (drawn from quotes within a pricing application) and passed along to a CRM or an order entry or ERP solution

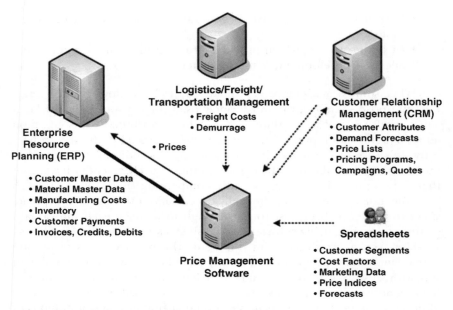

Figure 7.2   Typical Pricing Software Interfaces

2. Price list and pricing policy information sent from a pricing solution to an order entry or ERP solution
3. Information on customers, the product catalog, and historical transactions conveyed from CRM and order entry or ERP solutions to a pricing solution.

The level of integration between systems generally depends on waterfall data requirements and the availability, volatility, and volume of data.

Architecture.   Each software vendor creates its own unique platform. However, all systems must share certain elements to support the pricing domain:

- *Large-scale data management.* Effective pricing analytics requires processing huge volumes of transactions—in some cases millions of individual line items. Vendors have adopted the latest 64-bit computer and operating system capabilities as well as advanced data management techniques to support the needs of high-volume, mass-market, and consumer providers.
- *User interface.* Pricing management software appeared on the market after the emergence of browser-based, application development frameworks. As a result, pricing software typically adopts these web-based models.

- *Configurability.* Pricing is essential to a seller's relationship with a customer, and software vendors try to take this into account. While each industry tends to follow certain generally accepted approaches in dealing with customers, firms need some flexibility to accommodate their particular customer relationships and historical practices. Pricing software generally provides the configurability needed to meet these requirements.
- *Integration capabilities.* An essential quality of pricing management software is its ability to be integrated into different platforms. A steady stream of data needs to be shared between pricing management and other enterprise information systems. For example, to support customer-specific pricing, a current list of all clients is required. If companies attempt to enter this information manually into the pricing system, then discrepancies can result. By using an automated interface between the order entry or ERP solution and the pricing management systems, these potential problems can be avoided.

Industry Alignment

As pricing software vendors progressively enter new sectors, they adapt their products to meet the specific needs of these sectors. In 2010, manufacturing was still attracting the greatest competition, while sectors such as telecommunications and financial services represented relatively untapped territories. Although the alignment continues to change, Figure 7.3 shows the current industry-specific capabilities of the major software vendors.

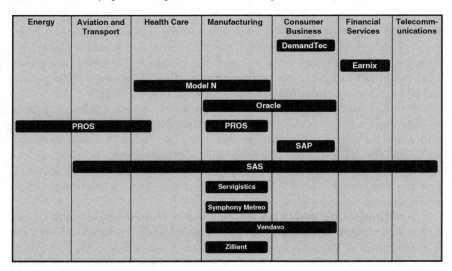

Figure 7.3   Pricing Software Vendor Industry Alignment

Source: Deloitte Consulting LLP, Pricing Software Technology Assessment Release 5.0, November, 2009.

The History of the Pricing Software Market

Pricing first developed as a simple way to quantify the value of goods or services for the purposes of an exchange. As business and economics matured, mathematics and statistics were utilized to perform quantitative studies on market behavior. Analysts were able to use statistical models and applied science to forecast customer demand for different products over time. With the advent and rapid evolution of digital computing, these modeling theories have provided businesses with the means to make smarter pricing decisions and to respond to competitor actions, market fluctuations, and inventory challenges with increasing effectiveness.

The earliest pricing software offered ad hoc tools that helped set prices in niche markets. This software evolved into advanced suites capable of facilitating the pricing process holistically. In this section we discuss the historical development of this market.

The Birth of a New Science

In 1978, shortly after deregulation in the U.S., the airline industry began to focus intensely on improving yield, which led, in turn, to the development of pricing as a science. The discipline of revenue management (RM) gained traction as it developed new methods for increasing sales revenue, maintaining profitability, and strengthening competitiveness in a highly complex marketplace. RM models analyzed transactional data to forecast future demand and facilitate decision making on the pricing and promotion of available product inventories across specific channels or geographically distinct markets. These models became more valuable as they increased in flexibility, enabling airlines to incorporate seasonal adjustments (such as demand variability), special events, and no-show rates. New forecast tools could accurately estimate the number of booked passengers who would fail to appear by the time of departure. This allowed the airline to sell empty seats while minimizing the risk of overbooking.

Post-deregulation, more advanced computer systems became available to passenger airlines in the 1980s. The first of these was SABRE, which was rolled out for American Airlines by its IT division, Sabre Decision Technologies (SDT). SDT pioneered technological advancements that spread throughout the airline industry and led to the broad array of software systems used today for RM, pricing, flight and crew scheduling, cargo tracking, and other operations.

Similar systems were built by Delta and United in the 1980s, and other RM software providers emerged to develop commercial systems globally, such as Decision Focus, Inc. (DFI), Aeronomics, SAS, and PROS Revenue Management. Several mergers reduced the number of providers in the 1990s: DFI and Aeronomics combined to form Talus (which was later acquired by Manugistics). The technology boom among the passenger airlines helped spur the rise of electronic commerce in the travel industry—long before the internet supported access to the World Wide Web.

In the early 2000s, airlines benefited again from advances in computer technology that opened the door to a more holistic network approach to RM, superseding the per-flight-leg optimization models. This resulted in further revenue gains, although the necessary investment in data integration and hardware infrastructure were generally costs that only top-tier global airlines could absorb.

RM also paved the way for improvements in pricing-related decision making in a variety of other settings. New products or adaptations of RM systems were developed that benefited the hospitality (namely hotels and car rental companies), energy, life sciences, health care, automobile, retail, telecommunications, and media sectors.

The Influence of Electronic Commerce

In the 1990s, the internet came into wide use when online shopping was introduced. It took several years, though, for developments in broadband and internet security to make electronic (e)-commerce a reliable and trusted option for consumers. By 2000, many U.S. businesses were offering their services through the internet, and consumers could purchase goods securely using various electronic payment methods. In this new era of disintermediation, low-cost distribution channels were created through these e-commerce websites.

With advances in optimization science, variable dynamic pricing enabled different schemes to be used online. Customized prices could now be calculated for an individual or a business customer based on the buyer's purchasing history. Websites such as Orbitz, Expedia, Travelocity, and Priceline offered customers the opportunity to make online purchases of airline tickets, hotels, and rental cars while simultaneously offering them powerful tools for comparing prices. Other multinational e-commerce sites, such as Amazon and Staples, provided a broad online retail shopping experience with up-sell and cross-sell features that were adaptive to each customer's buying habits. The key enabler here was the development of highly scalable technology, both hardware and software, that supported the storage, access, and processing of huge volumes of data at the transaction level.

The Influence of Enterprise Application Adoption

As the RM market crossed the maturity lifecycle (see Figure 7.4), businesses adopted a new generation of software packages in the 1990s, replacing the legacy systems that had previously performed corporate functions.[1] These new offerings were developed as stand-alone applications, and their databases were rarely integrated into the customer's centralized data

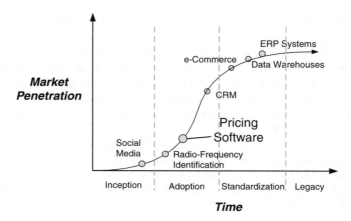

Figure 7.4   Pricing Software on the Technology Maturity Curve

source. Vendors began producing software packages that addressed common corporate functions such as accounting, reporting, order management, invoicing, procurement, and inventory management. From a cost perspective, software packages compared favorably with the rising expense of maintaining, improving, and enhancing legacy systems as well as migrating them from older computing platforms to the latest technologies.

ERP vendors emerged next and became the dominant players in the space, enabling companies to manage all business functions through one shared database, thus eliminating disparate software systems. Once information flowed reliably across business processes, other enterprise applications such as SCM, CRM, and human resources (HR) systems drew upon needed data from the ERP platform, making it the focal system-of-record. The adoption of these packages paved the way to richer data sources that would ultimately make it more viable to integrate the next innovation: pricing software packages.[2]

The Growth of Pricing Management

In the past two decades, pricing has been an important component of RM science. Since the early 2000s, the evolution of enterprise solutions has expanded opportunities for firms to apply pricing technology. This has had a dramatic impact on the software market. Now, instead of merely selling RM products, vendors have started featuring packages called, for instance, "Pricing and Revenue Management" and "Pricing and Revenue Optimization." These vendors have gradually been able to reposition their practices with this new pricing software.

Over the past five years, retail and business-to-business industries have seen performance improve by refining methodologies associated with price execution, enforcement, and optimization. These advances accelerated as early adopters drew the attention of their peers by their impressive financial gains—comparable to those recorded by travel companies in the early days of their industry.[3] While software vendors have used standardized methodologies to ease adoption across different sectors, each still presents unique pricing challenges. Vendors have thus had to sharpen domain expertise in vertical markets. Competition among vendors has become fierce, but the low adoption rate and market penetration of pricing management applications suggests there is still room for growth.

The Pricing Software Landscape

Providers tend to offer pricing technology and expertise in three different categories: yield management, general retail, and business-to-business commerce. In the latter two categories, the number of software releases remains high as providers continue to add new features as they jockey for position. In the past, pricing solutions required extensive customization to address the nuances of each industry. However, software vendors today have dramatically increased their product configurability to reduce the labor involved with implementation and to deliver value in less time. To some degree, this has had a stabilizing effect and has softened the organizational stress that comes with incorporating software updates.

The value offered by packaged pricing applications is becoming increasingly well recognized, so the market presence of these software companies will likely expand as business-to-business companies look for pricing to improve margins and sales force effectiveness.[4] In time, the ad hoc tools and spreadsheets that have been used to aid price setting will be replaced by more advanced software suites (see Figure 7.5). With these new tools enhancing their ability to manage processes holistically, executives, pricing managers, and sales leaders can shift their focus to improving pricing strategies and measuring the benefits.

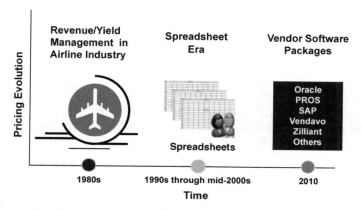

Figure 7.5   The Evolution of Pricing Software

The widespread adoption and maturity of ERP software has allowed many companies to shift focus and address pricing challenges more directly. With the increasing availability of relevant data, pricing improvement opportunities have steadily risen. This has enticed new vendors to enter the software market. The future of the market is uncertain; as of 2010, competing vendors were aggressively attempting to prove that their solutions had the agility and staying power to achieve broad enough adoption to ensure their survival (see Table 7.1).

Table 7.1   Key Characteristics of Pricing Software Vendors

Vendor	Founded	Acquisitions	Industries Served	Product Suite
DemandTec[®,a,b]	1999	Acquired TradePoint Solutions (2006) and Connect3 Systems (2009); IPO (2007)	Retail, consumer products	Consumer-centric merchandising and marketing: • DemandTec Lifecycle Price Optimization[TM] • DemandTec End-to-End Promotion[TM] • DemandTec Assortment and Space[TM] • DemandTec Targeted Marketing[TM] Consumer-centric sales and marketing: • DemandTec Trade Effectiveness[TM]
Earnix[c]	2001		Banking, insurance	Earnix platform: Earnix Optimizer for Insurance Earnix Optimizer for Banking
Model N[d]	1999		Life sciences, high tech	Life sciences and high-tech revenue management application suites
Oracle[®,e]	1986	Acquired Retek and Seibel (2005)	Manufacturing, retail (including brick-and-mortar stores), catalog and web-based retailers	Oracle Price Management Suite: • Oracle Price Analytics • Oracle Price Segmentation (with Dataminer) • Oracle Price Planning and Optimization (product not released) • Siebel Dynamic Pricer Release 8.0, eBusiness Suite Oracle Advanced Pricing Release 12 • Siebel Deal Management Release 8.0, eBusiness Suite Oracle Deal Management Release 12 (released April 2008)
PROS[f]	1985	NYSE IPO (2007)	Travel, hotel and cruise, manufacturing, distribution, services	PROS Pricing Solution Suite: • Scientific Analytics • PROS Deal Optimizer • PROS Price Optimizer • Pricing Optimization

Vendor	Founded	Acquisitions	Industries Served	Product Suite
SAP for Retail[g,h]	1996	Formerly KhiMetrics, acquired by SAP (2005)	Retail, consumer packaged goods	SAP for Retail: • SAP Price Optimization • SAP Promotion Optimization and Merchandising Layout • SAP Markdown Optimization
Servigistics[TM,i]	1999		Automotive, heavy equipment, high-tech	Servigistics Pricing Management
Symphony-Metreo, Inc.[j,k]	2002	Symphony acquired Metreo (2006)	Pharmaceutical, automotive, consumer products, manufacturing, high-tech, distribution	Symphony Metreo Enterprise Pricing Suite (EPS)
Vendavo[®,l]	1998	Reseller agreement with SAP (2005)	Chemicals, manufacturing, high-tech, distribution, mills products, consumer goods	Vendavo Enterprise Pricing Suite for: • Price and margin analytics • Price optimization • Price setting and administration • Deal execution
Vistaar[®,m]	2000 (introduced its first product in 2006)		High-tech, manufacturing, medical devices	Price Management Software for: • Price strategy • Price setting • Price execution • Portfolio planning • Price performance management
Zilliant[n]	1999		Manufacturing, high-tech, distribution, industrial, commercial services	Zilliant Margin Insight[TM] Zilliant Margin Manager[TM] Zilliant Margin Maximizer[TM]

Note:

[a]Hung LeHong, ``DemandTec Acquires TradePoint to Expand into Deal Management,'' Gartner Article ID no. G00145440, December 14, 2006, http://www.demandtec.com/c/document_library/get_file?uuid=8ff01639-add8-4422-a14e-432bbd15c432&groupId=10128.

[b]DemandTec website, http://www.demandtec.com/about-us.

[c]Earnix website, http://www.earnix.com/aboutEarnix.asp.

[d]``About Model N,'' Model N website, http://www.modeln.com/company/aboutModeln/.

[e]``Retek Inc.,'' Hoovers, Inc. website, http://premium.hoovers.com/subscribe/co/boneyard/factsheet.xhtml?ID=jrtyjfffffffff.

[f]Michael Dunne, ``MarketScope for Price Optimization and Management Software for B2B,'' Gartner Article ID no. G00169583, July 31, 2009.

[g]``KhiMetrics, Inc.,'' Hoovers, Inc. website, http://premium.hoovers.com/subscribe/co/boneyard/factsheet.xhtml?ID=rfxkstffffffffff.

[h]SAP, ``SAP Acquires Khimetrics to Further Extend Its Retail Market Leadership,'' press release, November 22, 2005, http://www.sap.com/about/newsroom/press.epx?PressID=5261.

[i]Dunne, ``MarketScope for Price Optimization.''

[j]``Symphony Technology Group Acquires Metreo; Acquisition of Leading Pricing Solutions Company,'' Business Wire, January 30, 2006, http://findarticles.com/p/articles/mi_m0EIN/is_2006_Jan_30/ai_n16034453/http://www.allbusiness.com/company-activities-management/company-structures-ownership/5365289-1.html.

[k]Symphony Metreo website, http://www.metreo.com/company/default.asp.

[l]Dunne, ``MarketScope for Price Optimization.''

[m]Dunne, ``MarketScope for Price Optimization.''

[n]Dunne, ``MarketScope for Price Optimization.''

Building a Business Case for Pricing Technology

As with any improvement initiative, when implementing new pricing technology management must be able to justify the costs, enumerate the benefits, and forecast a return on investment (ROI) and payback period. Companies can be wary of implementing new pricing technology because it can be costly and resource-intensive. But if they properly assess the proposed solution in advance and determine its goals carefully, then it should yield substantial and lasting returns.

Targeted Benefits

Any improvement program should be driven by critical business imperatives, not solely by a desire to replace an existing technology. It must also be unencumbered by false assumptions. Technology, no matter how advanced, will not achieve the benefits that can come with systemic organizational improvement of pricing capabilities (including the supporting processes and policies). But picking the right technology solution should help companies in their efforts to realize those benefits faster, increase returns, and sustain the improvements over the long term. Besides helping to strengthen the bottom line, new technologies can:

- *Deepen insights into customers and sources of profitability.* Sophisticated applications can help a firm in setting and managing pricing policies more effectively by arming the sales force and marketing organization with detailed information that can help them better understand customer segments and the performance of individual buyers. They can also suggest how to focus the product portfolio more effectively and identify ways to steer customers to more profitable purchases.
- *Make deal negotiations more profitable.* Pricing initiatives can reveal elements that increase or erode profits, and they can also provide the sales force with critical data on customers and product profitability to help give individual representatives leverage during negotiations. In addition, the underlying information system can be used to enforce adherence to pricing processes and policies through automated workflows.
- *Increase speed and accuracy in pricing administration.* Large organizations struggle to handle thousands of customer-specific price points and still respond quickly to changing market conditions and opportunities. Bringing prices under the management of an automated information system can make possible the rapid approvals and mass changes needed to support business decisions.
- *Strengthen optimization capabilities.* The ability to model and test optimized price points can result in increased revenue, margin, and even market share.

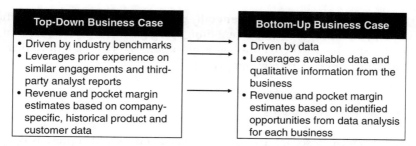

Top-Down Business Case		Bottom-Up Business Case
• Driven by industry benchmarks • Leverages prior experience on similar engagements and third-party analyst reports • Revenue and pocket margin estimates based on company-specific, historical product and customer data	→	• Driven by data • Leverages available data and qualitative information from the business • Revenue and pocket margin estimates based on identified opportunities from data analysis for each business

Figure 7.6   The Differences Between Top-Down and Bottom-Up Benefits Estimates

- *Sustain cultural change.* Organizations that implement effective pricing processes and make the necessary organizational adjustments that must go with them are more likely to continue improving margin over the long term.

All these potentially substantial benefits must be considered. But while some are quantifiable, others are intangible, which complicates making a business case with them. In practice, a hybrid estimation of top-down, applied benchmarks and bottom-up, projected improvements is required (see Figure 7.6). Top-down estimates are typically stated in terms of return on sales (ROS) or actual profit improvement. Reasonable benchmarks include 1 percent improvement in ROS and a 1–5 percent increase in pocket margin. Combining these estimates with some transactional analytics on actual data should result in a range of benefits that can help build a strong business case.

Costs

Pricing software implementations vary according to type and company size and comprise both start-up and ongoing costs. Based on a 2008 survey of 219 companies completed by AMR Research, the companies spent $4.3 million, on average, for pricing initiatives.[5] Figure 7.7 shows how these expenses are typically allocated among cost categories.

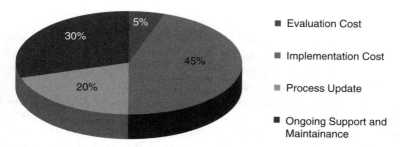

Figure 7.7   Typical Pricing Technology Implementation Cost Breakdown

Software evaluation, which generally represents about 5 percent of the total implementation cost, is a one-time charge associated with assessing and selecting the pricing technology application that best matches a firm's needs. This exercise typically comprises:

- evaluation resources
- readiness assessments.

Implementation costs are also one-time occurrences and represent by far the largest expense for the total implementation. They include:

- software purchases
- implementation resources (internal and external)
- rollout charges.

The process update category covers the one-time costs incurred when firms redefine the pricing processes and policies that will be supported, or enabled, by the new technology. These costs cover:

- process redesign
- change management to align the firm and its customers with the new processes, policies, and technology
- training.

Ongoing expenses represent approximately 30 percent of the total implementation cost (see Figure 7.8) and comprise:

- software licensing
- system upgrades and enhancements
- data loading and troubleshooting
- ongoing user support and training.

Risks

Senior managers tend to assume that once an organization is armed with more data, new processes, automated information systems support, and potentially redesigned organizational structures, it will make more profitable pricing and selling decisions. However, not all stakeholders in the process may share this optimistic assessment. They may legitimately point to potential hazards posed by a proposed transformation. These risks should, in fact, be taken seriously as they can impact the cost and speed of the implementation as well as the effectiveness of the solution. The top five risks faced by organizations when transforming their pricing processes and infrastructure along with potential mitigation strategies follow.

Lack of Clear Vision, and Poorly Defined Priorities. Management rushes through the planning stage without clearly defining and prioritizing key opportunities and primary business objectives. Or the team focuses too much on responding to gaps in business capabilities without determining which ones are most critical to achieving the goals of the transformation. Mitigation:

- Create a separate initiative to focus on identifying desired project targets (through a transactional pricing assessment process).
- Use proven analytic strategies and techniques to identify business opportunities that can be quickly capitalized on.
- Ensure key stakeholders understand current market realities thoroughly and focus on the areas offering the greatest opportunity to affect margin.
- As part of the project charter, or during the software selection process, establish a clear understanding between IT and other business stakeholders of what the conceptual design of new business processes and supporting systems should look like.
- Involve all user groups affected by the initiative early to gain consensus on the approach and solution before making the software purchase.

Limited User Adoption. A system that is not used, or is used incorrectly, will obviously not yield the expected business benefits. For example, sales representatives may be overwhelmed by a new system if they are shut out of the early development process or if they lack the proper documentation, training, and help desk support after the system's implementation. Other problems in user adoption might be unclear functionality, a poor user interface, and irrelevant data. Any of these factors will hamper the acceptance and usage of the new system and processes. Mitigation:

- Involve key sales, marketing, pricing, and finance personnel early and continuously throughout the development process.
- Work with business leaders who are forward thinking and understand the mission of the project.
- Use pilot user groups to help drive process improvements.
- Use user teams to help refine the interface design, and overall navigation and application flow.
- Involve pilot user groups in functional reviews.
- Incorporate new data elements into existing information management processes.

Weak Data Quality. Pricing systems rely on good data for analytics and optimization. Poor or inadequate information in pricing and deal management results in a cascading series of problems (e.g., wrong prices being placed on customer invoices or miscalculated price points). Mitigation:

- Understand the business processes that capture data and where those data are saved.
- As soon as data needs are identified, sample extracts should be made and validated to determine whether the information is accurate and complete; cleanup should be assigned to a separate team to complete remediation of data quality issues before the deployment of new pricing systems.
- New data capture processes should not be created to resolve gaps in current systems; instead, existing processes and systems should be modified, enhanced, and improved.
- Ensure error handling for interfaces between systems is robust, problems are reported quickly, and failed data transfer transactions are automatically recycled.

Inadequate Planning for the Complexity of Business Process Transformation.   Mitigation:

- A manageable and modular implementation plan should be developed that delivers benefits quickly and focuses on the areas of greatest opportunity.
- A limited test of the system—a *proof of concept*—should be run to obtain organizational buy-in and to confirm the suitability of the software package, while deepening the skills of the team that will implement and support it.

Measuring Success

Implementation should be executed against a clearly defined vision of how success will be determined. Firms must decide, in advance, what measurements will be made, so that the necessary reports can be generated, processes designed, and remediation steps taken in concert with the implementation itself. With proper planning, management will receive the kind of periodic feedback it needs to ensure that the promised, quantifiable benefits are being achieved.

Metrics.   Firms need to settle on the metrics that are most critical for measuring the effectiveness of their improvement initiative. These may vary, but here are some important ones to consider:

- pocket margin increases
- reduction in number of pricing errors
- shortened lead time for deal approval

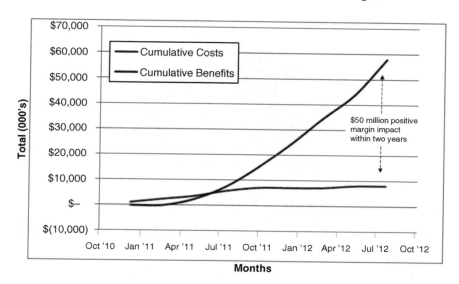

Figure 7.8   Pricing System Cost-Benefit Analysis

- increase in deal/win ratio
- higher rates of compliance with new processes and policies, deal guidelines, and so forth.

Return on Investment.   The ROI for pricing improvement initiatives is typically extremely attractive. Figure 7.8 depicts a sample cost-benefit analysis over a two-year period for a representative consumer packaged goods company.

Payback Period.   Cost recoupment can be achieved in less than 12 months for nearly 50 percent of pricing initiatives, and almost three-quarters pay back their costs in less than 24 months. The graph in Figure 7.9 shows the distribution of payback periods for a sample of pricing technology implementations. This time frame is significantly shorter than that which can be achieved in most other technology implementations because the focus is specifically on margin improvement. Thus, pricing software tends to pay for itself and also carries the most obvious metric that validates its worth.

Selecting Pricing Management Software

A global chemical manufacturing company established a rigorous request-for-proposal (RFP) process with pricing software vendors. After three months of demos, sales pitches, and reference checks, the lead of the RFP team summarized his frustration by saying, "I can't tell them apart. They are all the same."

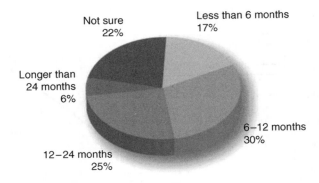

Not sure
22%

Less than 6 months
17%

Longer than
24 months
6%

6–12 months
30%

12–24 months
25%

Figure 7.9   Average Payback Period for Pricing Software

Source: Noha Tohamy and Heather Keltz, ''Building a Bulletproof Business Case for Pricing Improvement Initiatives,'' AMR Research Report no. 21745 (Boston: AMR Research, 2008) (reproduced by permission).

And this is true to a certain extent. For the most part, the solutions available today provide similar functionalities. At the same time, the rapid pace of software releases means vendors can quickly—albeit briefly—leapfrog their competitors with each new solution. Firms should engage in a comprehensive evaluation process to compare the attributes of each offering to determine which one best suits their needs. This process, comprising five key steps, is shown in Figure 7.10.

The approach is similar to that taken by companies choosing most new technology solutions. However, pricing software does present some additional considerations. As an emerging technology, it often lacks the toolsets for configuring advanced applications, thereby forcing more features to be hard-coded. In addition, pricing software vendors offer a wide range of specialized solutions based on industry and functional capabilities (e.g., analytics, optimization, deal management, and pricing management), so companies have to determine which ones offer the most value according to their needs.

When exploring the use of commercially available pricing technology, companies should ask the following questions:

- Does the technology match the scope and requirements of the problem at hand?
- Are our processes and pricing strategy driving the selection of the solution rather than the other way around?

Define Scope and Approach

Define Requirements and Prepare for Vendor Demo

Conduct Vendor Demos and Follow Ups

Develop Final Vendor Recommendation

Initiate Procurement Process

Figure 7.10   Pricing Software Evaluation and Selection Process

- Can existing tools and systems be improved to meet needs more cost-effectively than a new system that will generate significant selection and implementation expenses?
- Will existing IT systems and capabilities complement or complicate pricing technology implementation and use?
- Are current processes robust enough to be implemented in the new software or do some internal issues need to be resolved first?
- Have employees in IT and across the business been trained to implement, use, and maintain the proposed pricing technology?

Defining the Scope and Approach

As with any software selection process, firms need to define the geographical and functional scope of the evaluation, determine the assessment criteria, and validate the metrics for pricing. A typical approach for this phase is depicted in Figure 7.11.

Preparing for Vendor Demos

During the first part of this phase, a company will determine (and weight) the pricing-related business requirements for the application, identify the processes that will demonstrated, and if appropriate create an RFP. The

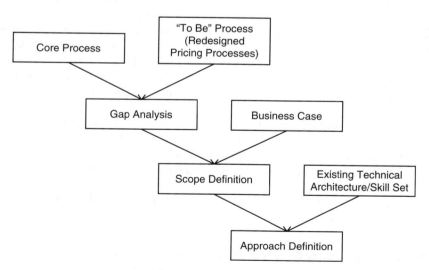

Figure 7.11   Scope and Approach Definition for a Software Selection Project

business requirements document will define the most critical expectations. It will:

- identify the functionality required
- help the team ensure this functionality is accounted for in the system selection
- note potential enhancements that a vendor can make if the application initially fails to meet requirements.

Defining the requirements for pricing software can be challenging for several reasons. First, an unusually wide range of business processes must be included, various governance issues must be identified and resolved, and numerous functions must buy-in to the proposed transformation to be supported by the software. Second, pricing applications often change how a sales force is compensated and how it prioritizes its daily workflow as the processes and metrics are redesigned to improve profitability. And, finally, the implementation of a pricing system can affect relationships with customers as deal management processes and prices themselves are likely to change. All of these factors are critical and must be considered.

In the second part of this phase, a firm should do its pre-demo preparation and create an evaluation framework. Firms often ask selected vendors to demonstrate the most difficult business scenario (*use case*) they can envision. While this approach may seem like a rigorous way to differentiate sellers and their solutions, it often fails on two counts. First, vendors' salespeople are trained to demonstrate use cases even when the functionality can't work in a production environment—a practice sometimes referred to as bending the software. Most salespeople can create a demo to fit virtually any scenario, which further perpetuates the false impression that all pricing solutions are the same. Second, difficult use cases are often not particularly representative of a firm's typical processes. Thus, asking vendors to demonstrate unlikely scenarios may result in a firm's overlooking the seller that may in fact offer the best solution. To avoid such pitfalls, firms should:

- assemble the RFP with the most common use cases for the business
- build a cross-functional team to evaluate the software
- create the assessment framework before soliciting responses to the RFP to create an impartial structure by which to evaluate the proposed solutions
- ask the vendors to work with the firm's IT group to base their demo on internal data.

Conducting Vendor Demos and Follow-Ups

An effective demonstration should show how the application works in general as well as its look and feel. However, as noted above, the talent of the vendor in making a compelling presentation can skew the evaluation. An impressive demonstration on a great user interface may win a vendor top rating on *all* criteria.

While usability is an important selection criterion, many others must be considered and weighed before a purchasing decision is made. To maintain its objectivity, the evaluation team should be reminded not to judge the functionality of the software by its user interface alone and to refrain from comparing applications before all demonstrations are complete.

Given the artificiality of the demonstration environment and the ability of vendors to influence customer assessment, companies can find it difficult to understand a software's true capabilities. However, there is an effective approach to consider. Once the vendor demonstrates a company's most common use cases, the company can present two fresh situations: an entirely new case and the modification of an existing one. The vendor's team can then be required to make the adjustments on the spot, witnessed by the evaluation team. This exercise forces a vendor to address issues of actual versus demo-only functionality, usability, and configurability. While it may require additional time during the selection process, the company should gain:

- better insight into the platform and technology
- an understanding of what it takes to configure and customize the software
- a sense of the software's integration capabilities and the level of support it will require to achieve integration with the company's systems
- an opportunity for the IT department to get under the hood of the application to make a qualitative assessment
- hands-on experience working in the vendor's platform.

An international consumer products company showed how this approach can work effectively. The company was selecting a pricing software vendor and included a use case that required the creation of regional English-language price lists in Australian dollars. During the follow-up, the top vendor candidates were asked to enhance this capability to support multiple languages and currencies. They were further required to add a new use case to support index-based pricing. According to a member of the evaluation team, ''Vendors hated it.'' But the company was the clear winner in the process. Because of its extra vetting, the company was able to find a pricing software solution well suited to its needs.

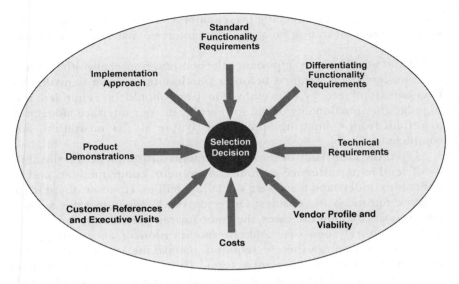

Figure 7.12   Vendor Selection Scorecard Criteria

Developing Final Vendor Recommendation

To settle on a software provider, firms must score each application according to the assessment framework specified during the preparing for vendor demos phase. Numerous criteria are typically considered (Figure 7.12 shows sample scorecard criteria).

Initiating the Procurement Process

During this phase, companies negotiate the details for procurement, licensing, pricing, and payment. While this is similar to other enterprise software purchases, all aspects of the relationship between the company and the software vendor should be considered:

- software licensing
- implementation services
- technical and implementation team training
- user conferences
- technical support and service-level agreements
- annual maintenance
- core system enhancements and customizations
- ownership of data and intellectual property
- warrantees and performance guarantees
- vendor references or success stories demonstrating qualifications.

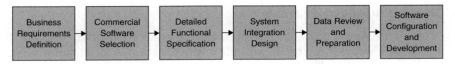

Figure 7.13 Stages of the Software Development Lifecycle (SDLC)

The Pricing Software Development Lifecycle

There are six distinct stages in the software development lifecycle (SDLC) (see Figure 7.13). These stages are common to all types of software but, because of its multifaceted nature, the pricing SDLC can be more complicated and difficult to navigate.

While many pricing projects are initiated by C-level executives, they directly affect Pricing and Sales, and often involve Marketing, Finance, IT, and even Human Resources. Here are the common questions frequently asked by these functions' representatives:

- *Pricing and Marketing.* What functionality will I have with this software? Will it replace or augment current pricing systems? Will the software make my job harder or obsolete?
- *Sales.* Is this system easy to use? How will it help me determine the right price? How can it match my market experience? Does this system take into consideration the nuances of my accounts and my territory? Why should I trust my commission-based income to software?
- *Finance.* Is the information accurate and complete? How does the system tie into our financial records? How will we make profit improvements?
- *IT.* Why do I need to install and support a new system? What legacy systems will be affected by the new pricing software, and how will they need to be reconfigured? Does the software create data redundancy?
- *Human Resources.* Are the employee compensation plans aligned with the goals of the software?

The greatest risk to successful adoption of any new software comes during the rollout. When new systems or processes are put in place, the implementation team often does not take into account the needs of certain constituent groups or fails to anticipate what effects could occur downstream. This type of oversight can undermine the implementation, even causing it to fail completely. An effective approach to help address this risk is to engage all stakeholders from the beginning of the SDLC.

The Business Requirements Definition and the Commercial Software Selection stages of the SDLC were covered in the previous section, "Selecting Pricing Management Software." The subsequent stages are described below.

Detailed Functional Specification

While defining the business's requirements for the application will establish *what* it will do for the organization, the functional specifications describe more specifically *how* the software will fulfill the needed tasks. Any gaps in the application's capability need to be addressed by either further enhancements or customizations; otherwise, these gap requirements will need to be satisfied outside the software.

This stage of the SDLC will likely present significant challenges because of the numerous functions involved. The impact on Sales can be felt personally by employees, as the pricing improvements brought about by the application can affect compensation. Team leaders should communicate the importance of this stage to the project's success—and as an opportunity to align the organization around policies, processes, and goals that will lead to greater profitability—which benefits everyone.

At a large metals distribution and processing company, various groups were consulted about a new software package. Salespeople shared their concern that the pricing package might adversely affect their compensation, which traditionally had been based on revenue rather than profit. The business's profitability had been taking a hit, however, because salespeople had become overly focused on locking up deals, no matter how low the margin was. By identifying this problem, the company was able to design a system-supported, revised commission structure that reflected its new focus on margin lift. This successfully encouraged the right behavior from the sales force.

System Integration Design

This stage identifies points where integration is needed to satisfy functional requirements, or where certain gaps or issues need to be addressed. Once this is accomplished, then the potential solutions can be designed. Three common issues generally arise in this phase of the pricing SDLC. The first involves resolving what is to be done with legacy pricing tools. In some organizations multiple spreadsheets have been integrated into the current systems along with processes to support them. In a pricing transformation, all the components that uphold the current processes, no matter how small, must be identified. The omission of one spreadsheet on a single user's desktop can result in pricing errors and cut deeply into profits.

The second issue involves how the new pricing software is integrated with existing ERP, CRM, rebate management, and contract management systems. While many packages currently on the market can exist as standalone products, most organizations prefer to integrate the pricing information they produce into existing systems. A seamless integration can make adoption easier.

The final challenge presented by this SDLC stage is the sheer volume of pricing data and the need to capture and transmit it instantaneously. Interface design can be difficult, and the system can't be taken down over a weekend to carry out the conversion lest it affect the sales team's ability to negotiate deals, or even worse, negatively impact the customer directly. An additional layer of planning must, therefore, be woven into the process to allow the integration to be handled while the system is online.

Data Review and Preparation

While theoretically straightforward, many organizations find this stage among the most challenging of the SDLC stages. It requires an organization to identify systems of record for every data element, while assessing the availability, quality, volatility, source, and governance attributes of all information. The data must then be consolidated or converted into useable formats. The two factors that complicate this effort for pricing are the volume of transactions and the quality of the data.

In most pricing transformations, the software requires multiple years of historical data, which can amount to millions of transactions. Collection alone can be a challenge. In addition, *normalizing* the information requires an intimate understanding of the data, the originating system, and the complex procedures needed to cleanse it. Often, the cleansing can't be based on formulas or algorithms, but requires people to review and interpret special codes that were used by individuals to overcome system challenges. This stage is critical to the ultimate success of the project because it enables the validation of the new prices and pricing analyses. If users suspect the quality of the data in the new pricing system is flawed in any way, then they will reject the software before it even has a chance to go live.

Software Configuration and Deployment

In this final stage of the SDLC, the software is configured and can be customized to meet the requirements outlined in the Detailed Functional Specification stage. Appropriate actions are then taken to integrate the software into existing applications as determined in the System Integration Design stage.

Several factors make this last SDLC stage challenging: the importance of validation, vendor limitations, and the nature of the change associated with the implementation. First, pricing professionals and salespeople must rigorously analyze newly generated prices and test every element of the new system-supported pricing processes before the software is deployed.

Poorly inspected and unvalidated prices may find their way to the market, which could not only undermine organizational adoption of the software, but also have a disastrous impact on profits. In addition, pricing software vendors tend to be relatively small, with still-maturing capabilities (e.g., unsophisticated toolkits and limited training and support resources to accompany a rollout), so organizations must acknowledge and plan how to overcome these limitations.

Many projects fail because the organization does not manage the changes well. A successful transformational strategy should include a plan to communicate clearly the purposes and benefits of the software to all stakeholders. Constituent groups must be trained to use the new tools and the revised policies and processes that go with them. Salespeople may also have to learn to think about pricing in new ways. Is an optimized price to be considered the starting point for negotiation, the floor price, or the target price? What corporate policies will govern quotes above or below an optimized price? How should a pricing professional interpret the software's analytics and leverage that information into action? Teaching individuals how to use the tool is as important as building it.

One advantage of installing new pricing technologies is that their impact is measurable. By sequencing implementation by region or product category, an organization can measure the delta between those who are and aren't using the new optimized prices (test versus control groups), while monitoring changes across time periods. A carefully designed testing plan can allow an organization to quantify the return on its investment in the software by profit, revenue, and market share.

Future Trends in Pricing Technology

In the early 2000s, numerous vendors pitched their competing pricing software. This number dwindled over the next several years as a result of acquisitions and simple market fallout. Some vendors experienced substantial growth, but this was moderated by the economic downturn of 2008–2009, when many technology vendors saw new opportunities either lost or delayed.

Where is the market headed? Many companies recognize pricing as an untapped area of opportunity, so demand is likely to continue increasing. Moreover, major ERP vendors have focused on acquiring pricing solutions to bolster sales as their mainstream products have experienced a drop in demand. All told, relatively few companies have been contracting to date in this emerging marketplace. The future is expected to be active to say the least. Three key factors will fuel this growth:

1. *Mindshare of company leadership.* Executives in nearly every industry are catching on to the fact that improvements in pricing can materially impact their operations. As mature organizations rethink

their go-to-market strategy, they are reconceiving their entire approach to pricing—as well as the need for more sophisticated technologies.

2. *A growing ecosystem.* Pricing has caught the attention of the academic, analyst, and consulting communities. Graduate programs in pricing are becoming more prevalent. Leading industry analysts are devoting significant resources to the discipline. Major consultancies now have entire practice areas that focus exclusively on pricing and profitability management. The increasing dedication of intellectual resources to this area has led to a more intensive examination of supporting technologies. This, in turn, is pushing the market to even greater innovations.

3. *Software maturity.* Pricing technology has now matured sufficiently to support a vast amount of transactional and segmentation data. Vendor software packages are routinely being integrated into enterprise-wide solutions, encouraging their spread through many industries.

To prepare for and help encourage this growth, providers are focusing on three major areas, as follows.

> A consumer durables company realized that poor internal practices had led to a confused presentation of its brands, product offerings, and price points. As part of a major transformational initiative, new pricing software was implemented with revamped supporting policies and processes. This successful program enabled the company to interact with the market far more effectively and profitably, while retaining the flexibility to capitalize on new opportunities as they arose.

Product Features and Tools

All pricing software solutions share similarities in their core areas—analytics, optimization, and execution (a scatter plot or bubble chart can, after all, be drawn in only so many ways). So, to differentiate themselves, vendors are devoting a lot of their R&D efforts to addressing usability. Application toolkits (configuration and customization) are receiving substantial attention, giving companies a means to distinguish competing solutions from one another. Feeding transactional information and master data (customer and product) into each software tool efficiently is critical if advanced analytic capabilities are to function fully. Moving this information into pricing and ERP software is relatively straightforward. More complex is the integration of the pricing software itself into an order management workflow. In the coming years, vendors are expected to address this market need by expanding functionality to handle end-to-end order management processes, particularly in the business-to-business space.

Wireless PDA support has also received attention. Sales representatives who use these devices in the field can connect to centralized pricing and data systems to access and share information in real time. Eventually, these capabilities will become a standard requirement for retailers and large distributors. CRM integration—particularly for sales force automation (SFA)—is another area receiving a lot of attention. In each case, vendors are upgrading or customizing functionality largely because of input from existing customers. These new or improved capabilities offer immediate benefits as they can be quickly shuttled into the sales process to benefit deals currently in negotiation.

Industry and Geographic Expansion

Companies need to understand the maturity of the modules and feature sets that most interest them. They must also know where the software packages they are considering have been previously deployed. A company that uses significant promotions in its business model might be very disappointed when it discovers that the promotions capabilities described by the vendor were tailored for a very different sector. How industry pricing practices vary is a factor that must be fully explored during the software selection process. Many current vendors have matured in only one or two industry segments. However, some are attempting to break out of these silos to go after their competitors' business in new segments. Business-to-business vendors represent a notable exception to this trend. They have yet to find a way to cross over into the business-to-consumer space—and vice versa. The pricing fundamentals of these two industries are so different that a breakthrough solution that can meet the requirements of both will have to be found.

On the international front, the battle between software vendors to determine who can get into these markets first is officially underway. Companies in Europe, South America, and the Asia-Pacific region are proving an attractive market for pricing software. Vendors are currently limited, however, in their ability to develop even a small sales and delivery capability outside North America. A number of companies are looking to systems integrators to assist their international expansion strategies. These companies must realize, though, that in the short term at least they will receive limited technical support from vendors as it is predominantly provided during U.S. working hours.

New Delivery Models

An emerging opportunity for pricing software vendors involves providing software as a service (SaaS) or a hosted solution. For example, a large automotive company recently implemented a solution in a hosted environment under a leased agreement with the vendor. Many RFPs now ask software providers to describe their capabilities and qualifications in this area as firms are becoming more comfortable hosting their most sensitive data externally. A few smaller vendors have actually modeled themselves as SaaS businesses. The larger providers will likely follow suit; not presenting themselves as solely SaaS providers, but rather offering clients a hosted option and the flexibility to lease the software versus acquiring a perpetual license.

Overall, the future is bright for commercial pricing software vendors. Despite being affected by the 2008–2009 recession, their growth rates are expected to rise dramatically over the next decade. As in most new software spaces, the weaker vendors will quickly fall off the radar. A select few will become the de facto short list for companies to consider along with the pricing tools resident in the ERP applications of vendors such as SAP and Oracle. Spreadsheets will remain the dominant form of pricing management in the short term, but the end of their preeminence in the pricing arena is in sight as pricing software continues to take hold.

Pricing Technology Selection and Implementation Recommendations

Moving from problem definition, to solution selection, and then implementation can be a difficult process for an organization. Decisions made early in the selection phase are critical if the organization is to capitalize on opportunities to improve processes, pricing effectiveness, and margin. Here are some key points that organizations need to get right.

- *Start with small wins*, such as finding and correcting price leakage, to fund initiatives that will provide long-term benefits. Early successes can also help build internal credibility and confidence in new systems, processes, methods, and people.
- *Create a phased implementation approach* to keep costs in line with the benefits realized. Consider investing first in diagnostic and analytic tools that will identify the elements contributing to existing profits and costs, help locate points of price leakage, and assist in identifying small and quick wins, which, as stated above, can help fund later phases.
- *Establish improvement objectives with realistic metrics* early in the project to help manage the expectations of leaders. Decide in advance which metrics will be looked at and how they will be responded to. Be realistic about estimating resource and time requirements. Talk about what thresholds could trigger an adjustment in the timeline or resources for the project.
- *Ensure the final pricing software selection is handled internally* with specialists being used only to define and facilitate processes, apply insights to define requirements, and understand true product capabilities.

By ensuring the team acts as the final decision maker, an organization can avoid having individual members second-guess the approach when issues arise.

- *Communicate recommendations on the software solution promptly* to gain consensus and ensure buy-in.
- *Understand the technology and support implications fully* as they can produce the greatest stumbling blocks during the implementation process. A company's IT team must fully grasp the effort required to configure, modify, and customize the software. When an internal system is designed to support the new software, it must be flexible enough to adapt to changing business conditions. It must also support the needs of the various functional groups within the organization that are impacted by pricing. Data quality must be assured and the ramifications of all proposed process, policy, and technological changes should be considered in advance.

Endnotes

1. Robert L. Phillips, *Pricing and Revenue Optimization* (Stanford: Stanford Business Books, 2005).
2. Phillips, *Pricing and Revenue Optimization*.
3. Phillips, *Pricing and Revenue Optimization*.
4. Michael Dunne and Robert P. Desisto, "MarketScope for Price Optimization and Management, 2008," Gartner Article ID no. G00153034, March 20, 2008.
5. Noha Tohamy and Heather Keltz, "Building a Bulletproof Business Case for Pricing Improvement Initiatives," AMR Research Report no. 21745 (Boston: AMR Research, 2008).

Integrating Tax and Regulatory Policies with the Pricing Strategy

*A fine is a tax for doing something wrong. A tax is a fine for doing some-
thing right.*

—Unknown

When companies set out to improve their pricing and profitability management, their view often extends to only pre-tax income, even though focusing on after-tax income would enable them to keep more of the profits they generate. These companies fail to investigate the regulatory costs and potential tax consequences, both direct and indirect, tied to prospective sales. Why does this happen? The most obvious reasons include lack of expertise and poorly designed policies; for example, compensatory schemes that reward personnel based on pre-tax calculations (i.e., earnings before taxes [EBT]).

Unfortunately, one reason companies fail to include tax in their management of pricing and profitability is because the leadership team incorrectly views tax and regulatory compliance teams as cost centers that deal with expenses that are not controllable. Another reason is that some companies have traditionally restricted Tax to working on financial transactions and have not integrated the function into the general operations of the business.

Regardless of the cause, the result has been that many enterprises are taking a hit to their after-tax profits. Companies are legally permitted to organize themselves and to structure their transactions to achieve operational and tax benefits as well as cash flow benefits; failing to take these steps means companies are unnecessarily leaving money on the table. From a competitive standpoint, not integrating operating and pricing

A professional services firm learned how costly it can be to price a consulting engagement without first evaluating the tax implications of the workflows being provided. The firm's Southeast Asian subsidiary provided computer programming support in conjunction with services rendered by a second subsidiary that resided in a nearby country. Ultimately, the second business unit became responsible for making the final deliverable to the client. This is where problems arose. The services firm hadn't realized it was creating a nonrecoverable value-added tax (VAT) liability by the way it structured the delivery of service. The charge assessed to the second subsidiary represented more than 10 percent of the fees earned for the programming work. This VAT had not been negotiated with the client, which resulted in the service firm's having to absorb the tax liability, effectively eliminating most of the profit on the engagement.

initiatives with tax and regulatory planning is a peril that should be avoided—particularly in this era of decreasing margins.

Consider a hypothetical scenario. A multinational corporation manufactures and sells consumer electronics products. To distribute these products, the company needs to execute transactions around the globe through various legal entities as well as through joint ventures with foreign-owned third parties. If the company fails to integrate its operations and tax planning, then it may retain as little as 60 percent of the potential after-tax income. However, if the company does make full use of its tax department, then it may realize 80 percent or more of the potential after-tax income. While management examines supply chain and distribution channel issues, another team could evaluate the tax regimes of the jurisdictions in which the company currently—or might potentially—operates. Based on the combined analyses of its functional groups, the manufacturer might find that it could reduce its operating costs by relocating supply chain and distribution activities to new jurisdictions—while still meeting the company's strategic needs.

This chapter will focus primarily on why income and other tax considerations should be taken into account when establishing pricing policies and will demonstrate the need for firms also to consider regulatory requirements when making these critical decisions.

The Convergence of Tax and Pricing Strategy

Jurisdictions and Taxation Regimes

When formulating pricing policies, companies must sort through the many jurisdictions that impose taxes through a wide variety of regimes.

This complex task is complicated further by frequent rule and rate changes. Despite these challenges, business leaders must take the necessary steps to understand their company's position. To start with, a company's taxable income base must be evaluated in the relevant jurisdictions. Here are some key issues that should be considered when assessing each applicable regime:

- Is it territorial (i.e., does it apply to transactions falling within certain jurisdictional borders) or is it residence-based (i.e., are taxes levied upon the income of a resident corporation regardless of the jurisdiction where the income was earned)?
- What is the nature of the regime (e.g., income, sales, use, value-added, excise, or property taxes, along with licensing requirements and duties)?

Tax laws can influence how a company conducts its business in a variety of ways, including how information is captured on an invoice, where title (for goods) is transferred to customers, and where contracts with clients are negotiated and executed. Companies need to examine these issues *before* a transaction has been negotiated and executed as it is far more difficult to structure a deal tax-efficiently, or to negotiate with a tax-levying body for reduced rates or exemptions after the fact. Fewer options are available for tax personnel when they have to play catch up.

Companies should mandate that tax assessments be conducted routinely in any relevant decision-making process. For example, tax analysts can periodically check sample sales transactions to analyze their impact. If they find areas of concern (e.g., intercompany sales that have transfer pricing and customs valuation issues), then they can develop case studies to share with Sales and Operations personnel. These would show:

- Factually, what occurred (e.g., goods were sold through multiple related entities located in different countries prior to being shipped to the customer)
- What should have occurred (e.g., the goods could have been purchased from one unrelated party and sold to another unrelated party using a single distributor; service fees could then have been paid to entities that performed related procurement services)
- The financial benefits of pursuing this more efficient approach.

Through these case studies and other forums, organizations can educate their sales personnel on basic tax concepts and show how their actions can unwittingly create tax issues that significantly reduce the return expected on a transaction.

Companies often fail to take advantage of tax laws that offer significant benefits for businesses that engage in specified activities. For example, the

U.S. Congress encourages corporations to innovate and manufacture products in the United States by establishing laws that provide tax credits for research and development (R&D) expenditures and a deduction for U.S.-based manufacturing operations.[1] To take advantage of these and other tax-incentivizing laws, companies should determine whether other jurisdictions might offer more favorable environments for the company to carry out certain activities.

Treatment of Tax Departments within a Company

In the U.S., tax departments were traditionally seen as silos whose primary mission was to keep the corporation compliant with federal income tax laws and to assist financial reporting and other personnel in preparing the quarterly and annual corporate statements (i.e., by calculating the provision for income taxes).[2] Over time some companies may have added international and provincial income tax specialists to the mix. Depending upon where their headquarters were domiciled, these experts may also have assumed further responsibilities for sales, use, and franchise taxes as well as VAT and VAT-related assessments.

Many businesses that had customs experts tended to place them outside the tax department (e.g., with Logistics, Procurement, Transportation, or Trade). This practice can interfere with a company's ability to develop a comprehensive, integrated tax strategy. Until recently, this problem was compounded by resource limitations that too often prevented tax from engaging in the sophisticated analysis and planning of global transactions that would enable a company to realize incremental benefits related to pricing.

Figure 8.1, from a growth strategies study, shows how executives rank the importance of various activities in managing their firm's globalization objectives. Moving from the top of the left-hand axis down, the first three activities, predictably, are tied to the growth of the business. Respondents rated "Tax Savings" last in importance. Fortunately, while this ranking may still be a common one, various factors are coalescing to give tax a greater role in strategic planning. Over the past decade as computers have become more powerful and software functionality has improved, tax analysts have been able to engage in more complex analyses. In addition (as we will discuss later in the chapter), companies are increasingly seeking new ways to improve after-tax margin as older methods such as cost-cutting are losing effectiveness.

However, significant obstacles continue to hamper the integration of tax with pricing. The sheer complexity of tax laws, jurisdictions, and regimes tends to discourage internal cooperation and so, too, do practical, organizational issues. Sales, for example, uses granular metrics about the products and services being sold, whereas tax typically receives aggregate numbers to complete compliance forms. It is hard for the two functions to

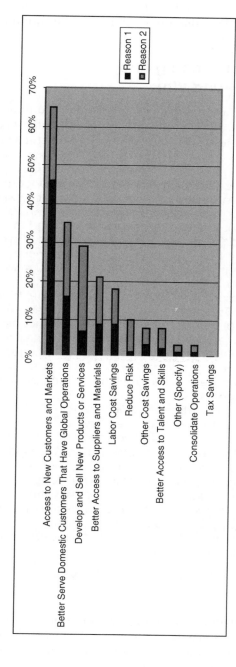

Figure 8.1 Priorities of Globalization Objectives

Source: Deloitte Private Company Global Growth Survey, 2008.

talk if they don't utilize the same data sets. Yet as companies continue their efforts to improve their profitability and competitiveness, the focus on after-tax margin will lead them to establish a closer working relationship between these vital areas.

How to Integrate Pricing and Tax Functions—and Why

Connecting pricing and tax policies may sound daunting, esoteric, and costly to implement. But if firms wish to increase after-tax profits, then they must achieve at least some level of integration between them.

Consider two hypothetical competitors: Mesa Department Stores and Donner Home Furnishings. Both have sales strictly within the U.S. They have different tax situations because of various factors, including where the companies are headquartered and the location of their respective distribution channels. Donner is based in a more business-friendly state that assesses lower corporate income taxes, and (unlike Mesa) it has a China-based operation through which it channels its imports to increase its operational efficiency.

For these reasons, Mesa's effective tax rate (ETR) is 39.5 percent, while Donner's is 36.5 percent. As a result, on an after-tax basis, Donner has additional cash equal to 3 percent of its income to use as it sees fit. Critically, the lower ETR will permanently benefit the company as long as the relevant tax regimes remain unchanged. Mesa may well have options to generate more after-tax cash from its operations, but it will require a better blending of its business and tax policies to achieve them.

According to an article in *AMR Research Outlook*, in environments where pricing is undisciplined and unstructured, the initial benefits of pricing management can result in a margin increase of 2–7 percent of sales on a pre-tax/EBT basis.[3] Assuming an ETR of 38 percent for a U.S.-based company that does not have international operations, the pricing improvements will net, roughly, 1.24–4.34 percent of sales on an after-tax basis.[4] If Mesa Department Stores undertakes a pricing initiative to increase its competitiveness with Donner, but does not conduct the proper tax analysis, then even a small overlooked tax detriment could end up producing a negative cost-benefit ratio after implementation.

Are there companies integrating tax and operational decisions into their pricing policies today? Unequivocally, the answer is "yes." But, to be truly effective, this integration cannot be limited to tax's simply analyzing how a specific transaction is priced.

Consider this hypothetical example. The tax department of Better Health Pharmaceutical Company routinely reviews contracts, whose financial implications are material to the operations of the firm, before they are signed. In one instance, tax concluded that the negotiation and execution of a contract would create a permanent establishment (PE)[5] in a higher-tax foreign jurisdiction. The sales team correctly assumed that creating a PE would be a bad outcome because it would subject the firm to additional foreign income taxes. Unfortunately, Better Health could not explore other options. The buyer had imposed time constraints on the negotiations. Thus, tax was unable to do the necessary analysis that might have equipped Sales to make the tax implications for the firm legitimate negotiating points. There was also no time to propose alternate contracting arrangements that would have avoided creating a PE. As a result, Better Health was unable to close the deal.

Aligning the Tax Model with Business Requirements and Strategy

To achieve an advantageous relationship between tax and pricing, organizations should align their tax model with their business requirements and strategy. An operational framework that identifies points in the decision-making process where tax can assess the organization's potential tax exposure and liabilities, while still advancing the strategic goals of the business should be created. Because organizations can be subject to a range of taxes, duties, and regulatory costs, the framework should identify the different intersection points where the tax department will weigh in. This should always happen at the earliest possible stage of the deal negotiation or activity in question.

Tax can be extremely helpful in aligning an enterprise's legal structure with its business operations. Figure 8.2 shows the issues that must be taken into account when looking at a company's current operating model and legal entity structure. Pricing initiatives can be an important reason to perform this kind of review.[6] The team assigned to the task—which should, of course, include tax personnel—will need to address the legal structure and, based upon the factors in Figure 8.2, craft a solution that takes into account:

- the number of business units involved
- the types of activities to be performed within the business units
- the form of conducting business (e.g., corporation, partnership, branch)
- the jurisdictions where the business units will be located.

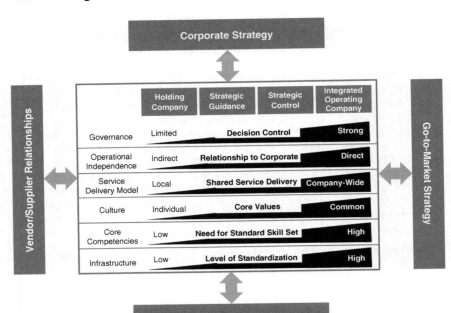

Figure 8.2   Operating Model Design Considerations

Once the key elements of the business are identified, the organization can create a tax-efficient operating structure for the principal company, which might place Sales (and other shared services), intellectual property (IP), and production units into legal entities to consolidate operations and to increase the after-tax margins generated by their activities. Design considerations (see Figure 8.2) must be integrated with business operations, product flows, and each of the steps needed to increase core business efficiency. In addition, the company needs to analyze relevant business issues thoroughly as well as U.S. and foreign tax considerations directly affecting the company's operational reorganization. Failure to do so (and to plan accordingly) could trigger tax audits and require subsequent adjustments in several jurisdictions, increasing the company's overall ETR.

The fundamental approach to identifying key business processes for integrating Operations and Tax[7] (see also Figure 8.3) are as follows:

- Identify product pricing leakage then determine pricing and business process changes that can address the problem.
- Review the functions used by employees of the principal and their contribution to the manufacturing activities.
- Evaluate arm's-length pricing to compensate the principal for its activities and risk.

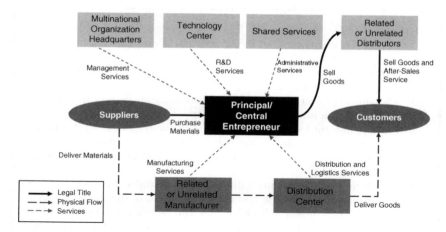

Figure 8.3 Identifying Key Business Processes for Integrating Operations and Tax

The primary goal is to use the enhanced understanding of the key business processes to create synergies between Operations and Tax to structure the company's core, income-generating activities and to allow for the efficient repatriation of cash (i.e., cash movement from foreign subsidiaries to the home country of the business). This can be a challenging task, but it will benefit the company's bottom line over the long term if well executed.

CASE STUDY: Improved alignment between tax strategies and business processes lowers ETR and improves profitability

Consider the case of a hypothetical company. Midland Generators produces some of the world's top diesel engines from its factories in Germany, the U.K., and the U.S. Midland also sells maintenance contracts to provide onsite assistance to service its engines. A newly hired CEO noticed that Midland's ETR was almost five points higher than that of its competitors. The CEO created a VP of Tax position within the organization and brought in an experienced professional to fill it. The VP began a review by asking the tax department to examine the organization's current manufacturing and distribution structure. Staff members examined product flows (especially those of the generator parts) to gain a better understanding of who Midland's clients were and where they were located. The team also reviewed the organizational structure of the company to evaluate its present tax efficiency. The results of the initial investigation were:

- The product flows indicated that parts made in the U.K. and the U.S. were shipped directly to Germany, where the engines were assembled.

(continued)

(*Continued*)

The VP assigned her team the added task of investigating how inter-company pricing of parts was handled between the subsidiaries, and if the pricing conformed to the income tax rules on transfer pricing between the countries.

- Midland's customers were located predominantly in nations that had excavation and mining activities in South America. Because the manufacturer did not have any legal entities in the region, the VP had her department review the contracts and interview the company's sales and operations personnel to determine the tax consequences of current operations.
- Part of the IP that enhanced the value of Midland's engines resided in U.S. patents covering the fuel efficiency pieces of the engine design. In recent years, however, both the U.K. and Germany had reduced their income tax rates. The VP decided that Midland should investigate its global funding and dissemination of IP. An analysis was performed to determine how the cost of developing future intangible assets could be shared with the non-U.S. affiliates engaged in manufacturing and selling the products.
- The VP's team found that Midland had assumed tax costs tied to its engineers and maintenance personnel serving long-term assignments in South America. These added costs had not been taken into account by Sales when pricing the contracts. This naturally contributed to margin erosion.

After the investigation was complete, Tax made several recommendations to Sales to change critical business processes, including:

- Mandating training for all Sales personnel to educate them on prohibited activities (to avoid the creation of a permanent establishment in each country where transactions occurred).
- Ending the execution of contracts by sales personnel. Agreements would now be forwarded to the office of the organization's General Counsel for review.
- Mandating that contracts with a value exceeding $10 million would be reviewed, in advance, by Tax to analyze the potential liabilities imposed by the terms. Areas where tax savings could be achieved would be communicated to Sales, which could then modify the agreements or change pricing.
- Requiring that all contracts specify that the client would reimburse the additional income tax expenses incurred by engineers and maintenance personnel from their overseas assignments, or the price quoted to the client would cover these extra costs.
- Incentivizing Sales personnel to meet after-tax return on investment (ROI) targets.

(*continued*)

In addition, Tax created a new entity (within the larger corporate structure) in a low-tax European jurisdiction to coordinate both development activities and IP use outside the U.S. as well as to share the costs of developing new IP. This entity would also earn royalties from the sales of engines incorporating the new IP.

After initial resistance, Sales agreed with all the recommendations and implemented new policies and procedures to support them. These were communicated to employees throughout the organization. The decision to implement the changes reduced Midland's ETR by 3 percent annually and affected roughly $500 million in sales made to South America. As an added benefit, the organization was able to reduce its costs by several hundred thousand dollars, as clients assumed the incremental tax liabilities incurred by Midland's employees working for them.

Maximizing Global Profit Drivers

The varying rates of income tax across different jurisdictions has led multinational organizations (MNOs) to lower their ETR by coordinating the location of their business operations with jurisdictions that provide a competitive tax regime. To do this, international tax and transfer pricing issues must be thoroughly reviewed to determine the most advantageous options from both a business and a tax perspective.

Though the benefits may seem obvious, some internal resistance may need to be overcome before new policies can be set. Too often, senior managers may lobby to have income flow through their areas, though this may not, in fact, be best for the company. For example, if the incremental profit of a multinational's manufacturing or distribution subsidiaries is earned in a jurisdiction with residence-based taxation[8] (e.g., the U.S.), any benefits that accrue from improved pricing management will be earned within the country in which those subsidiaries reside or in the country where that income is repatriated. Those profits become subject to local income tax laws. In most industrialized and developing countries the tax rates range from 25 to 35 percent. A coordinated effort between Operations and Tax should be undertaken to ensure that a company's ETR is not being adversely influenced by the senior manager or managers with the most clout. Instead, the company should analyze its operating structure and determine which affiliates should own interests in its IP and help fund R&D activities. If the company determines that there are business reasons to implement changes, then the company should also develop new compensation structures to alleviate the concerns of senior managers affected by any operational reorganization.

Not all tax efficiencies need come from changes in the legal structure. Consider the previous example where Mesa Department Stores and

Donner Home Furnishings were described as having an ETR of 39.5 and 36.5 percent, respectively. Regardless of whether the pricing policies being evaluated (or some other mechanism) successfully decrease the percentage of income taxes paid, the goal should be to reduce the company's ETR without reducing the pre-tax margin (unless the organization is in a period of contraction). Several mechanisms can be used to do this without reducing sales income. Mesa, for example, could negotiate with the state or states where its manufacturing and distribution centers exist to receive a reduced income tax rate in return for employing a certain number of people over a mandated threshold. While this action may not be a pricing decision per se, Mesa's tax department can communicate the potential impact to the sales organization. For example, if the company has established a certain after-tax margin as the goal for each sales transaction, and the revised business structure reduces the overall product costs, then this cost reduction should give salespeople additional latitude to lower a price, if necessary, to secure a deal.

Domestic Production Deduction.   In the U.S., another vehicle for reducing a firm's ETR (without cutting sales) involves taking advantage of the domestic production deduction (DPD).[9] The DPD gives preferential tax treatment to income generated by the sales of products manufactured in the U.S. This deduction was phased in gradually between 2005 and 2010, 2010 being the first year when the maximum deduction (equal to 9 percent of taxable income related to a qualifying sale) applied. The deduction produces a 3.15 percent[10] reduction in the ETR applicable to the sales of qualifying goods that fall under this regime. Table 8.1 demonstrates the mechanics of this calculation.

The DPD does have some requirements, such as demonstrating on an item-by-item basis that a significant portion of the product was manufactured, produced, grown, or extracted by the taxpayer in the U.S. When an

Table 8.1   Example of the Domestic Production Deduction (DPD) for $200,000 Income Related to U.S.-Manufactured Products in 2010

	Produced by Taxpayer	Purchased for Resale
Sales	$1,000,000	$1,000,000
Costs and Expenses	($800,000)	($800,000)
Net Income	$200,000	$200,000
DPD(at 9% in 2010)	($18,000)	$0
Taxable Income	$182,000	$200,000
Tax @ 35%	$63,700	$70,000
Effective Tax Rate	31.85%	35%

Note: This example assumes that the DPD is not reduced or eliminated by statutory limitations (e.g., overall taxable income and wages paid attributable to domestic production).

organization decides to take advantage of this regime, it must ensure that it is executed and communicated properly throughout the organization. Relevant information must be shared, particularly with the Sales department, which must price the manufactured parts and service elements of a contract where DPD applies separately to achieve the target after-tax income.

Income Taxes on Employees.   Income taxes should be considered at the individual level for companies that have a tax equalization policy[11] with their employees (an arrangement that typically increases a firm's overall tax costs). Without proper planning and identification of the costs when pricing a transaction, margin can be easily diminished. For example, consider a hypothetical engineering services firm that signs a contract with a port authority of an Eastern Mediterranean country. Twenty engineers, all residents of Germany, will be assigned to the engagement. When moving people (resources) like this across jurisdictions to satisfy contractual obligations, firms must consider many variables to assess the tax impact. These include:

- What jurisdiction or jurisdictions will the employee be working and living within?
- How long will the employee be physically located in a foreign country?
- How will reimbursable expenses of the employee be handled?
- What changes in compensation will be received by the employee for this assignment (e.g., housing allowance, educational reimbursement to pay for language-appropriate schools for children, cost of flybacks to the employee's home country)?[12]
- Is the employee on secondment, where payment for the employee's services will come from the firm's subsidiary at which he or she is located?

Although many companies are good at estimating the costs of the individual items, the tax-equalization amounts that they pay (which are typically calculated after returns are filed) need to be included in the pricing of the engagement contract as well. Companies may initially believe that all expenses will be passed through to the client, but this will occur only if they are all identified and negotiated before the agreement is finalized. The client may maintain that these tax-equalization obligations are between the service provider and its employees.

Using the illustration given, an administrator for the port authority would feel some control when negotiating costs related to, for instance, flybacks and food and entertainment allowances an engineer would receive, because these items are readily understandable. But the administrator would need to be an expert on both local *and* German income tax laws to understand how these regimes might apply to this contract, how they interact with each other, and any treaty relief that might exist between the two countries. Only then would he have a frame of reference to understand what might be fair in a tax equalization agreement. If the engineering firm can reasonably estimate its costs to reimburse the employees for their incremental personal income tax liabilities from the engagement, then it may be simpler for the firm to reprice the services fees to cover these costs, rather than trying to negotiate for the client to assume them.

Indirect Taxes.   Indirect taxes (e.g., sales tax, VAT, duties) can also be affected by pricing decisions and therefore should be integrated into a company's pricing strategy. Although indirect taxes will primarily affect the buyer of goods and services, savvy customers know what the tax costs and implications are for a given transaction. If the buyer notices something amiss, then this can create unnecessary tension and result in the possible loss of a sale. As an example, professional services firms often prefer to bill centrally from one country, while performing their services in the countries where they have located their service centers or centers of excellence.[13] In one actual case, the client realized that the seller had structured the delivery for the workflows and the billing of the engagement in a way that would result in nonrecoverable VAT. So the client asked the seller who would be responsible for paying for these costs (they amounted to more than 15 percent of the total price of the engagement).[14] After an uncomfortable discussion, the seller decided to change the jurisdiction of the billing location to avoid the nonrecoverable VAT. This move, in turn, required the seller's tax department to determine how best to repatriate the monies from the engagement.

VATs differ from sales taxes typically found in the U.S. in key respects. Sales taxes are imposed on the end consumer, but are collected by the retailer that sells the good or provides the service. VATs, on the other hand, are imposed at each stage of the supply chain (e.g., a vendor will collect one from a customer at the point of sale [output VAT], while the tax amount the vendor paid when purchasing the inventory [input VAT] may be refundable). Consider this scenario. A lumber mill fulfills orders for raw materials (shelving) for a carpenter (the buyer) who builds bookcases. If the carpenter subsequently sells a bookcase to a customer, then he must charge VAT at the prevailing rate. However, the carpenter can also typically reclaim the VAT *he* paid on the shelving. When he makes his corresponding VAT filing, he can offset these two amounts and remit the balance to the tax authority. Table 8.2 compares the ways that a VAT versus a sales tax regime apply to the manufacture of a product.

The VAT incurred on certain purchases may not be eligible for credit. Similarly, specific sale types (mainly services) may be exempt from VAT,

Table 8.2   Sample Calculations Representing Differences Between a VAT Regime and a Sales Tax Regime

VAT@10%	Price ($)	Input Tax ($)	Output Tax ($)	Payment to FISCUS (net) ($)
Raw Material Supplier	100	0	10	10
Manufacturer	150	(10)	15	5
Wholesaler	250	(15)	25	10
Retailer	350	(25)	35	10
Total Net Tax Collected				35

Sales Tax@10%	Price ($)	Tax ($)	Payment to FISCUS (net) ($)
Raw Material Supplier	100	0	0
Manufacturer	150	0	0
Wholesaler	250	0	0
Retailer	350	35	35
Total Net Tax Collected			35

Note: FISCUS is a tax-collecting agency.

but the vendor will not be allowed to recover the VAT incurred on related purchases. Thus, suppliers who must charge the tax to exempt customers should consider the financial impact that these charges will have on their customers.[15]

VAT compliance is an area where *tax leakage* often occurs because of the complexities involved with capturing and documenting all the inputs and outputs. In the example above, the carpenter is responsible for tracking each order of raw materials purchased, the amount of VAT paid on those materials, each order sold, and the amount of the tax collected on those sales. If the taxes are not managed and reported, with documentation, on a timely basis, then this may result in the loss of recoverable VAT monies and reduced after-tax margin on the sales.

VATs are also imposed on the importation of goods, which can be a reason to find a jurisdiction with a more favorable import rate. Exports, on the other hand, are typically exempt from these taxes.

If a company plans to implement a more operationally efficient supply chain that may result in reduced income taxes, then it must consider the effect that the structural changes will have on VAT and duties as the impact can be very different on these indirect taxes. First, the definition of a related party (two parties who are joined by a special relationship prior to the deal, such as subsidiaries of the same company or a general partner and the partnership it has an interest in) transaction may differ between the income tax and customs' regimes, as it does in the U.S. Under U.S. rules for the former, 50 percent ownership is the threshold for a related-party sale, while for customs purposes the ownership level need be only 5 percent. Even when a sale is considered a related-party arrangement for both regimes, the methods of supporting an *arm's-length* (between unrelated parties) agreement are often quite different for customs and income tax.

On imported goods, the U.S. Internal Revenue Service (IRS) wants to ensure that a transfer price is not higher than an arm's length price (resulting in incremental profits being earned outside the U.S. tax jurisdiction and thereby reducing taxable income that will be generated in the U.S.). When a U.S. subsidiary of a foreign corporation resells product that it purchases from its foreign parent and shows zero income on its U.S. tax return, the IRS will likely recalculate the intercompany price of the sale of the product between the foreign corporation and its U.S. subsidiary. This will result in the IRS making an assessment on the profit it calculates for the intercompany sale.

On the flipside, the U.S. Customs and Border Protection (CBP) agency seeks to prevent value declarations below the arm's-length amount to ensure the U.S. Treasury collects the proper amount of duties. Most countries have some form of governmental import–export agency, generally referred to as *Customs*. In the U.S., the CBP (the largest component of the Department of Homeland Security) has three major roles with respect to facilitating trade to and from the U.S.: (1) helping to secure the country from acts of terrorism, (2) ensuring that goods are legitimate (e.g. legal to possess), (3) and preserving trade compliance by the enforcement of import laws and making sure that the appropriate duties and fees are paid. An importer should never assume that its transfer price is de facto acceptable as the *transaction value* for customs purposes, although it may provide a good starting point for determining the import value.[16]

Though an arm's-length principle is used in both cases, the approaches for determining the pricing of a product may differ between the U.S. income tax and customs laws. Using transfer pricing rules, taxpayers look to establish the best method to determine an arm's-length intercompany charge for income tax purposes.[17] On the other hand, the CBP has a hierarchy of six methods to be used in establishing dutiable value.[18] Other jurisdictions around the world have their own rules for determining the appropriate transfer price and customs values, though many are similar. Again, when a company changes the jurisdiction where it operates, even if its income tax rate has been reduced, it needs also to examine duties and indirect taxes before adjusting pricing.

Free trade zones and bonded warehouses offer ways to reduce the cost of duties. The agreements governing the free trade zones specifically outline which goods will qualify for free or reduced duty, how country of origin rules will be satisfied, and other documentation requirements. Sellers should investigate whether a supply chain can be channeled through a free trade zone. Bonded warehouses are physical storage sites established by the relevant customs authorities. These facilities allow for the storage of quota goods, the deferral of payment for duties, and, in some situations, the avoidance of levied duties on goods entirely. Both free trade zones and bonded warehouses can potentially eliminate the concern about duties and allow the enterprise to focus solely on the tax implications of a transaction and adjust pricing accordingly. Additional compliance issues will be explored later in this chapter.

Taxes and Bundling.   One of the most complex issues involving pricing and taxes arises when different products, or products and services, are bundled together and represented in a single line on an invoice. Many jurisdictions tax products and services at different rates. If the items are not separated on an invoice, then the tax jurisdiction will typically apply the higher rate to both items.

Bundling can also include the physical manner in which products are shipped. Consider a laptop that is being exported to a foreign jurisdiction. If the computer has software loaded on its hard drive at the time of transport, then it will be subject to additional indirect tax charges—a laptop with software loaded on it is more valuable than the same one without it. The incremental value created by the installed software will likely result in more duties, VAT, and so forth being assessed on the transfer of the property. Although in many circumstances the tax costs tied to bundling will affect only the third-party buyers paying for the goods, not addressing this issue may cause angst within an organization when the bundled transactions are for intercompany sales. The solution, however, can be simple. In the example above, the computer can be shipped to its destination and the customer can download the software separately over the internet.

Sellers must also consider compliance as they are typically responsible for calculating the amounts owed and must remit the collected funds to the tax authorities. The subject of pricing and compliance costs will be discussed in detail later, but clearly, bundling can cause problems during an audit by a sales tax body because the applicable tax rate multiplied by the sales of a particular class will not equal the total remitted to the state. Different components of a particular sale may be taxed at different rates (e.g., goods and services) and there may be exempt items. In addition, it is often difficult to allocate income between classes when months or years have passed between the transaction and the audit.[19] Addressing these issues before being contacted by the tax authorities is obviously far more cost- and time-effective for an organization.

Integrating Tax Planning into Sales Negotiations

By proactively combining tax planning with pricing, decision makers can systematically capitalize on opportunities to improve profitability when negotiating and executing sales agreements. For example, a firm could change the location of where title is passed on the goods that it sells to utilize foreign tax credits. Under U.S. tax law, a credit is allowed for taxes paid to a foreign jurisdiction in an amount equivalent to what the U.S. liability would be for the same level of income. Some countries historically have had tax rates in excess of the 35 percent established by the U.S., so paying income taxes to these countries would generate more foreign tax credits than allowed by U.S. laws. In addition, various differences in the net earnings subject to the foreign tax may result in an ETR in excess of 35 percent in a foreign subsidiary.

To utilize these *excess credits*, additional foreign source revenue needs to be generated. A way to accomplish this is by changing the title passage of an export to a country other than the U.S. Depending on the circumstances, roughly one-half of the taxable income attributable to this sale may be taxed as foreign source income.[20]

A U.S. boat manufacturer builds its boats in Louisiana. A French customer wishes to buy a boat from the manufacturer for $1 million. The boat manufacturer has $100,000 of foreign tax credits that it has not been able to use previously under U.S. tax law, but would like to take advantage of before they expire.[21] The manufacturer could change the delivery (and title passage) point from New Orleans to Le Havre. Typically, no additional foreign income taxes are incurred when a seller transfers a title to the international jurisdiction where the product is shipped. Most countries only tax sales that occur within their jurisdictions.

If the sale of the boat results in $200,000 of taxable income, with one half of that attributable to foreign sourcing of income, then the company's unused excess foreign tax credits can be used to reduce its U.S. tax liability related to the *foreign* part of the sale. One advantage of using this option is that it will cause minimal changes in actual operations (though the foreign title passage generally alters shipping and insurance terms of the sale). Table 8.3 illustrates the mechanics of this calculation.

The additional costs incurred by the manufacturer to ship and insure the product from its loading docks in New Orleans to the location where title passes, Le Havre, should be transferred to the customer. The customer would be unlikely to object as the overall charges would be similar if the title had passed in New Orleans—the

(continued)

Table 8.3   Changing Title Passage to Generate Additional Foreign Source Income to Address an "Excess Foreign Tax Credit" Position

Foreign Title Passage: Sales of U.S.-Manufactured Products

Sales	$1,000,000
Costs and Expenses	($800,000)
Taxable Income	$200,000
U.S. Tax @ 35%[†]	$70,000
Foreign Source Income @ 50%[‡]	$100,000
Excess Foreign Tax Credits Available	$100,000
Foreign Tax Credit @ 35%[§]	$35,000
Net U.S. Tax After FTC[¶]	$35,000
U.S. Effective Tax Rate	17.50%

[†]$200,000 Taxable Income *35% Tax Rate.
[‡]$200,000 Taxable Income *50% Foreign Source Percentage from Foreign Title Passage.
[§]$100,000 Foreign Source Income *35% Tax Rate, Limited by Foreign Tax Credits Available.
[¶]$70,000 U.S. Tax Liability Less 35,000 Foreign Tax Credit.

customer would have needed to ship and insure the vessel anyway. In addition, the customer would have added time to defer payment until the transfer occurs.

All of these issues must be considered by the company during negotiations with the buyer. In addition, the company must decide whether the deferral of income is acceptable in return for gaining the tax credits. Because contracts can be difficult to amend, a change in title transfer may not be feasible (or acceptable to present to the client). However, if the company has a large number of soon-to-expire excess tax credits, it may be more motivated to make concessions to get the buyer to accept the modification. Often, changing contractual terms regarding title passage on intercompany sales overseas is easier than negotiating with third-party buyers.

Sales Compensation and Tax Planning.   As with other aspects of pricing processes and policies, sales compensation guidelines can thwart well-conceived tax planning. For example, consider the ramifications if, as discussed above, an organization decides to transfer title to the goods it produces abroad to take advantage of its excess tax credit position. This policy change might result in the sales team's not receiving credit in the same manner that it would with a U.S. title passage. If the organization pays quarterly sales bonuses based upon these "U.S." transactions, then what incentive is there for a salesperson to sign a contract that creates foreign source income?

Title transfer is not the only situation where a sales team can undermine tax goals. Many corporations have set up HubCos that operate as centralized purchasing and distribution companies. If the sales team does not understand how to use the structure correctly, then there can be costly consequences. For example, in one MNO, sales personnel were selling through the HubCo but making independent decisions on how the goods were to be shipped based on timing and logistical costs. What this meant was that Sales was sometimes having orders transported directly from warehouses (located in different jurisdictions) to the customer and bypassing the HubCo. This created additional VAT liabilities for the MNO of potentially tens of millions of Euros. To avoid this problem, organizations should ensure both that their salespeople are properly educated about the use of HubCos and that an appropriate incentive and rewards system is established that reinforces the right behavior.

Managing Pricing and Compliance Costs to Maximize Returns

There is a common cost of business related to both taxes and governmental regulations: compliance-related expenses. These include:

- Obtaining business licenses and permits
- Retaining multiple documentation to substantiate positions
- Calculating amounts owed to the tax authorities and other regulatory bodies
- Paying the parties who perform the calculations, fill out the necessary forms, and defend audits.

While some of these costs, such as procuring a business license, apply to all revenue streams, others apply only to certain jurisdictions or business lines (or combinations of the two). In some situations, firms may find that it makes sense to allocate these costs to specific products, services, or distribution centers in particular jurisdictions. For example, a retailer that decides to sell alcoholic beverages will have to meet jurisdictional requirements (e.g., participate in state-approved employee training) and will incur expenses (e.g., licensing fees) directly attributable to the new offering.

By examining profitability at a granular level, management can see what each product and service brings in, and how changes in compliance costs may affect the business if it enters a new market in a new jurisdiction. Management can then set prices that incorporate these added expenses instead of throwing all compliance and regulatory costs into the selling, general, and administrative (SG&A) expense bucket, where their allocation across all sales can be less meaningful for decision making.

VAT regimes raise some of the most complicated compliance issues—and can, as a result, expose companies to onerous tax liabilities or leakage because of the different rules and rates that apply according to the jurisdiction involved. U.S. companies are more likely to find that they have created a VAT registration liability as opposed to an income tax liability (through the creation of a permanent establishment), because a lower threshold of activity is needed to generate the former. For this reason, companies need to be particularly careful as they transact business around the world. When addressing VAT rules for a sale, companies must at least determine:

- Whether the constituent parts of each transaction being sold are goods or services, or both
- In which jurisdiction (country) the VAT will be levied
- If the supplier or the buyer will be responsible for VAT accounting
- Whether there is a VAT registration obligation for the seller
- Whether any VAT simplifications apply
- What the VAT invoicing requirements are
- The proper rate to apply:
  - Is the transaction subject to the standard VAT rate?
  - Does a reduced or zero rate apply?
  - Is the transaction exempt from VAT?
  - Does the transaction fall outside the scope of VAT?

Some ERP systems have the capability to help manage this process, but they require continual updating. Where should the costs to perform this updating be charged? Does the nature of the organization's business suggest that these compliance costs should be allocated to particular revenue streams? Not all revenue streams are subject to VAT regimes; for example, products produced in the U.S. and sold locally.

Organizations must keep in mind that to be VAT compliant and to take advantage of refundable VATs, they may need to register with the appropriate tax authorities. In some cases, more than one entity or jurisdiction (or both) might be involved in the creation of the product, depending on the entity's supply chain and legal structure, so multiple VAT registrations and filings may well be required. The example in Figure 8.4 shows the large number of potential VAT *triggers* that could exist in a typical supply chain in a single jurisdiction.

For pricing purposes, sales personnel must be kept up to date on changes in VAT laws that could affect the cost of sales to both the buyer and the organization. They must also be educated in how VAT is triggered, and why nonrecoverable VAT costs and expenses are allocated to specific revenue streams.

Compliance costs can also include the expenses involved with obtaining visas and creating the necessary filings (e.g., income tax) that organizations

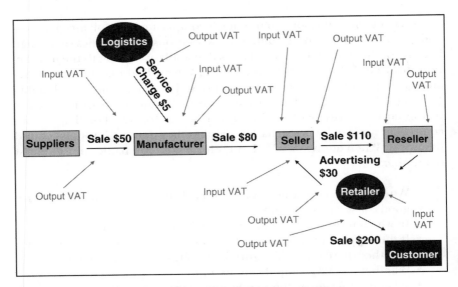

Figure 8.4   VAT Trigger Points in a Typical Supply Chain

bear on behalf of their employees. As noted earlier, when workers are sent abroad on long-term assignments, these costs should be estimated accurately to price the affected product or service properly. Organizations selling services should be especially wary of contracts that cap expense reimbursement based upon a percentage (e.g., 10 percent) of total fees. Travel expenses and tax-equalization payments can quickly eat through the funds in a negotiated reimbursement scheme.

Another hidden cost for companies can arise from the use of customs brokers. The CBP licenses, regulates, and empowers brokers to assist exporters and importers in complying with U.S.-government requirements applying to exports and imports.[22] Approximately 16,000 licensed brokers operate in the U.S., and many more around the world are regulated by their resident countries. How can customs brokers affect pricing? The key factor is the number a company employs. A rationalization review could reveal that using a large number of brokers is less effective than maintaining relationships with only a few. A more streamlined process might produce compliance savings, while also allowing the company to leverage its purchasing power with the remaining brokers (i.e., negotiating for reduced fees through economies of scale). A company can significantly lower import costs by streamlining operations and reducing brokerage fees.

Compliance Benefits

Tax departments have not traditionally had access to the granular data captured by pricing models. But with better organizational alignment between Tax and Pricing, the former can use the information to file more complete and accurate tax returns. If a company has already completed a transactional pricing assessment, then that data set should be shared with Tax, which will be able to improve its ability to track sales amounts and costs related to particular jurisdictions instead of relying upon the product-level rollups that it often receives. The information can also help determine if policies established for tax purposes are being followed. For example, the profit waterfall may indicate that a product has been shipped directly to a customer instead of going through a distribution chain, thereby increasing tax exposure for the company.

Although the cash benefits are difficult to quantify, making this transactional data available to the tax department should allow for a more efficient compliance process. Combining this action with better management of the company's jurisdictional exposure should further improve its margin.

Navigating Regulatory Environments When Making Pricing Decisions

Regulations vary considerably across geographical boundaries at both national and regional levels. State, federal, and international laws can present considerable challenges to firms when they implement pricing programs and structure transactions. For this reason, firms must seek regulatory interpretations from their legal counsels before making any major pricing decisions.

In general, regulations affecting pricing fall into four major categories: international and domestic trade agreements, restrictions, and certifications; collusion and price fixing; bundling; and price discrimination. All the laws influencing regulation cannot practically be cited here, but we touch on the general principles in the following.

International and Domestic Trade Agreements

Regulations affecting sales price present the greatest issues flowing from international trade agreements. Taxation, tariffs, and transfer prices have already been addressed in this chapter. Companies must, however, evaluate the impact of product costing and trade agreements when considering pricing. In the health care and defense industries, for instance, the U.S. government has a best price requirement for its purchases. This requires analytics and oversight to understand the impact of favorable prices earned through discounts to large customers, so that these prices do not inadvertently trigger a requirement to lower the price offered to the federal government. Furthermore, pricing contracts often contain language that references best price guarantees.

The North American Free Trade Agreement (NAFTA) and other trade agreements have provisions that impact price and tariff requirements. For instance, if product shortage occurs at one location, then compensating by providing product from another location can have a considerable impact—particularly if the agreement specifies discounts or exemptions from taxes or duties based on where raw materials are obtained, where the product is produced or made, and where the product is sold. Violations of agreements like these can instantly make a product price uncompetitive. This is particularly true when the violation results in products being sold at or below cost (also known as *predatory pricing*), which is considered anticompetitive behavior and is illegal in many countries.

Collusion and Price Fixing

The second major regulatory concern involves collusion and price fixing. In most countries, it is illegal for competing entities to work together to set the price for a product in the marketplace. In a free market economy, competition generally leads to lower prices. Companies that engage in price fixing can prevent this from occurring. The penalties for companies engaging in these behaviors are severe. Obviously, organizations must continually make employees aware of these laws as well as the harsh penalties attached to any violations. Management must also put in place internal controls to prevent violations at any level of the company.

Bundling

Bundling in and of itself is not illegal, though this is a commonly held misconception. In fact, bundling is a valuable and appropriate strategy for increasing the number of goods sold within a category. Food service companies do it regularly, and the practice is common with electronics retailers too (e.g., buy a Nintendo Wii and receive two games). In general, products that are intimately linked can be bundled, as long as this does not create an anticompetitive outcome. Bundles are considered illegal if they result in an anticompetitive *tying* situation, where the market strength of the initial product is sufficient to impact the competitive situation in the market of the second product. In *United States v. Loew's, Inc.* (1962), the purchase of rights for popular films for television was conditioned on customers also buying the rights for less popular films. The ruling held that forcing television stations to acquire these lesser films precluded them from purchasing rival or alternate products and therefore was anticompetitive.[23] Subsequent court cases have further clarified the situations where tying is illegal. Bundles, therefore, must be considered carefully for legality, but can be used in a variety of situations to improve overall sales and profitability.

Pricing and Antitrust Regulation

Companies must remain up to date on all laws and regulations governing anti-competitive practices and monopolies to make sure all transactions are conducted according to these laws and regulations. Legislation such as the Clayton Antitrust and the Sherman Acts define these prohibited practices. They further stipulate that mergers and acquisitions must be reviewed by a regulatory body to ensure the proposed combined organization does not significantly limit competition in the marketplace or produce a monopoly.

Other legislation such as the Robinson-Patman Act is designed to protect the consumer from both monopolistic and discriminatory behavior. The Sherman and the Clayton Antitrust Acts also address these practices and prohibit manufacturers from controlling the market, forcing out competition due to their size, and manipulating prices to resellers. Robinson-Patman further specifies that a company cannot sell a product to competing companies at different prices except under specific exceptions such as a real difference in cost to serve or expiring inventory. In all cases, however, if companies can match the same service level and requirements, the price under which the product is sold must be the same. This can limit the amount and type of discounts that may be provided to a variety of customers. Both the Sherman and the Clayton Acts address elements of price fixing. They prohibit the restriction of supply, exclusive dealings, and collaboration between rivals to increase the price of a good.

Again, continuing education of all affected Pricing, Sales, and corporate functions must be maintained, so that employees are kept apprised of the relevant laws, and policies must be developed and enforced to ensure these laws are followed.

The complex issues surrounding the tax and regulatory environment require careful attention and the support of counsel and tax professionals to prevent, to the extent possible, litigation, audits, and investigations. Moreover, careful attention to these complex issues can improve both pricing processes and cash flow. All too often organizations don't take these critical factors into account when making pricing and profitability decisions, which leads to substandard outcomes. Despite their complexity, these concepts must be incorporated into the foundation of the organization.

Where to Go from Here?

The regulatory environment provides an overarching framework for pricing and profitability decisions, and it can impose significant restrictions. Actions cannot be taken unilaterally by salespeople. Instead, all pricing processes, policies, and decisions must be reviewed for legality and to prevent significant and potentially costly pricing mistakes from being made. As we have discussed, regulation and licensure affect pricing in a variety of ways depending on the type of product or service as well as the sales jurisdiction.

Regulatory issues must become a standard part of the pricing equation; otherwise, what appears to be a solid pricing policy can be undermined by unforeseen taxes, fees, and charges, as well as by compliance costs. Incorporating regulatory considerations throughout the pricing and profitability management lifecycle is critical for maintaining—and improving—the competitive position of a business.

With a little education, improved policies, and a closer alignment of the tax and pricing functions, companies can make profit improvements to the *real* bottom line: after-tax net income. By taking certain steps, companies can incorporate tax considerations more effectively into pricing processes, policies, and strategies. These include determining:

- Current tax and regulatory attributes and strategies for using these attributes most effectively
- Tax and regulatory regimes that apply to the current supply chain or delivery system
- Where jurisdictional boundaries are crossed and how this would affect the types of regimes identified
- Where the best opportunities are for savings (at a high level)
- How best to use transactional data to aggregate transactions and to verify the cost savings amounts.

Here are some key points firms should consider when addressing the costs related to tax and regulatory regimes:

- The materiality of certain taxes and how they affect an organization's competitiveness. Business conducted in just a few jurisdictions within a single country will rarely present the complex issues that large MNOs must confront. The more tax regimes from different jurisdictions come into play, the greater the exposure.
- Where taxes and regulatory costs should be incorporated into the pricing picture: jurisdictional, regional, product, or transactional level.
- What modeling techniques should be applied to evaluate the company's potential after-tax position when considering modifications of the supply chain.
- How to conduct an ongoing assessment to ensure that the business's tax activities are keeping pace with operational changes (e.g., manufacturing companies that have had their operations and equipment sold off to a competitor, but continue to generate revenues in the form of royalty payments from IP upon which the former operations were based).
- The current jurisdictions where filings are being prepared should be reviewed to determine if a nexus or PE can be eliminated, thereby reducing exposure.
- Whether the business would benefit by consolidating the customs brokers being used under the organization's current operating model.

Endnotes

1. Internal Revenue Code: I.R.C. §§41 and 199.
2. International Financial Reporting Standards (IFRS) and Generally Accepted Accounting Principles (GAAP) provide rules and guidelines for financial reporting purposes. When compared to the tax rules of a jurisdiction (e.g., those propagated by HM Revenue and Customs in the U.K.), there will be some differences in the way that income is calculated that will be of either a temporary (reverses over time) or a permanent nature. The tax provision process helps to calculate those differences for IFRS and GAAP reporting purposes and apply those differences to either the IFRS and GAAP earnings statement or the balance sheet as appropriate.
3. Laura Preslan, "Price Management: Conventional Wisdom Is Wrong," *AMR Research Outlook*, February 2, 2004, 1.
4. After-tax numbers calculated as follows:

$$2\% \times (1 - 0.38) = 1.24\%$$

$$7\% \times (1 - 0.38) = 4.34\%$$

5. A permanent establishment is defined as a fixed place of business through which the business of an enterprise is wholly or partially carried on. This definition is used within virtually all modern tax treaties in establishing the ability to tax unincorporated activities. *Nexus* is a similar concept used by states for assessing taxes related to income generating activities.
6. Others might be related to financing and repatriation of earnings.
7. In instances where businesses are owned (directly or indirectly) by U.S. shareholders, additional review is required to analyze the Subpart F rules of the Internal Revenue Code to determine if the desired benefit can be achieved.
8. Residence-based taxation is where taxes are assessed on all of a person's or an organization's income (regardless of source and location derived) under the principle that these taxpayers should contribute to the public coffers where they reside because that is where they receive public services. Source taxation connects the jurisdiction providing the opportunity to earn the income with the right to tax profits earned from that opportunity.
9. Internal Revenue Code: I.R.C. §199.
10. The 3.15 percent ETR reduction is determined by multiplying the 9 percent deduction factor by the U.S. statutory rate for corporations of 35 percent.
11. A tax equalization policy is a set of rules a company establishes to create a *tax neutral* effect for its employees that work outside of their home jurisdiction. As an example, a U.S. citizen or resident who takes a one-year assignment in the U.K. would typically be subject to double taxation. To tax equalize this employee, the company might compare the total amount of income taxes (for all jurisdictions) that the employee was legally obligated to pay against a hypothetical amount of what the employee would have been liable for if he or she did not take the assignment. The difference between those two amounts would result in a true-up or tax equalization payment between the employer and the employee.
12. These items, which are included as additional compensation for the assignment, are often taxed in both the home and the host countries.

13. Service centers are often proficient in providing programming, data processing, and so forth, which are integrated into deliverables to clients. They can contribute to the start of a workflow or add value to the engagement at various points along the process flow.
14. The MNO originally planned to bill from its U.S. legal entity to the client's U.S. legal entity. The services were performed by a South American subsidiary of the MNO for a South American subsidiary of the client. The services provided were subject to VAT.
15. Items for which the VAT is non-refundable vary by jurisdiction (but typically include vehicle costs and business entertainment). Categories of services that are often exempt from VAT include postal services, education, medical care, financial services, and insurance.
16. Also, in the U.S., Section 1059A of the Internal Revenue Code ties the inventory price for tax purposes to customs value in many cases.
17. Transfer pricing methodologies include comparable uncontrolled price method (CUP), resale price method (RPM), cost plus (CP), comparable profits method (CPM), and profit split (PS).
18. The six methods' hierarchy for determining the *transaction value* for customs purposes is: (1) transactional value actually paid or payable, (2) transaction value of identical goods, (3) transaction value of similar goods, (4) computed value (cost plus expenses), (5) deductive value (resale less profit, transportation, and other expenses), and (6) fallback value.
19. For example, a computer manufacturer sells hardware and a maintenance contract to service that hardware directly to consumers. Some states will apply different sales tax rates to different classes of sales (e.g., goods versus services). In the case of a bundled sale where the price of the hardware and the maintenance contract are combined on the invoice, the same rate will likely be applied to both items. At the end of the year, multiplying the sales of hardware by the sales tax rate for goods and adding that to the maintenance contract sales by the applicable rate for that class will likely not equal the amount of sales tax remitted.
20. Internal Revenue Code: I.R.C. §863(b).
21. Unused (excess) foreign tax credits can be carried forward for up to a period of 10 years by a U.S. company before they expire. Failure to use the foreign tax credits within the carry forward period may have financial statement consequences if a tax benefit for the credits was taken in a prior period. If a company is unable to utilize the foreign tax credits, it is possible to claim a deduction for the foreign tax as an alternative to achieving some tax benefit, albeit less than the benefit derived from the foreign tax credit.
22. U.S. Department of Homeland Security, CBP website, http://www.cbp.gov/xp/cgov/trade/trade_programs/broker/brokers.xml.
23. *United States v. Loew's, Inc.* (1962), accessed from http://supreme.justia.com/us/371/38/case.html.

Pricing as a Sustainable Competitive Advantage

Great things are done by a series of small things brought together.
—Vincent van Gogh

Why Taking a Holistic Approach to Pricing Matters

Big Track Automotive (a fictional company, but reflecting a typical situation and solution that can apply to real companies) sells high-performance engines around the world. Boosted by a loyal customer base, some high-profile endorsements, and top ratings from leading consumer magazines, Big Track grew for 10 straight years. To improve profitability still further, the company decided to spend a significant amount of money to implement a new pricing software package. Using sophisticated mathematical models, the software identified key price points that would optimize the price–volume trade offs for each customer segment. The company projected that implementing these prices would add millions of dollars to the bottom line. Senior management signed off on the changes and looked forward to a banner year.

Twelve months later reality hit. The CEO was astounded to discover that profitability had not increased at all. An investigation revealed why: the sales force had been giving discounts on more than 30 percent of the company's best-selling products, canceling out the projected revenue increases. When asked why they offered so many discounts, the salespeople claimed that customers wouldn't buy at the company's targeted price. Unfortunately, the team responsible for implementing the software didn't have the budget to
(continued)

(*Continued*)
train the sales representatives to sell at the higher prices, nor did it have the authority to change their incentives. The CEO eventually realized he would either have to spend more time and money to align the salespeople with the new pricing models, or abandon the price improvement effort altogether. Unfortunately, a global recession had recently started, and Big Track didn't have the funds to make the necessary adjustments. Ironically, if the company had correctly implemented the program, it would have been better able to weather the recession. Instead, the company was forced to abandon the effort and never recovered its initial investment.

Big Track's situation reflects the two dilemmas faced by many companies undergoing pricing improvement initiatives: (1) how to achieve the greatest return on investment; and (2) how to sustain the initial benefits over the long term. As one CFO of a global manufacturer told us, "the 5 percent of revenue we took to the bottom line is big in absolute terms, but it is very small relative to the benefits we could achieve if we could just maintain the behavior after the consultants leave."

Indeed, as we've demonstrated throughout this book, a consistent focus on pricing and profitability can yield impressive results. While some improvement opportunities offer one-time benefits, the vast majority of them tend to be recurring and to compound over time. Yet an uncoordinated effort or a failure to make the required organizational or process changes, will not only undermine the original business case, but also likely cause an organization to sacrifice margin improvement that could have totaled 10 or even 100 times the initial benefits realized.

How can a company increase its chances of success? We believe the answer lies in the approach it takes. Each of the six competencies discussed in the previous chapters can provide value individually. But these benefits can be super-sized if the improvements are coordinated with advances in the other five competencies. In fact, they must be coordinated—a company's overall performance could actually worsen if changes are made in one of these interdependent functions without considering the others (see Figure 1.4 on page 16). For example, a firm that tries to upgrade its price-setting process could actually damage profitability if it does not simultaneously improve its price execution. As Big Track discovered, sales representatives must be properly trained and incentivized, or they will tend to offset price increases by issuing bigger discounts to favorite customers. Similarly, an organization that undertakes a pricing improvement project without considering its tax implications might suddenly find itself hit with higher fees or required payments to regulatory bodies. These extra charges could mean that the organization sacrifices its additional margin entirely, while still being left with the bill for revamping its price-setting process. However, coordinating the improvement efforts across multiple competencies can have an accretive effect, as we demonstrate in the case study below.

Bringing it All Together: A Case Study

The first year is an achievement. The second year's a duty.
An executive with a global beverage distributor during
an author's interview.

The following case history, while fictionalized, nevertheless reflects the typical experiences of various global companies that have successfully implemented holistic pricing transformations. Finding itself faced with new stresses on its business, Chocolate Delight, a global confectioner, invested millions of dollars to strengthen its pricing capabilities. The company had been facing increasingly aggressive tactics from rivals as well as rising cocoa, production, and distribution costs. Management believed that optimized pricing would offer the confectioner its best chance to improve profitability in the current environment.

To accomplish this, Chocolate Delight would need to address some complex issues. To start with, the sheer size and diversity of the company's functional units (predominantly located in Europe and North America) posed challenges. In addition, the company, which sold to customers around the world, had to factor in widely varying global market dynamics. The preferences for chocolate differed drastically between Europe and North America; so, too, did willingness to pay and quality standards, which forced Chocolate Delight to establish drastically different pricing strategies in the two markets. For example, in some European countries the firm had established a leading position for a line of boutique, high-end chocolates. But its more accessible, less expensive brands had only secured a limited market share.

In the U.S. the reverse was true: the boutique product lines weren't successful but the cheaper candy bars had some success. The confectioner had established some successful candy bar lines while also supplying chocolate product to many packaged-good companies for cookies, cake mixes, and other products. But the boutique chocolate lines were showing limited profitability.

The CEO, who had seen the consequences of failed pricing efforts earlier in her career, organized teams led by some of her most talented leaders in each competency. Each functional group was able to discuss its needs and make suggestions. Integration issues were identified and resolved. When there were disputes, the CEO made the final decision. After three months, the team settled on an approach. The group decided that it would need to draw on advanced analytics, new pricing technology, and better data management. In addition, organizational resources were committed to support the new strategy and ensure effective execution.

Because the company now operated in so many countries and jurisdictions, the CEO also tasked her tax function to examine day-to-day operations for additional savings that could be generated through increased efficiencies. Each team was then given three months to devise a plan laying out its activities and milestones. The VP of Marketing was appointed overseer, and he reviewed and managed the day-to-day development of the execution plan.

Integrating Advanced Analytics, Pricing Technology, and Data Management

Because the chocolate company had already engaged on a multi-year initiative to implement an expensive ERP system, management was careful to integrate this into its thinking. A new pricing software application had been selected so the project team laid out a plan to ensure it would complement, not interfere with, the larger ERP project.

Before the new pricing application was implemented, Chocolate Delight's technology team methodically determined the functional and technical requirements that would be needed. It also identified gaps in current capabilities. For example, the organization needed to capture accurately the fluctuations in commodity prices (i.e., sugar and cocoa, which were key ingredients) to understand true product costs and, ultimately, to calculate true profitability. The team worked with the software vendor to develop additional functionality to support these requirements. Meanwhile, the price execution team gathered two years of historical transaction data on chocolate sales worldwide. Some data integration issues were resolved in the process, which allowed the group to assign the national and local media spend to the right brands and markets at the transaction level.

The group conducted TPA-type analyses and identified short- to medium-term pricing improvement opportunities. For example, they recommended differentiating price points based on the SKUs sold in each sales channel, including grocery, convenience, and club stores. The advanced analytics team added behavioral and market data to model price elasticity and expected changes in purchasing behavior based on price adjustments. They also optimized the product mix suggested for each retailer and region based on their desired price points.

The analytics team had to contend with some special issues that complicated their assignment. The cocoa market was subject to high price volatility, so the group had to determine how much to raise prices (if at all) to accommodate higher costs. It also had to keep in mind that some customers and brands were more elastic than others. For example, rising food costs in the U.K. led consumers to be less willing to spend on chocolate, particularly the premium brands. On the other hand, the growing health-conscious sector in the U.S. had led to an increased demand for the dark chocolate products.

Taking these factors into account, the analytics group calculated the new prices and identified potential margin improvements. The company also mobilized a team to work directly with the sales force to improve price execution. But that effort would become part of a more fundamental organizational realignment.

Achieving Organizational—Especially Sales—Alignment with the New Strategy

After an extensive internal review, the management team identified the alignment of Sales as the greatest organizational priority. A number of issues were identified, including the need to give extensive training to employees and reconfigure their incentives programs.

The retail purchasing agents buying from Chocolate Delight were generally quite sophisticated. These agents routinely approached sales representatives with a wealth of data regarding the quantities and pricing offered by all of their suppliers as well as their own market and consumer demand forecasts. They were tough, informed negotiators, so Chocolate Delight decided that a *high-touch* approach would be needed to prepare the sales force for the difficult conversations that the new pricing guidelines would inspire.

The changes in processes, operational policies, and guidelines (price execution) required a detailed and thorough review of each sales representative's accounts, including the number and amount of each type of discount used (e.g., rebate, volume discount, and payment terms) on every transaction for the previous year. The analytics group used this historical data to create negotiating models for each customer with targets for each form of discount. A support team then went into the field with the sales representatives armed with spreadsheets of pricing data to explain to the customers the reasoning behind, and impact of, the changes. The analytics group expected resistance from the sales representatives and expected to hear a list of reasons justifying their past behavior and explaining why the new targets would be unachievable. However, something completely unexpected happened. Instead of exhibiting defensive behavior and a reluctance to change, salespeople appeared with smiles on their faces and even showed up before their personal evaluations were scheduled. They were looking forward to their individual reviews and weren't embarrassed by the numbers projected on the wall for their superiors to see. The representatives expressed appreciation for the attention they were receiving and the personal help they were getting to improve. The company had never given them performance guidelines before beyond the simplistic mantra of "sell more."

For the first time in their career, representatives could see how their individual actions, no matter how small, affected the performance of a very large corporation. And for the first time, employees began operating with a sense of ownership. They started to make decisions that were based on the long-term success of the entire enterprise, instead of the size of their own individual commissions. Notably, at this point in the manufacturer's pricing improvement program, the sales incentives had not yet been changed; many representatives were motivated to adjust their behavior solely by the increased transparency of the process. The combination of the price analytics and price execution competencies had made the true profitability of each transaction as well as its effect on the company's overall performance much clearer.

As discussed in Chapter 6, "Achieving Effective Organizational Alignment and Governance," aligning compensation and incentives is critical to the success of any pricing improvement initiative. But, as this chocolate manufacturer discovered, additional benefits can be achieved depending on when the issue of compensation (re)alignment is tackled. During the first round of implementation, which focused on a small pilot region, only vague references were made to changing the pay of sales representatives at some point during a future rollout. No specifics were offered. Of equal importance, the pricing and profitability data used for the pilot customers had been separated from the core data used to calculate commissions and other sales incentives.

Thus, while many sales representatives could see how the new system might be an advantage to them, others still wondered how they would benefit personally. The unspecified changes and unknown time frames, noted above, led some in the sales organization to doubt the sincerity and the longevity of the changes. Employees believed the company had failed to think through all of the details.

Management heard these concerns and made the necessary adjustments. For the next rollout, the team was better prepared to address the doubters. The issue of compensation was addressed at the same time as the other changes were taking place in analytics, execution, strategy, and technology. New compensation plans were communicated from the first day. The price analytics team was able to simulate the effects on each individual sales representative's accounts (including projected compensation) based on the targeted discount levels each was given. The field support team was able to review and adjust the targets based on the representatives' feedback on the simulations. The demonstration changed how the sales force viewed the new dashboards and tools: it made them real. Suddenly, they could understand how to use the new waterfalls and other pricing analyses to configure a deal that was good for both the company and their own paychecks. They trusted the data and believed it provided a single version of the truth because both their compensation and the company's actual profit were based on it.

Ensuring Optimal Price Execution

Like many companies, optimized prices for each of Chocolate Delight's products were established centrally (i.e., by corporate) and negotiations were done in the field. A certain amount of discounting was allowed. There was a natural tension that had evolved over the years between the two functions; the field team believed the list prices didn't reflect the realities of its markets, and the centralized corporate team believed the field team was giving away too much during the negotiation process. Each blamed the other for the suboptimal results of their pricing decisions. Both were right.

To strengthen pricing management, the company realized it would have to improve (and better integrate) both optimization and execution activities. First, the corporate team began using econometric models to calculate list prices. Consultants were brought in to refine the forecasting models and formulas still further. This eliminated the argument from the field team that prices were wrong to begin with. No longer could Sales claim that the target prices were too high or didn't reflect current market conditions. The mathematical formulas used to calculate and optimize the list prices were as good as they could possibly be. The sales representatives realized that these calculations—and the massive amount of data that fed them—could actually help them be more effective in their negotiations.

Second, because the price setting and price execution analyses were conducted in tandem, the company could clearly see, in advance, how the adjustments would affect their customers. For example, if the combined impact of price increases (from the optimization effort) and discount reductions (from the execution phase) would potentially result in too drastic a change for a major retail customer, then the team could develop a schedule to introduce the price increases gradually. Furthermore, the negotiation *guardrails* that were honed as part of the price execution improvements helped ensure the price changes were not undermined during negotiations. The clarity and precision of these policies made it easier on the sales representatives to make better pricing decisions and to negotiate deals that supported the new corporate margin targets.

Finally, and most important, the simultaneous work on execution created a feedback loop between the corporate group assigned to optimize prices and the field sales group that actually negotiated with customers. The representatives monitored the actual prices and quantities realized with buyers and sent this behavioral data to the econometricians to compare to the predictions of their optimization models. If the two sets of numbers were too dissimilar, then the corporate team could decide either to reset prices again or to get the field representatives back in line with the policies. In other words, the centralized group could continuously tweak its model to improve its accuracy, which produced more responsive and dynamic pricing overall.

As Chocolate Delight discovered, its efforts to improve pricing analytics and execution enhanced the pricing requirements and system configuration phases and so better addressed the true needs of the business. Managers referred to their TPA phase as a mirror that reflected what did and did not work in the company's previous approach to pricing management. Because the company had the results of these analyses while defining system requirements, it was able to create a system that more effectively supported the improved pricing processes. The internal assessment team was also able to better identify the analyses the software solution truly needed to produce. And because the group was strengthening pricing analytics amidst the technology implementation, it was able to detail more precisely the specific requirements, data fields, and calculations that were needed to support the business.

In the case of Chocolate Delight, handling optimization and execution together brought another benefit. As one executive commented, "the greatest cost of a software implementation is reimplementation. We did it right the first time and avoided costly rework."

Getting Tax Involved

As part of its holistic approach to pricing improvement, the CEO made a key decision to invite Tax to sit in on the cross-functional discussions. This was a first. The tax department had never previously been involved in a pricing transformation. But as the global scope of the operation unfolded, it became clear that the pricing and profitability management improvement team would benefit from its input.

For example, Chocolate Delight had some business-to-business customers with whom it negotiated long-term contracts. After conducting an analysis, Tax recommended coordinating business operations, where possible, with jurisdictions that provide a competitive tax advantage. The recommendations included a suggested re-evaluation of the delivery points for shipments in Europe (when the current shipping contracts expired). The company had current plans to consolidate distribution centers, so it was proposed that tax rates be included as a consideration. Finally, because Chocolate Delight lacked the necessary internal expertise, Tax suggested obtaining outside assistance to negotiate the proposed site for a new, expanded plant with the various jurisdictions (national, provincial, and local). This would potentially enable the company to take advantage of government-sponsored credits and incentives tied to hiring new employees (e.g., training grants). The outside experts could also help obtain other income and property tax abatements. By recommending these long-term operational changes, Tax helped Chocolate Delight achieve major cost savings. Sales also benefited because the lower production costs gave them more room to negotiate prices with major customers.

Tax and Legal also set up training for sales representatives to explain how critical contract terms could affect the overall profitability of deals (added customs duties, taxes, and other levies). A new policy further required that all sales contracts be approved by Legal and referred to Tax for further review if the dollar value reached a certain threshold. These combined savings significantly benefited the company. The policy also stopped sales representatives from agreeing to disadvantageous terms in their efforts to close deals, which had been a persistent problem.

Assessing the Benefits

As Chocolate Delight discovered, taking a comprehensive approach to pricing and profitability management benefited the company more than focusing on a single competency. The firm was able to treat the initiative as a portfolio with various elements, some of which were used to subsidize others at different points in time. For example, Chocolate Delight recognized that its sales team would require daily coaching and follow up to maintain momentum and to quell any unreasonable resistance to the proposed changes. But at 100 interactions per day, this high-touch approach was time-consuming and resource intensive. So the company strategically scheduled the execution efforts to follow a more benefit-rich TPA effort. The rewards from the TPA were used to fund the execution improvements (particularly sales training), essentially allowing the company to move ahead with new steps in its pricing program, while other, slower-developing benefits were being realized.

When Chocolate Delight assessed the results of the pricing and profitability initiative, the leadership team agreed it had been an overwhelming success. Not only had all the individual functions achieved their goals, but also the integration with the larger ERP project had worked seamlessly. Most important, profitability had increased year over year (YOY) by nearly 10 percent, despite higher expenses in the cocoa market.

The chocolate manufacturer's CEO had another reason to be pleased. The holistic approach to pricing had required the VPs from Sales, Marketing, and Finance to work together in a way they never had before. This brought other long-term benefits:

- Employees began to think about what could be done strategically, rather than focusing solely on their own operational functions. The entire organization now saw possibilities instead of limitations or obligations.
- The company as a whole became more aware of competitors. Chocolate Delight could react more effectively to the activities of its rivals by using the tools of effective pricing management—including the knowledge that different functional areas could unite to take effective action.

- The CEO's leadership and her decision to create an integrated approach drawing on leaders from all the critical functions reinforced internally how important the initiative was to the company. Moreover, by putting the right people with the necessary skills on the pricing team, the CEO ensured that the essential pricing analysis was done right and also that *all* of the strengths of the company were leveraged effectively.

Emerging Trends in Pricing and Profitability Management

In the years ahead, both large and small customers will continue to push the limits of current business models and expectations to capitalize on the power and complexity of pricing and profitability management. Sellers have found that, to stay competitive, they must learn to operate in many arenas, while staying current with new technologies and meeting increasing customer expectations for products.

Significant trends in the pricing arena—internal and external—are emerging, which are driving companies to further develop their capabilities. Here are some of them.

Multi-Channel Integration

In business-to-consumer businesses, the traditional views on the role of stores, catalogs, websites, and call centers are changing at warp speed. Consumers expect a company to offer them the opportunity to transact business across all channels or their loyalty is quickly lost. For example, most large pizza delivery companies now accept orders from walk-ins, by phone, or over the internet.

Suppliers realize, too, that trade promotion investments aimed at only one channel will likely have limited impact and sustainability. The risks of failing to provide an integrated experience across multiple channels can impact customers, retailers, and suppliers. Consumers will continue to be curious and active only if they can explore all of a retailer's channels. If the products and prices are not consistent across the store, catalog, and website, then the retailer risks a significant drop in customer satisfaction and price perception. And, of course, a decline in sales will also affect suppliers.

In fact, shareholders now expect companies to maximize each interaction point in each channel to maximize performance. To achieve true multi-channel integration, however, a company must knock down long-standing organizational silos and align performance metrics with *total company goals*. Companies that take the comprehensive approach to pricing that we have laid out will not only avoid channel conflict, but also be able to capitalize on multi-channel improvements. They will have the ability to understand how customers are shopping through the available channels and to track demand down to the category and item level. Businesses can use that knowledge and advanced analytic capabilities to model customer behavior across all channels. This can help in optimizing trade promotion events and everyday pricing to improve consumer confidence and price perception.

A major outdoor supplies company made significant investments to adopt a truly integrated multi-channel experience for its customers. The company installed Internet kiosks in its stores, ensured that its print catalogs directed customers to the company's website, which, in turn, referred buyers to the local store in their area. Online discounts coupons could even be printed and brought into the store for use with purchases. The company's integrated strategy was markedly successful: online visitors spent, on average, 22 percent more in their stores than offline-only customers.

Personalization of Customer Interaction

Companies need to consider every interaction a customer has with them. These interactions can be as simple as a call to customer service, a discussion with a sales associate, navigation of the company website, or perusal of a catalog. Each of these touch points offers the company an opportunity to build brand loyalty and create a more personalized experience for the customer. With more information, sellers can develop customized promotions based on the segment in which the particular buyer is assigned.

For example, a computer company can sell a laptop to a consumer through an online store. During the order process, the buyer may be asked to opt-in to receive tailored promotions and product offers throughout the year that specifically fit his or her known preferences (e.g., must-have accessories, extended service offers, specials on new desktop models). Similarly, an airline can send flyers for midweek or off-season specials to destinations that a customer has expressed an interest in. Or an electronic greeting card company can make use of self-reported family and friend birthdates to target specially priced gift promotions.

Some companies are now reaching out to their customers to create new access points through social networking sites, creating a truly unique, proactive, and highly personalized connection with their customers.

While some organizations may still hope this move toward personalization goes away, this is unlikely to happen. These organizations will likely discover that their competitors have been making significant investments to better orchestrate these consumer interactions. Moreover, the organizations that tie advanced analytic pricing capabilities to clearly defined strategies and supporting customer segments will clearly be in a better position to win. Over the longer term, they will likely continue to pull ahead of the competition by growing market share, and not simply by buying it through deep discounting and aggressive promotions.

Increased Price and Product Transparency

It's right around the corner: the day customers can open their mobile phone, scan a universal product code (UPC) in a store, and, within seconds, be looking at product features, customer reviews, and the best retailer pricing, along with a map and directions to get to the store. They will then be able to upload the price that's in front of them and, within seconds, that price will be in front of tens of thousands of other customers who may be looking at that same item. While some retailers may throw up their arms and surrender, others will look at how they collaborate with manufacturers, wholesalers, and retailers to change the playing field and offer unique items that can't be so easily compared.

The organizations that will be most affected by this type of *mobile pricing basket* are those that have been slow to develop a real relationship with their end consumers and have trained buyers to look for sales, promotions, and the best price. For these organizations, charging the lowest price in the market or having the most aggressive promotions in the Sunday newspapers are the only way they can survive. A me too strategy in which an organization simply adopts the price of a competitor has been a somewhat safe approach in recent years. However, as shoppers find more information at their fingertips and are able to compare an item's price across retailers, these organizations will find it increasingly difficult to compete.

But those sellers who have invested in developing a meaningful relationship with their customers will find it easier to hold their ground. They do not simply measure sales and profit, customer count, and month-over-month competitions. They look at factors such as category growth across key customer segments, attachment rates and pull through, brand trade-offs, and promotion effectiveness. With an integrated pricing discipline, they are able to take these insights and model countless scenarios to find the right price and volume tradeoff that will help them achieve their financial targets. They welcome this transparency because it illuminates the gaping holes in their competitors' capabilities.

The Choice to Be Green Doesn't Mean You Are out of the Red

Many sellers believe they can tap evolving consumer tastes by developing lines of eco-friendly products. The companies that have gone *green* have done so for many reasons, including to:

- generate buzz and improve brand image with consumers;
- open up new markets and product categories to reach greater audience segments; and
- boost overall profitability.

Car companies, airlines, manufacturers of household cleaning products, and even financial institutions have all started green campaigns and have been acknowledged, and even rewarded, by the market. But to achieve these gains, companies must carefully consider several issues. For instance, how do the new green products fit within the overall assortment strategy? How will they reach those customers whom surveys suggest resist these types of products or initiatives because they are perceived to be less convenient, less effective, or more expensive? How will sellers position these products within the overall price ladder?

Simply developing a more eco-friendly product or energy-saving manufacturing process doesn't mean customers will flock to a company's products. Companies must create a clear value proposition that the consumer will understand and adopt. New green offerings can also cannibalize similar items and product categories rather than being additive to the profit-and-loss statement. A related trend emerged in early 2000 when companies clamored to establish private label products. To their chagrin, firms discovered that rather than increasing overall sales, in many cases they had actually deflated their national brands.

Despite these caveats, the potential upside to eco-friendly products suggests companies should give them strong consideration. Those sellers that have achieved some financial success in this area did so by first establishing a clear pricing philosophy related to the green products' entry into their overall assortment. They painstakingly mined data and ran what-if scenarios to establish clear pricing ladders to help steer customers to an overall profitable mix. Clearly, there are customer segments that will pay more for green products and products made with recycled materials. By leveraging an integrated pricing approach, sellers will be able to identify win-win outcomes in both the short and the long term.

That Will Be $0.00, Please

Businesses have historically used *free* in only limited ways—by giving away samples, for example, or by offering free products to drive sales of related accessories (e.g., the now well-known razors and blades model). Free has rapidly expanded from a marketing tactic to a wide, sustainable business model. The trend may have started in the technology industry where the internet and other tools gave free access to information with near-zero distribution costs, but consumers are now increasingly expecting low or free pricing for traditional (physical) products as well. The recent shifts in customer behavior and expectations are turning economies into an entire *culture of free.*

Subscription-based businesses offer versions of their products at no charge, often subsidized by customers paying for premium content, in the hope of upselling them. Product manufacturers offer give-aways as loss leaders to build awareness and loyalty and to lock in the sale of profitable products. In some instances, cars are offered for free (for a time) in exchange for the advertisements splashed over them. This free trend will require companies to transform fundamentally their thinking about their business models.

The bricks-and-mortar businesses that can figure out how to apply free business models to their physical products profitably will have a significant marketplace advantage. Many of these models depend upon sophisticated segmentation to work because often a small number of highly profitable customers will subsidize an unprofitable majority. A company with this model must have extremely reliable pricing and segmentation data, and the ability to analyze it appropriately, to make these high-stakes decisions.

Lessons Learned: Getting Pricing on the Executive Agenda

Companies face a marketplace, today, where the pace of change is accelerating, where competitors can easily gather intelligence on their pricing and product strategies, and where consumer expectations are steadily increasing. Companies must factor all of these considerations into their planning. If they don't, then they will simply not be able to compete effectively. A U.K. publisher may seek to milk hardcover sales of a bestseller by delaying the release of the paperback edition in the U.S. Yet a customer in Dallas can simply go online to a virtual U.K. store to order the paperback edition and be happily enjoying her purchase days later. Though market dynamics are clearly changing, companies still show surprising resistance to adjusting their traditional sales and pricing strategies. Obviously, this is not a formula for success.

The same dynamic shows up in the way firms deal with new competitors. Daily newspapers, for example, have long been aware of the competition they receive from television news, but they realized too late the threat posed by the explosion of free content on the Internet. Now, because their leaders were slow to respond, many are struggling to remain profitable, while others have simply folded. Companies must find ways to respond to fluid market conditions, so they can better position themselves against competitors while still fulfilling customer needs.

To meet these challenges, businesses must strengthen their operational planning by implementing more effective pricing and profitability management. The multi-functional, multidisciplinary pricing competency can have a profound impact on the strategic and financial position of a business—but only with the active involvement of the company's chief executive. The CEO alone has both the authority and the companywide perspective to ensure that the right decisions are made, and that a carefully picked leadership team is able to answer questions such as:

- Who should handle pricing, and what kind of team is needed to execute it effectively?
- Do we need more resources, or just better ones?
- Is pricing a once-a-year obligation (e.g., publication of an annual price list) or is it a strategic activity (e.g., using price to drive customer behavior)?
- Do we need to sacrifice one region, product, or business for another in the short or long term?

Fortunately, CEOs have shown increasing willingness to emphasize pricing management as other options have fallen out of favor. Over the past two decades, for example, cost-cutting has reached its limits as a means for improving competitiveness and profitability. Campaigns to slash overhead have too often led to under-investment in areas critical to the long-term stability and growth of a business. In contrast, pricing has proven to be one of the most powerful levers a CEO can pull. It can have a transformational effect on a business, and as we have demonstrated throughout the book, pricing initiatives pay off with both immediate and long-term benefits.

Executives are also giving a higher priority to this critical competency because capital markets and the analyst community are increasingly looking at pricing when evaluating a company's performance and determining its valuation and stock price. Generally, businesses are expected to demonstrate that they are increasing both volume and market share while improving profitability. The only successful way to meet these often conflicting demands is to take—and sustain—a holistic approach to pricing.

Pricing initiatives also have other, more subtle benefits. A CEO can use a major pricing initiative to transform the mindset and morale of an organization. While cost-cutting may be presented as a way to keep a company lean and competitive, too often it has, instead, reflected a defensive response to market pressures. Pricing management, on the other hand, empowers employees. When it is done correctly, the work force can be united around shared strategic goals with employees gaining a new understanding of how their actions directly impact the overall success of the organization. In addition, as an organization buys into the new strategy, different functions begin working more cooperatively. With a strong communication plan and proper incentives, people will see clearly that as they improve the organization's bottom line, they will also enhance their own.

As we have noted throughout the book, when firms take a holistic approach to pricing and profitability management, this doesn't mean all six competencies must be improved at once. It simply means they should be coordinated and assembled into a strategic plan that is customized for each firm. The degree of improvement within each competency, and the sequence of the efforts, will depend on numerous factors, including current capabilities, market dynamics, leadership priorities, sales culture, and the firm's appetite for investment. But, if a business aims to create more value for its shareholders and customers through smarter pricing, then it must be the company's chief executive who leads the way.

Of course, changing market conditions will force organizations to shift priorities from year to year. But the need to emphasize pricing will remain constant. As an improvement lever, it exceeds all others in its dollar-for-dollar return on investment and its ability to strengthen performance in so many critical areas of an organization.

A senior executive noted of his company's pricing transformation, "the integrated approach allowed us to *surround* the problem." In other words, the company didn't focus on making a single improvement; rather, it attacked its pricing problems on all fronts by coordinating the efforts of cross-functional teams. Only a truly comprehensive approach to pricing and profitability management will drive the desired results in today's complex market *and* help sustain them over the long term.

APPENDIX

What Is Value and Why Is It So Difficult to Measure?

From a business perspective, *value* is represented by the benefits a buyer receives from an offering and its features. The definition is necessarily broad, because the concept of value does not have a universally accepted method or theory that prescribes a consistent approach for determining it. Measuring and understanding how customers value a particular product or service continues to be a challenge for many organizations today. And capturing that value through the mechanism of price can be an elusive science.

Why have companies continued to face this challenge? Several theoretical concepts on value have been posited over time, but economists have identified flaws in each. As a result, the concepts don't provide a practical, repeatable, and universal approach for calculating a precise value for a given offering. Consider the paradoxes associated with three example value theory concepts:

Value Theory Concept	Definition	Paradox
Value defined by production inputs	Value is the sum of production and labor inputs	A DeLorean might require $1 million in labor and parts to build today, but would a rational buyer value it at $1 million?
Value defined by scarcity	Value determined by lack of resource availability	If luxury brand bags were produced in the same limited quantities, but sold in the center aisle of discount retailers, would they have the same value?

(continued)

Value defined by benefits received	Value determined by advantages conveyed, both economic and intangible	How would one value a limited resource, such as crude oil, if only considering the benefits received?

These examples highlight the difficulties that prevent the literal application of these theoretical concepts in practice. However, learning and adopting ideas from each can enable an organization to formulate an approach for determining value that is pertinent to its own customer base and industry.

Value Defined By Production Inputs

One of the most mechanical ways of thinking about value for any offering is simply the sum of its labor and production inputs. On the surface, it appears logical to value something based on its components and the labor required to transform the inputs into a market offering. Early classic economists such as David Ricardo argued that the labor and production inputs were better proxies for value than the utility of the offering, providing the example that water, despite its high value in supporting sustainable life, has little exchangeable or expressed value between buyers and sellers.[1] Ricardo later acknowledged that this perspective applied most appropriately to commodities, and that exceptions do exist whereby value can be ascertained from other factors.[2] Consider the value of a souvenir from a honeymoon or a prized family heirloom: calculating only the sum of the raw inputs and labor would understate its true value to the owner.

While it is unrealistic to use production inputs alone as an indicator of value, the practical message from this for pricing organizations is that one useful way to think about value is to understand what is required to create and support an offering. While many organizations have a strong sense of cost of goods sold, a deeper understanding of all of the costs to take the product to market and to serve a customer can be lacking.

Value defined by production inputs can be useful as a lower bound—the minimum value a product or service must provide to be viable in the marketplace. A second value theory concept, value defined by scarcity, infuses the influence of supply and demand to provide another perspective on measuring value.

Value Defined By Scarcity

Value defined by scarcity parallels the basic economic concepts of supply and demand. If a product or service required little to no effort or monetary consideration to obtain, would it have any value? Do goods that are more difficult to access have relatively greater value than their likely substitutes? For example, would diamonds become less valuable than pearls if pearl divers all suddenly refused to get in the water? Or if pearl suppliers controlled the flow of new pearls in the marketplace to preserve scarcity, intentionally keeping perceived value high?

That assertion, that as resources become scarcer, customers' willingness to pay and the related value they place on the good or service increases, implies a demand curve. The timeless DeBeers "A Diamond is Forever" marketing campaign not only promoted longevity and symbolism in long-term relationships, but also discouraged a secondary market for resold diamonds, which ultimately maintained scarcity in the marketplace.[3] Generally speaking, scarcity also has a tendency to evaporate in market entry scenarios, where competition impacts valuable products once in high demand (formerly patented or produced by only a select few in limited quantities) that have become commoditized by oversupply.

Similar to the value defined by production inputs concept, scarcity is difficult to use as a standalone method for calculating value. At what point does crude oil become sufficiently scarce and prohibitively expensive to discourage consumption? While likely impractical in its purest form, the message here is that a pricing organization should consider how scarce the good or service it offers is in the marketplace from the perspective of the customer. While this concept begins to incorporate some facets of customer demand on value, the next theory, value defined by benefits received, incorporates the tangible and intangible benefits customers experience to further extend their involvement in determining value.

Value Defined By Benefits Received

Value defined by benefits received expands the perspective of value defined by scarcity and encompasses how customers derive advantages and satisfy needs from a good or service. For example, one potential benefit of purchasing a scarce good in high demand, such as a designer handbag, is the perceived exclusivity or intangible value of the satisfaction of owning something others can't easily acquire. Here the value isn't necessarily due to the fact that the good itself is scarce, but is derived from the intangible value a customer attributes to the offering.

There are seemingly countless ways a customer benefits from, and therefore values, a company's product or service. Three key examples are: application of the benefits, convenience and immediacy of experiencing the benefits, and value associated with intangible benefits. To illustrate the first application of the benefits, consider a box of baking soda. The benefits received might rely on what the consumer plans to do with the product. For instance, baking a special cake for a child's birthday party would likely convey a different value than deodorizing a refrigerator. Often companies don't have insight into how customers ultimately use their products, and therefore can't differentiate offerings based on end use.

Convenience and time to benefits might also influence the value of a product or service. For example, an ice cold soda offered to a baseball fan in his bleacher seat on hot day is much more valuable than one he has to wait in line for at the concession stand. Similarly, $6.99 sandwiches at a local deli are much more valuable when the customer is hungry right before lunch than after the customer has devoured one.

Intangible value loosely encompasses the perceptions about a particular product or service along the lines of reputation, brand, and quality. An annual study conducted by Millward Brown Optimor estimated the brand value alone of Coca-Cola at nearly $58.2 thousand million in 2008.[4] The determination of intangible value can be particularly challenging because it is individualistic in nature; for instance, two friends may view and value a brand very differently. Despite the difficulties, understanding the benefits a customer receives from an offering is a critical concept in measuring value because it helps the pricing organization understand where it can capture value through pricing.

Trekking the Elusive Path to Measure Value

There are many theoretical concepts on value. But companies can't stay in business based on theory alone—they strive to capture the value they provide through effective pricing. However, measuring value is difficult and sometimes seems more like an art than a science. The concepts described here can be used as guideposts for turning theory into practice. Understand the production inputs required and how scarce the given product or service will be in the marketplace. Balance those factors with an understanding of the benefits, both tangible and intangible, to catalog where your product or service is providing value, and attempt to quantify them through research or price testing. Then, determine how much value should be captured versus conferred to the customer in determining the price. A pragmatic approach using the perspective these concepts offer will help pricing organizations navigate the elusive path to measuring value.

Endnotes

1. Makoto Itoh, *The Basic Theory of Capitalism: The Forms and Substance of the Capitalist Economy* (Basingstoke: Palgrave Macmillan, 1988), 17.
2. Itoh, *Basic Theory of Capitalism*, 17.
3. Edward Epstein, ''Have You Ever Tried to Sell a Diamond?'' *The Atlantic Magazine*, 2, 1982, http://www.theatlantic.com/magazine/archive/1982/02/have-you-ever-tried-to-sell-a-diamond/4575/.
4. Lindsey Partos, ''Coca-Cola Brand Value Tops $58.2bn, claims report,'' *Food Navigator USA.com*, May 13, 2008, http://www.foodnavigator-usa.com/Financial-Industry/Coca-Cola-brand-value-tops-58.2-bn-claims-report.

INDEX